Voeks

On becoming an educated person

W. B. Saunders Company

Virginia Voeks

Professor of Psychology
San Diego State College

On becoming an educated person: the university and college

third edition

1970
W. B. SAUNDERS COMPANY
PHILADELPHIA · LONDON · TORONTO

W. B. Saunders Company: West Washington Square
                           Philadelphia, Pa.   19105

                           12 Dyott Street
                           London, WC1A   1DB

                           1835 Yonge Street
                           Toronto 7, Ontario

On Becoming An Educated Person

Print No.:   1   2   3   4   5   6   7   8   9

To My Students

who have been an inspiration and have taught me much

and

To My Beloved Husband

who has made this book and much else a reality,

this book is dedicated with affection and esteem.

Preface
to the third edition

SINCE FIRST this book was published, much has happened in our world. On the happy side, extensive research has been carried out by men and women of patience and integrity. Exciting new findings have been reported. Lacunae in our information have been filled. New ideas have been put forth. Old ideas have been explored and developed. Much of this has been incorporated in this new edition.

You who have come to regard this book as a stand-by in your endeavors will be pleased to find the old familiar passages still included. This, though, is a new book written from the increased wisdom of scholars in many fields, and much work on the part of the author.

You will find here much that is new: new facts and ideas related to ideas in the first and second editions; new principles extending and supplementing the old; new topics and references. The book has been brought "up to date."

There are new sections on creativity, a new section on learning other peoples' languages, a new section on educational television and on teaching machines, new sources of information on becoming an educated person.

Especially for those of you with access to the library of a large modern university, a bibliography is given to aid obtaining additional facts and ideas on the topics covered in this little book. A special thanks goes to Mrs. Antoinette Crane for her great assistance in typing.

"On Becoming an Educated Person" carries the subtitle "The University and College." This new edition is for those individuals and all the others not at universities and colleges who yet care about this crucial human enterprise.

VIRGINIA VOEKS

San Diego, California

To those embarking on a new voyage toward becoming educated

Most especially to college and university students

WHETHER THE CHANGES into college life are abrupt or gradual, there are changes in kind. Life is and will be quite different, both while you are in college and (as a result of your education) after you have left college. To give you perhaps a better notion of how you might best use what you already know and how you can best educate yourself in college and afterwards, I have written a little book.

Partly this book contains the notes of a person who experienced not so long ago much of what you may experience in college. You can learn where many pitfalls lie and avoid them. You can learn where enriching experiences lie and seek them out. You can more quickly and enjoyably attain your goals as educated persons.

Partly this book contains wisdom of others who have become highly educated persons. Bits from their lives, their experiments, their thoughts I have put down so that you too can profit from the joys and help these others have offered.

Partly this book is my way of talking to you, of including you in this wonderful human endeavor of becoming educated, sharing — if you like — things which were and are very precious to me.

I hope very much that my endeavors aid your endeavors and that you become the person you most want to become.

I think things go best if you start at the beginning of this book, but you can start anywhere you choose. There is a table of contents, remarkably complete. In addition, Mr. Sturges has prepared an excellent index to enable you to find quickly any topic herein of especial concern to you.

VIRGINIA VOEKS

Preface
to the first edition

THE DREAMS we build and the life we lead sometimes differ by staggering amounts. This need not be. We can reduce that gap and build a life which accords quite closely to our dreams.

This book is written with the hope that it may help you do that and, most particularly, help you make the reality of your college years approach more nearly the once-bright dream you had for them.

Going to college is extremely complicated. Studying is itself a set of complex skills. Even the nature of these skills is hazy to most of us; hazier yet are ways whereby those skills can be developed. What does comprise skillful studying? A wealth of opportunities surround us; but their very number can be sorely baffling. Why are we in college anyway? What did we hope to become through our efforts here? We hardly know. And there are other perplexing difficulties. We attempt to study, but distractions hamper and disrupt us. What can be done about this? We start to take a test, but become jittery and blank out. How can we ever get over this? We read material with painstaking care, manage to stay calm on the test, and still we do poorly. What went wrong? About the time we graduate, we begin to have some fairly neat solutions to those problems. But that is rather late.

In the following pages, these problems are considered and some ways are offered for at least partially resolving them. Perhaps this can free you from some of the usual trial and error, so you may profit more fully from your years in college.

The chapters have no formal summary. Instead the book is so written that you can use its table of contents as a summary and also as a preview of the chapters.

References to some of the pertinent experiments are included in the footnotes. All of these experiments were done with people — except for two studies done with white rats and one with guinea pigs, exceptions explicitly noted in the text. The references are not intended to prove the various propositions offered here. Rather, they are intended to give you some idea of the sorts of data which, when combined with other information available, lead to the conclusions presented. They are offered also to give you some sources through which you can learn more about the phenomena discussed in this little book.

Many persons have helped in the preparation of this book. Persis Sturges assisted with the typing; Kent Willson and John Wolff constructed the graphs; Persis and Duane Sturges compiled the index. I am deeply grateful to them. I should like to express my appreciation also to my family and other friends — especially Sidney, Gwen, and Ira — who helped in many ways too intricate to catch in words.

Virginia Voeks

San Diego, California

Contents

chapter 1

The nature of an
educated person

A. Statement of the Problem

A species who can go to the moon is a fantastic species. A species who can enable millions to watch this trip as it is happening, and see men while they walk on the moon, and hear men on the moon talk is almost incredible — especially if you think about it. A species who can go to the moon cannot necessarily do everything. But clearly, they can do a great deal more than many had thought possible.

A country whose people in a single decade reduces by more than one-third the percentage of those impoverished,[2] and does this yet again in the next seven years,[31] and gives to almost fifty million children a grade school or high school education and offers a college or university education to almost five million in a single year,[3] and voluntarily reduces its birthrate in an over-populated world (not just relatively, but a reduction in total numbers), a country which can and does do these and more, simultaneously, is a tremendous country accomplishing feats many would have deemed impossible for any group, no matter how large or how small it might be.

Much in the world is good. Much in the world is wonderful. Not all is well, though. In the universities and colleges too, much (but not everything) is excellent.

Then there is you. How about you? Could you too become more than you thought possible? Could you learn to live more effectively? Your use of current years lays the foundation for your many years of adult living. Could you use your college and university years to build habits and skills and knowledge even greater than you had dreamed, and beyond what you are now doing? Diverse roads lie open to you.

A professor in a remarkable novel by H. G. Wells speaks to his niece about this. He tells her universities are concerned, in the minds of many, with

"... imparting some sort of ultimate wisdom and mental habits unknown to the commonality, initiating them into a mastery of life. . . .

"Initiation. That is what you thought they were going to do for you. . . . That is what our poor befuddled, humbugged lower classes believe goes on up here to this day. They really believe that people who have been up here are mentally better than people who haven't. You cannot believe what they imagine! Education—at a University. Excelsior, and there is nothing higher. They look up to it with their mouths open. Crumbs fall to them. University Extension! Oh, generous, beautiful words! You, Stella, were to be one of those precious educated. The concentrated sort, not the extended sort. And now after two years you find you have got nothing whatever, nothing that makes you different, or stronger, or better. Eh?"

"That is what I'm telling you," said Stella.[53]

So it goes—the current tragicomedy played by college students and their professors. The major difference between Stella and many other college students is that Stella awakened after two years. Many awaken only after four, or not at all. Every spring, thousands upon thousands of black-robed figures docilely line up, parade down an aisle, take their sheepskins, and walk to their seats again, often with quizzical, sardonic smiles. To many of them college has been a farce — and a rather humorless farce at that.

Yet, in that same line are other students — radiantly afire with exciting discoveries and deeply serene with new resources. There are students who feel they have had experiences of great value, experiences of greater value than could be communicated well in any language (designed, as languages are, to convey best only the prosaic).

And you? In which group will you be marching when you graduate from college?

You rather hope, of course, that it will be the latter group. But hopes are not enough. Songs and folklore notwithstanding, wishing does not make it so — not even very intense wishing.

Let us try to see, then, how you can guarantee an outcome you will value. As you probably suspect, the outcome of college depends largely on you.

Where shall we start? Would you like some rules on how to study? Possibly you would. But before we ask "How should I study?" we should ask ourselves another question: "Why should I study? Toward what ends?"

In attempting to solve any problem, the wisest starting point is a careful answer to these questions: What precisely am I trying to do? Where do I want to get? The *probability* of your ever reaching a desired goal is increased greatly by knowing exactly what you are trying to achieve. Your *efficiency* in reaching a desired goal also is increased when you answer first "*What* am I trying to do?" and only then ask "*How* can I do it?"

The point seems obvious, almost like common sense. And yet, how many times have you searched for solutions to problems without knowing clearly what you were trying to solve? As with other problems, so it is with school and studying. Thousands go through school (the majority perhaps) without answering in any specific detail that first crucial question—What am I doing here? Often they fail to even consider the question.

Small wonder many graduates are bitter, sometimes sardonic and cynical. Everything has been rather pointless for them. They missed what they wanted from college—this they know. But what did they miss? And why? Even twenty years later they often wonder still just *what* it was they wanted, or what they want now. That, largely, is *why* they missed obtaining it. Vagueness as to your goals may cause you also to lose what you desire.

You deserve a better fate. You can have it too. A good bit of thinking is required; but the results warrant the time and effort.

First ask yourself: What sort of person am I trying to become as a result of these four years' activities? What am I aiming for? As you may have noted, these questions do not bear on college years alone, nor on your vocational life alone. Your whole life is influenced by your answer, or your failure to answer. Having asked yourself these questions, answer them in as much detail as you can.

These questions, and all other questions involving your scale of values, you must answer for yourself. No one else can do this for you—unless, perchance, he knows you extremely well, is an acute observer, is unusually astute, and is willing to spend considerable time on this project. Such a combination is not common, is it? And without that combination, the best someone else can do is state what *he* would try to do: i.e., what *he* values, or what other people value. That "best" will not suffice, for your scale of values and his may differ markedly.

Suppose we were to ask you: "What are you trying to do

by going to college?" Probably your reply would be: "Get educated, of course." That seems definite enough. But is it? The more one ponders this reply, the more one sees that the answer really is no answer at all. The question remains: What do you mean by "educated"? Until you answer at least that question also, do you really know what you are trying to do?

To be of real help in reaching your goals, your replies must be highly detailed and definite. One way to form more specific answers is by asking yourself not a single question, but a series of questions. After each reply, ask yourself: "And what do I mean by that?" Then answer that question as precisely as you can.

What *do* you mean when you say you want to become educated? To help you start formulating your own answer, here is one conception of "a highly educated person." You may think of other characteristics which are essential to what you mean by being "highly educated"; and you may deem nonessential some included here. These characteristics are merely possibilities. They might be the attributes you are striving to acquire in college. They are the sort of detailed answer which will help clarify your own goals and thus increase your chances of becoming, through college, the person you want to be.

B. Toward What Ends Are You Attending College? One Concept of an Educated Person

1. YOU COULD BECOME BETTER FITTED FOR A PARTICULAR VOCATION.

Virtually all students in four large classes we surveyed said they wanted to become fitted for a "better job." Many students listed only this goal. This raises some questions. Although one goal (and a goal which can be met through college), is this the *only* reason those students were attending college? Is it yours? Probably not. However, if vocational training is your only goal, you would be wise to consider taking a job or attending a vocational or technical training school, rather than a university or liberal arts college.

In two extensive studies of college dropouts*, the reason most often given by men[5] (and frequently by women[5, 14]) was indecision about a major or vocational goal. College and university work can help clarify what one's vocation and major might most appropriately be. So also can the counselling services. Nonetheless, dropping out may be an eminently sensible thing to do if your main objective is vocational training and you have no particular interest in any of the majors offered.

Is preparation for a particular job your *main* objective in college? Are other goals of as great or even greater importance to you? Do you, for example, care more about becoming a person who can be deeply happy regardless of his particular vocation? Is becoming a citizen who can effectively participate in a democracy of value to you too? You may wish to prepare for the large portion of your life not spent on a vocation, and for the large amounts of leisure accruing from our use of machines and our highly industrialized culture.

Your deepest concern perhaps is not earning a good living, but rather earning a good life. If it is, bear that fact in mind. Otherwise you will tend to evaluate any course or topic primarily in terms of whether it furthers your vocational training. At the extreme, you may even evaluate your

---

*Throughout this edition, as in the prior editions, all references are to reports of experiments or other systematic research except when otherwise noted, and all were done with people except those noted specifically.

whole college endeavor in terms of contribution to vocational skills. With such a narrow preoccupation, you will tend to overlook much of what you could be gaining. Even if you continue at the college or university, you will be apt to miss many (perhaps most) of the opportunities for growth afforded you. Perhaps already you have found yourself ignoring many things because "they have nothing to do with being a physicist," or laboratory technician, or whatever your vocational objective may be. Is that all you want to be?

The following goals would facilitate effective participation in most vocations. They also would facilitate your creating a satisfying life—regardless of your later vocation. They are what Sidney Gulick[25] has called "durable satisfactions": characteristics enhancing life regardless of one's job, regardless of one's age, year after year throughout one's lifetime. They are ways of earning a good life. You, we hope, will think of additional ones.

2. YOU COULD DEVELOP DEEPER COMPREHENSION OF THIS
   WORLD OF WHICH YOU ARE A PART, AND AN EAGERNESS TO
   GO ON LEARNING.

You could build a more complete fund of facts, concepts, principles, and ideas. You could develop habits of eagerly enlarging your fund, while in school and long after school is over.

A fund of information and ideas is a set of tools. Using them, you can do wondrous things: You can solve more reasonably the problems you meet; you can interpret more fully the events about you; you can predict more adequately and even partially control the events to come. Using them, you also can acquire more easily further facts and ideas. Facts, concepts, principles, and ideas can be extraordinarily useful tools.

However, if you merely collect and store them, facts and ideas are pointless. They are of no more value than a basement full of hammers, saws, and lathes, whose owner proudly displays them to visitors, but leaves them to rust the remainder of the time. Similarly, the mere possession of information is almost worthless.

Furthermore, possession of even a tremendous fund of information does not constitute being "educated," as we are using the term. To be educated, one must develop also the following attributes.

3. You could increase your ability to see interrelationships of all kinds and make new, more meaningful integrations.

"Integration" refers to a synthesis of materials. It is a sort of tying together of the concepts, data, methods, and ideas available from one source with those available from other sources—from other courses, books, and magazines, from newspapers, movies, and plays, from one's life in general.

With skill in making integrations, each new fact or concept makes old ones more meaningful and comprehensible. All aspects of the world are enriched whenever one discovers anything about any aspect of the world. To a person of such facility, a knowledge of literature contributes to his understanding of individual behavior (psychology), to his understanding of group characteristics (sociology), to his understanding of the areas of his world most extensively considered by philosophers, anthropologists, political scientists, economists. Similarly, an understanding of psychology or sociology, philosophy or anthropology, economics or political science can enable one to read literature with deeper appreciation and comprehension. Through making integrations, your fund of concepts and facts becomes valuable and useful.

The concept of "integration" is fairly simple. The process is not. To illustrate the integrations you could make and the effect of seeing these interrelationships, let us consider some parts of psychology and one bit of literature, Flaubert's *Madame Bovary*.

In that book, Flaubert paints certain episodes from Emma Bovary's childhood and adolescence. Suppose you understand many of the facts and principles of psychology and are skilled in making integrations. Then these portrayals take on deeper color for you. You go between and beyond the lines and see vividly, deeply the effects of these experiences on Emma. You put these together with your knowledge of psychology and get new views of the world about you. The effects of her impoverished home, devoid of beauty to Emma, but providing materials from which the child created elaborate dreams of life-to-be—these you would see keenly. No longer are those pages stuffy descriptions, dull background information. They are laden with gripping drama—when you know and use your knowledge of psychology. You understand more fully what is resulting from Emma's creation of that world of fantasy and from daydreaming as an habitual response to frustration. Much else too you see more clearly and understand more deeply: how Emma responds to the discovery that the dashing prince she married is neither a prince nor dashing—and never will be . . . how the world strikes her when she finally does get a home of her own . . . how her husband (and life) look to her when she moves into this "new" home, the home which was to be a sort of castle, elegant, exciting, and peaceful, but which actually is shabby, despicably ordinary.

How these later experiences affect Emma, you foresee and appreciate more keenly when you know the common results of living in fantasy and integrate this knowledge with the material of the novel. If you add to this an understanding of the relationship between frustration and aggression, you will understand with greater acuity the murderous actions to which Emma later resorts. You understand better, also, the world in which you live.

This is the merest hint of how a book takes on added significance and richness when you integrate a knowledge of psychology with the portrayals of a novel. Through such integrations, you catch more of the author's ideas; you build more ideas of your own; you notice more aspects of the world described; and you see more completely what is happening in your own world. You read with deeper appreciation and enjoyment than you otherwise could, for new dimensions have been added.

Literature becomes more meaningful when you integrate it with your knowledge of psychology. Similarly, psychology becomes more meaningful when you integrate it with your knowledge of literature. You can better comprehend psychological concepts, principles, and facts if you have read reflectively such a book as *Madame Bovary* and have developed skill in seeing interrelationships. To illustrate this, let us look at a sentence from a psychology textbook.

"One's vocational and marriage choices are based, in large part, on fantasy."[48]

Now there is a statement which looks trivial, almost puerile—until you start to think about it and relate it to your other knowledge. Suppose in the course of your thinking, you recall Emma Bovary and *her* marital choice based on fantasy. How did that work out? You remember how she repeatedly compared her husband with her dream and found Charles always sorely lacking, the dream always better, far better. You remember her disappointed bitterness when the dream exploded. You recall the way she spoke and acted after she discovered her husband was no gallant knight, no extraordinarily gifted man. You recall how she humiliated and taunted him, goading him for years to try the near impossible; and you recall how Charles became, as a consequence, ever less like her dream. You remember Emma's ensuing conquests, her ruthless exploitation of other men—men who might be princes, but never were.

"One's . . . marriage choices are based, in large part, on fantasy."[48] Do we have clues here concerning an underlying difficulty in many homes? Could this account perhaps for some of the disrupting flashes of rage, the damaging onslaughts, we have often witnessed but seldom understood? The sentence from the psychology text *combined* with a knowlege of "Madame Bovary" gives one new leads concerning the nature of the world. That is one result of "making integrations."

"One's vocational . . . choices are based, in large part, on fantasy."[48] If one chooses a vocation in terms of a dream of the job, would not the results resemble those so tragically illustrated in Emma Bovary's marriage? Does this give some clue to why many people are sorely disappointed by their vocations, rebellious toward their employers, beset by feelings of betrayal? With similar bases for their choices and for Emma's, we should expect similar results. This may afford new insight concerning one way to avoid the disillusioned bitterness and conviction of betrayal common in our world.

The foregoing does not mean we can prove the statements in a text by finding parallels in literature. One cannot do that, but what one can do is truly remarkable. By integrating materials from literature and other fields of life with text materials, you can illustrate the statements in the text. You can bring out their meanings. You can see more of the possible implications. Dry facts become alive; new ideas are born.

4. YOU COULD BUILD WIDER, DEEPER INTERESTS AND
   DEVELOP THE HABIT OF CONTINUALLY EXTENDING YOUR
   INTERESTS.

Such habits go far toward precluding the boredom and lostness we observe all about us and (oftentimes) within us. Bob is an illustration.

When alone, Bob habitually switches on the radio or television, though he finds most programs "stupid." He tries to read, but everything seems dull. That is not surprising, for Bob knows almost nothing about philosophy or astronomy, anthropology or botany, economics or geography, or any other broad area of investigation. He scoffs at these. He scoffs at poetry too. The lives of others (history and biographies) he deems stuffy. Occasionally he reads novels, but even they soon pall on him. Books as sources of joy do not exist for Bob. Listening to music, attending speeches, visiting art museums, writing — all these activities he labels "highbrow" and shoves away. What *can* Bob enjoy? By himself, Bob is bored and discontented. Why? He decides he is lonesome.

So he calls some acquaintances, urging them to "do something" with him. But when they do, Bob still is bored, often restless, and discontented. We could predict that. As is well known (well known to psychologists anyway), *the person who is bored alone, usually is bored also when with others.*

This is no jaded appetite! This is an absence of appetites. Bob's dilemma reflects (among other things) a failure to have developed hearty appetites in the first place.

Pitifully enough, Bob is not the extreme individual you might imagine. His dilemma is that of many. His dilemma may even be yours, though exaggerated of course. To better understand you, or what you might become, let us summarize Bob's predicament.

The general pattern is this: The individual has a deep restlessness. He complains to himself or his parents or his friends that there is "nothing to do." He labels many activities "stupid." When alone, he is listless and lonesome.

He is driven to seek others' company. But even when with other people and "on the go," the restless discontent, the insidious boredom creep up on him.

Life in general is pretty dull, he feels; or else (as he often phrases it) he is "missing life."

As an escape, he seeks thrills avidly—thrills from the excitement of breaking rules and customs, suspense from pinball machines or other gambling. But these do not satisfy his nameless craving. Soon he is restless and bored again, often even more "sunk" than before the episode. As a consequence he seeks thrills ever more frantically with the blind, unverbalized feeling they *must* relieve his tension and discontent.

Thrills do not cure the difficulty. They cannot, since a fundamental trouble of these people is a boredom within one's self and with most of the world, a boredom stemming in part from a paucity of deep interests. Ocassionally the individual has many interests, but the interests are shallow, and confined to a few areas only.

Bob's difficulty differs from that of many other people only in degree. Is he so different from you?

Can *you* be happy alone? Really happy? Or are such hours ones to be endured (not lived), as best one can? Must you flee from solitude to others? And when you find them, what then? Do you know that restless lonesomeness Bob has?

This boredom (or "restlessness" or "lonesomeness"—it has many names) sometimes is pointed to as characteristic of our culture. It is, however, a characteristic of many *people*, and *not* a characteristic of this civilization. It is not the inevitable fate of people born into this or any other society.

How can you avoid having a life like Bob's? (Incidentally, this condition is not improved by merely getting older!) One of the best ways is that suggested in the heading of this section: Develop wide and deep interests. This does not mean, of course, that you should abandon your current interests. Quite the contrary! Keep those, and develop them; but build new ones in addition. Establish the habit of continuously widening and deepening your interests.

A variety of deep interests does not inevitably result from going to college; or from traveling; or from any other set of experiences. Neither are we given these by other people—no matter how imperiously we demand that they make things interesting. Rather, possessing deep interests results from one's own efforts—from living in certain ways.

Live with intense eagerness for finding out about the world. When reading a text, for example, try to discover from it as much as possible about the nature of the world with which it deals—whether or not you suspect any of this will appear on a later test. When listening to a lecture, be alert for new facts and ideas. When riding on the subway or trolley, idly eavesdropping, try to gain new insights into how others think and feel.

Try observing more closely everything about you. What you learn in school can give you a wealth of clues to new aspects of the world worth watching and examining. Relate what you discover at any particular time to the rest of your life.

Be alive to beauties and little joys.

> "If those who seek happiness would only stop one little minute and think, they would see that the delights they really experience are as countless as the grasses at their feet or the dewdrops sparkling upon the morning flowers. . . . It would be wonderful to find myself free from even a small part of my physical limitations . . . to walk around town alone . . . to come and go without a word to anyone . . . to read the newspapers without waiting, and pick out a pretty handkerchief or a becoming hat in the shops. . . . I feel fortunate indeed that it has been possible for me to enjoy sculpture, poetry, happy make-believe in bleak corners of my limitations."[29]

This gratitude and alert awareness are part of "the miracle of Helen Keller,"[4] a human being whose life "defies the notion that man is a passive automaton whose sole purpose is to reduce tension by adaptive responses to threatening environmental changes."[4] *Your* life can be richer too. Life is not drab to one fully awake.

Share other people's interests with them — especially when their interests differ from your own (i.e., from those you already have).

Welcome topics falling outside your old interests. Often we say, "That subject doesn't interest me at all"; then we ignore the subject or look into it only grudgingly. Such an approach militates against new interests. New interests grow and flower only when we explore beyond our current confines.

Common today is an invidious misconception: When we know much, things lose their charm. But knowledge kills no charms. In fact, quite the opposite is true. *The more you know about something, the more fascinating it becomes.*

The more you know about botany, for instance, the more interesting botany becomes and the more interesting also the world becomes. Flowers retain all their old charm, while acquiring for you new beauty and new interest. You see parts you may never have seen before—the varied intricacies of veins in petals and leaves; the fragile beauty of little blossoms in the center of composite flowers, such as daisies, sunflowers, and cosmos; the intriguing array of pistils and stamens. You notice relationships between parts and their functions and begin to see the marvel of how life is sustained. You look at a flower and behold a whole new world of almost magical beauty.

Or you study astronomy—and the night sky, glorious when one knows nothing about it, becomes yet more glorious, marvelously fascinating. No longer do you see merely a jumble of faint lights. You see now the soft rose of Mars, the radiance of Jupiter, the glimmering whiteness from dwarf stars, thousands of times heavier than lead. You note the pulsing shimmer from some far-away star, a light now ending its journey of ten thousand years, or even more. You see a pinpoint of light and know it to be not one star, but an unfathomed swirling array of stars, comprising a vast galaxy clear outside our own. This is another world.

Fear not. You can know incalculable amounts about an area and still its charms endure. Far from being tarnished, they are enhanced by deepening knowledge. (The contrary notion is, we suspect, only a rationalization, a wobbly justification for intellectual loafing or a defense for one's *status quo.*)

Go out to meet your world. Discover as much as you can about everything you meet. Avoid insulations between you and life—the obvious physical, psychological, and social ones, but also the subtle insulations such as drugs. Live each hour with verve, a wide-awake perceptiveness, an eagerness to discover and learn and grow. No better way exists for avoiding later boredom and discontent. No route makes current years more deeply joyous.

5. YOU COULD DEVELOP AN INCREASING APPRECIATION
   AND LOVE FOR THE ARTS — INCLUDING SKILLFUL
   COMPOSITIONS OF ALL SORTS.

Sculpture, paintings, free verse, sonnets, novels, essays, interior decoration, food combinations, theories — new worlds wait your discovery. You can use these years to explore them, and more.

In our universities and colleges, there are music courses and musicians — symphony orchestras, marching bands, symphonic bands, choruses, choirs, glee clubs, opportunities to learn to play any of several instruments, individual lessons and group lessons. There are many kinds of art courses and artists, science courses and scientists, athletic programs and skilled athletes. There are architecture and clothes designing and on and on, worlds without end.

Everything (almost) our peculiar species can do which creates beauty, or knowledge, you will find offered at our universities and colleges. These are fascinating worlds. The opportunity is yours to learn about them and become better able to appreciate and delight in them — now and in the years of life ahead.

One world you are certain to touch is that of books. Have you considered the nature of books? Their magic is one boon available to all men. But few can accept it. A modern tragedy is that many persons, far from learning to appreciate books, actually learn to abhor them.

This is tragic, because books are more than useful tools, far more. They hold keys to other worlds, opening the way to exciting new realms of experience. They can be wondrously enlightening and stimulating, deliciously amusing, deeply refreshing. But all this has been better expressed (in books) by some of the world's most gifted men. Let us listen to them for a moment.

"The world of books is the most remarkable creation of man. Nothing else that he builds ever lasts. Monuments fall, nations perish, civilizations grow old and die out; and, after an era of darkness, new 'races' build others. But in the world of books are volumes that have seen this happen again and again, and yet live on, still young, still as fresh as the day they were written, still telling men's hearts of the hearts of men centuries dead."[10]

"All that mankind has done, thought, gained or been: It is in magic preservation in the pages of books." So Carlyle speaks, across the miles and years, to us.

Mark Twain provocatively reminds us: "The man who does not read good books has no advantage over the man who can't read them."

As you doubtless have observed, what people are like to you depends largely upon you and your interactions with them. As with people, so it is with books: What any book is like to you depends rather more upon you than upon it. When we pick up a book with the half-verbalized set, "I dare you to tell me anything sensible" or "I dare you to amuse me," we will find that book dull. One gets nowhere that way. Suppose on the other hand, we turn to a book asking, "I wonder what new ideas I can create with the help of this man and his book?" Or, "I wonder how this person has analyzed that problem?" Or, "What neat expressions will I discover here?" With such an approach any book becomes provocative and enlightening.

To find books interesting and worth reading, we must meet them half way, or even more than half way. We must read as a collaborator with the author—not as an antagonist, nor yet as a receptacle!

The same point holds for music, for paintings, for practically all aspects of the world. *How* to meet artists half way, how to collaborate with them, these you could learn in college.

In college you are certain to come in contact with students and professors who deeply enjoy various forms of beauty. Usually they will be genuinely eager to give you leads on ways you too can derive deeper appreciation and enjoyment from those aspects of the world.

Our worlds are filled with many sorts of beauty, could we but see them. You can go to college in such a way that you discover these new realms and learn to love them.

6. YOU COULD DEVELOP A DEEPER COMPASSION AND
   UNDERSTANDING OF ALL OTHER PEOPLE.*

Compassion and understanding of each other are two most distinctively human potentialities. Probaby you value those qualities in their own right. In addition, they lead toward goals you may also cherish: They enable you to live more joyously and more harmoniously with your fellow men; and also (delightful result) they enable you to be more at peace with yourself. Developing compassion and an understanding of many other individuals almost precludes extensive dictatorships, and is prerequisite to a true democracy.

Psychology, of course, can help you learn to understand people better, see more clearly their problems, their limitations, and their assets. So also can philosophy, economics, business administration, sociology, anthropology, physiology,

---

*See, for example, Anderson[1] and Schweitzer[46] for an extraordinary illumination of the nature and significance of this quality.

zoology, neurology, geography, political science, literature, art, and history. All of these and others too can help you understand people better. They can, that is, if you study these areas partly in an effort to gain deeper insights into the nature of your fellow men, their actions, dreams, and problems—and their achievements. These are far more remarkable than commonly realized.

Extraordinary achievements are the result not merely of great talent, as is almost invariably assumed, but of extraordinary effort, devotion, and a willingness to work extremely hard.[8, 9, 44, 45, 49] Long ago Edison notified us that genius is 99% hard work, 1% talent. Alexander Dumas pointed out: "I achieve the impossible working as none else ever works. . . ." Michelangelo remarked: "If people only knew how hard I work to gain my mastery, it wouldn't seem so wonderful at all." (To some, of course, it would seem more wonderful.)

Accounts by individuals sketching how they manage to paint, or write, or carry out illuminating research, how they manage to beautifully re-create music, to invent, or to live in any other way with grace and creative skill, make clear these are unspeakably difficult human feats when done superbly. They are triumphs of the human spirit.

Creative endeavors of all kinds are remarkable human feats. Recently we have acquired invaluable information[6, 11–13, 15, 18–24, 26–28, 30, 32, 35–40, 50–52, 55] better enabling us to understand in detail what creativity involves, what the creative person is doing, what these individuals are like. We can understand better these people, and those parts of ourselves.

In college and afterwards you not only will study about such people, you will meet many such individuals and can talk with them; you can learn first-hand to understand them, and what they are achieving. You will meet many different sorts of persons, with different skills, different information, different kinds of abilities, different kinds of achievements. You could develop better understanding of all these richly varied persons, and what they are doing.

7. YOU COULD GAIN A NEW APPRECIATION OF INDIVIDUAL DIFFERENCES.

The capacity to appreciate persons different from ourselves is not identical with compassion and understanding. Nor is it faintly synonymous with toleration. Valuing individual differences goes far beyond the "live and let live" philosophy.

When this characteristic is developed to a high degree, we appreciate the worth of each human being, we recognize the uniqueness of individuals, and (crucially important) we consider this uniqueness outstandingly precious. Instead of merely tolerating differences in people, we value these differences; we strive to maintain and encourage at least some aspects of the uniqueness of individuals. This is rare — even in our society — and is of great worth.

To deeply understand the worth of "valuing individual differences," we should have to study the natures of democracy and autocracy, and study also their importance. We cannot do that in this little book, but in many of your college courses you will have opportunities to examine these matters. Let us glance, however, at some of the repercussions in your world when people fail to value individual differences.

Don is a college student. He enjoys the writings of Molière, Proust, and Shakespeare. He appreciates the artistry of Shostakovich and Cézanne. Almost certainly Don will be labelled an intellectual and, in less happy times, "Un-American."

David writes poetry which to him is beautiful and is a joy to write. Some other people too find in it new and unique beauties. However, since his writing meets the unfulfilled needs of only a minority, it often is labelled "silly" and "highbrow."

Professor B is trying to introduce a new course. It is a course which perhaps only one person of a hundred deeply needs in order to better utilize his capacities. The welfare of thousands of people may be enhanced if that one per cent can develop their potentialities as fully as possible. Yet for introducing this course, Professor B is labelled "undemocratic" and "out of touch with reality." (Alice, of course, was deemed wholly mad by the Queen of Hearts and her entourage; but that was in Wonderland.)

These labellers would maintain that they themselves are strongly democratic. But are they really? Whitman wrote a haunting lament: "Democracy, the destin'd conqueror, yet treacherous lipsmiles everywhere, And death and infidelity at every step."[54] That is a poetic exaggeration; treacherous lipsmiles are not everywhere. Yet episodes like those in the paragraphs above do occur many times each day. And who, in such cases, is undemocratic? Is it really the labelled? Or is it the labellers?

The foregoing examples illustrate the opposite of valuing individual differences. In each case, the labellers fail to value individual characteristics. Further, they scoff at individual differences, attaching to them all manner of opprobrious adjectives. They try to make individuals conform to one pattern, their pattern. Consciously or unconsciously, they work toward making people into carbon copies of each other. Converting people into carbon copies appears outstandingly characteristic of Stalin's Russia, of Hitler's Germany, of all authoritarian regimes.

The essence of democracy, on the other hand, consists in part of a recognition of individual differences, a high evaluation of many of these differences, and actions in accord with this recognition and evaluation. Without these, all shreds of democracy die. With them, democracy can grow.

Valuing individual differences also makes it possible for you to be you. Suppose differences in people were minimized. Suppose everyone actually did conform to a comprehensive set of standards. Then, whether the standard for conformity was that of the current majority, or your own standard, or any other, *you* would not exist. You would be indistinguishable from everyone else. You, and all people, would be individuals only in the sense that oranges are individuals—they occupy different positions in time and space.

Were there few individual differences, life would be horribly boring. Can you imagine what that world would be like? Suppose there were a world with people as much alike as so many ants in a hill. Even if all the ants were like *any one of us,* would not life be infinitely monotonous?

You help create the social climate. If you value the results of there being many individual differences, and dislike the opposed results, it behooves you to develop your own appreciation for such differences and to actively encourage these differences. Your associates, in turn, can more readily appreciate individual differences when you do so. College work will furnish you many opportunities for perceiving the value of difference, and learning to act in accord with these perceptions. But here again, you must be alert for these opportunities to profit from them.

8. YOU COULD LEARN NEW SKILLS IN THINKING — AS CONTRASTED WITH MEMORIZING OR BLINDLY ACCEPTING "AUTHORITY."

Skill in thinking does not inevitably appear merely because you were born with that potentiality. Much practice is required in order to develop clear thinking.

Nor are you doomed forever to sloppy thinking merely because currently you are maladroit. Thinking can be impaired; and thinking can be improved.[7, 33, 34, 41, 42, 47]

Unique opportunities to practice these skills are furnished in college. While studying, for example, or listening to a lecture, or participating in a discussion, you could practice the skills which comprise clear thinking: skill in analyzing data and formulating a variety of alternative interpretations for the data; skill in evaluating hypotheses and devising sounder modifications of them; skill in identifying pitfalls in thinking; skill in avoiding these pitfalls; skill in seeing what leads to what. You could learn to doubt honestly and without fear. You could learn to ask pertinent questions of yourself and to derive your own answers.

Through practicing and developing these skills, you free yourself from having to rely so heavily upon other people's thinking (skillful or otherwise). You free yourself from being harnessed to their conclusions, when you are able to form your own conclusions with soundness and swiftness. You become a remarkably adept thinker.

9. YOU COULD ACQUIRE A GROWING ABILITY TO ASSUME RESPONSIBILITY FOR YOUR OWN LIFE.

To what extent do you rely on others' thinking and delegate responsibility to them? If you watch yourself and your own living, you may be quite enlightened by what you find. Note the variety of situations in which you wait for someone to tell you what to do and how to do it and insist upon having detailed instructions. When trying, for example, to decide upon a vocation, or to devise ways to study, or to smooth out difficulties in interpersonal relations, how often do you seek directions from others, instead of figuring these things out for yourself? Do not include here the times you seek information or collaboration, a pooling of skills. Include only the times you seek *conclusions,* asking that the decisions be made for you.

Sometimes we even seek solutions to personal problems, and then seek advice as to the proper choice among the conflicting recommendations. We may go so far as to assume it is the advisers' "fault" when things work out poorly for us—although we are the ones responsible for turning that part of our life over to them.

How we depend upon others even for our opinions. In this connection, there are many little investigations you could conduct. For example: In conversation, watch for such phrases as "Well, Russell Kirk said . . ." or "David Brinkley said . . ." or "My husband said . . ." and then note how often such statements are made *in place of* formulating any opinion of one's own or are made in order to "prove" some contention. "I read it in the newspaper." "I heard it on the radio." Ipso facto, truth; my job is done.

Our position often is not as different as we like to imagine from that of a dependent child. We have merely switched, and added, parents. We have adopted new authorities to do our thinking for us.

Like children, too, we want something but do not want the inseparable correlates of the something. Do we want liberty? But shrink from the correlated obligation of making our own decisions? Do we want the right to vote? But do not want to bother about getting pertinent information and thinking about it? Often we want the pleasures and privileges of being free adults, but neglect to develop the skills requisite for that freedom.

We want to live our own life, pursue our own goals, make our own decisions, but neglect the necessary skills of accepting responsibility and thinking clearly.

Insofar as we lack skills in thinking and in accepting responsibility, we have but two choices when facing a problem: (1) We can trust to luck and fate. (You know how that alternative works out.) Or (2) we can ask for instructions, waiting for others to tell us what to do and how to do it. These "others" may be clumsy thinkers too; they may be as poorly informed as we — or more so; they may know little about us and care little or nothing about our problem; but accept their advice and conclusions we must. We must accept their statements and interpretations for the simple reason that we have no other choice, unless we have learned the skills necessary for making our own decisions. Dismally oppressive though dictators may be, they would be indispensable — in private life and public.

To develop skill in being responsible requires continuing sustained practice. But to the extent you succeed, you become more fully human. You become more autonomous, freer. You can solve your problems more satisfactorily. You no longer need wait (often in vain) for someone else to tell you what to do. You will become increasingly adept in weighing the factors important to *you* and making your own decisions. You will develop a new ability to work independently, on your own initiative. You could even live your own life and have real freedom.[16, 17, 43]

10. YOU COULD EARN A GOOD LIFE, AS WELL AS A GOOD LIVING.

You know the nameless longings, the vague discontents which haunt men's lives in this culture of plenty. You have witnessed the strife based on misunderstandings. You have seen the bitter cynicism, the lostness, the sense of futility which wreck human living. These you can avoid. Yours can be a very different life.

Your world can be a fascinating place of challenging experiences and new delights. Through your college work and ways of living, you can develop new sensitivity to beauty in all of its many forms. You can build such a breadth and depth of interests that no hour could fail to touch some of them. You can learn the thrill of discovery and of creativity. Fresh worlds would open.

You can develop new skill in coping with your world. You can learn to think with greater clarity and speed. You can gain greater abilities to apply information, to see new relationships, to judge the reasonableness of arguments, and to solve myriad problems. You can build a more complete fund of concepts, facts, and ideas with which to comprehend your world, your fellow men, and yourself.

Your interpersonal relationships can have new peace and joyousness, based firmly upon these more complete understandings and a deepening, genuine sympathy which make life a joy to you and you a joy to others.

New skills in living and a new enthusiasm for life can be yours. You can earn a good life — regardless of what your job might be.

All these things can happen. However, college guarantees no such outcome, no such personal development. One can attend college in such a way that none of these attributes accrue. It has been done.

Colleges furnish opportunities. The best college imaginable can do no more.

C. Concluding Remarks

No college or university can give one an education. Becoming educated does not follow inevitably from anything done by anybody else. Becoming educated depends upon you and what you do.

Theodore Roosevelt once remarked, "What I am to be, I am now becoming." That is true for you too. What sort of person you later will be is influenced by every response you currently make. What you are like on Graduation Day depends upon all the habits you practice while in college: the way you study, the way you listen to lectures, the way you participate in other activites, the way you respond to your colleagues; in brief, the way you live each hour. And the way you do all these depends partly upon the clarity with which you recognize your own goals, whatever they may be, and the constancy with which you practice the skills comprising those goals.

This doctrine will be a horror to many people, and will be rejected by some of them as sheerest nonsense—for there are many people who, because of their own inner make-up, must believe that events are always due primarily to other people and their actions.

Actually, it is a happy circumstance that the outcome of college rests mainly upon you. It means your life is in your hands. You need not trust in luck, nor even in other persons' generosity, skill and wisdom. *They* do not determine whether you become highly educated nor what sort of life you have. You do.

Let us consider in more detail, now, some ways through which you can attain the goals sketched in this chapter and become a deeply educated person.

Bibliography for Chapter 1

1. Anderson, Erica. The Schweitzer Album. New York: Harper and Row, 1965.

2. Anon. Family income levels. Wall Street Journal, April 5, 1961.

3. Anon. The magnitude of the American educational establishment (1964-65). Sat. Rev. Lit., November 21, 1964.

4. Anon. Helen Keller (1880-1968). J. Amer. Med. Assoc., 205, 584, 1968.

5. Astin, Alexander W. Personal and environmental factors associated with college dropouts among high aptitude students. J. Educ. Psychol., 55, 219-227, 1964.

6. Berger, R. M.; Guilford, J. P.; and Christensen, P. R. A factor-analytic study of planning abilities. Psychol. Monogr., 71, No. 435, 1957.

7. Bruner, Jerome S. Learning and thinking. Harv. Educ. Rev., 29, 184-192, 1959.

8. Chambers, J. A. Relating personality and biographical factors to scientific creativity. Psychol. Monogr.: Gen. and Applied, 78, #584, 1964.

9. Chambers, J. A. Creative scientists of today. Science, 145, 1203-1205, 1964.

10. Day, Clarence. The Story of the Yale University Press Told by a Friend. New Haven, Conn.: Yale Univ. Press, 1920.

11. Dentler, R. A.; and Mackler, B. Originality: Some social and personal determinants. Behav. Sci., 9, 1-7, 1964.

12. Dreistadt, Roy. The use of analogies and incubation in obtaining insights in creative problem solving. J. Psychol., 71, 159-175, 1969.

13. Eisenman, Russell. Creativity, awareness, and liking. J. Consulting and Clin. Psychol., 33, 157-160, 1969.

14. Faunce, Patricia Spencer. Withdrawal of academically gifted women. J. College Student Personnel, 9, 171-176, 1968.

15. Frick, J. W.; Guilford, J. P.; Christensen, P. R.; and Merrifield, P. R. A factor-analytic study of flexibility in thinking. Educ. Psychol. Measmt., 19, 469-496, 1959.

16. Fromm, Erich. Escape from Freedom. New York: Farrar and Rinehart, Inc., 1941.

17. Fromm, Erich. Man for Himself. New York: Rinehart and Co., Inc., 1947.

18. Gershon, A.; Guilford, J. P.; and Merrifield, P. R. Figural and symbolic divergent-production abilities in adolescent and adult populations. Rep. Psychol. Lab., Univ. Southern California, No. 29, 1963.

19. Getzels, Jacob W.; and Jackson, Philip W. Creativity and Intelligence: Explorations with Gifted Students. New York: Wiley, 1962.

20. Gibson, James W.; Kibler, Robert J.; and Barker, Larry L. Some relationships between selected creativity and critical thinking measures. Psychol. Reports, 23, 707-714, 1968.

21. Guilford, J. P. Creative abilities in the arts. Psychol. Rev., 64, 110-118, 1957.

22. Guilford, J. P. Factors that aid and hinder creativity. Teachers Coll. Rec., 63, 380-392, 1962.

23. Guilford, J. P.; Merrifield, P. R.; Christensen, P. R.; and Frick, J. W. Some new symbolic factors of cognition and convergent production. Educ. Psychol. Measmt., 21, 515-541, 1961.

24. Guilford, J. P.; Merrifield, P. R.; and Cox, A. B. Creative thinking in children at the junior high school levels. Rep. Psychol. Lab., Univ. Southern California, No. 26, 1961.

25. Gulick, Sidney L. Consider the long view: A square report. Invited Address, San Diego State College Chapter of Phi Kappa Phi, (mimeo.), 1969.

26. Hoffman, L. Richard. Conditions for creative problem solving. J. Psychol., 52, 429-444, 1961.

27. Houston, J. P.; and Mednick, S. A. Creativity and the need for novelty. J. Abnorm. Soc. Psychol., 66, 137-141, 1963.

28. Israeli, Nathan. Creative art: A self-observation study. J. Gen. Psychol., 66, 33-45, 1962.

29. Keller, Helen. The Faith of Helen Keller. Kansas City, Missouri: Hallmark, pp. 20 and 24, 1967.

30. Kettner, N. W.; Guilford, J. P.; and Christensen, P. R. A factor-analytic study across the domains of reasoning, creativity, and evaluation. Psychol. Monogr., 73, No. 479, 1959.

31. Kihss, Peter. Nonwhites said to gain in income. New York Times, May 3, 1969.

32. Krop, Harry. Effects of extrinsic motivation, intrinsic motivation, and intelligence on creativity: A factorial approach. J. General Psychol., 80, 259-266, 1969.

33. Landa, L. N. O formirovanii u uchashchikhsia obshchego metoda myslitel-noi deiatel'nosti pri reshenii zadach. [On the formation in pupils of a general method of thinking activity in the solution of problems.] Vop. Psikhol., 5, 14-27, 1959.

34. Lyle, Edwin. An exploration in the teaching of critical thinking in general psychology. J. Educ. Res., 52, 129-133, 1958.

35. Maier, Norman R.; and Burke, Ronald J. Studies in creativity: II. Influence of motivation in the reorganization of experience. Psychol. Reports, 23, 351-361, 1968.

36. Maier, Norman R.; Thurber, James A.; and Janzen, Junie C. Studies in creativity: V. The selection process in recall and in problem-solving situations. Psychol. Reports, 23, 1003-1022, 1968.

37. Mednick, M. T. Research creativity in psychology graduate students. J. Consult. Psychol., 27, 265-266, 1963.

38. Mednick, M. T.; Mednick, S. A.; and Jung, C. C. Continual association as a function of level of creativity and type of verbal stimulus. J. Abnorm. Soc. Psychol., 69, 511-515, 1964.

39. Merrifield, P. R.; Guilford, J. P.; Christensen, P. R.; and Frick, J. W. The role of intellectual factors in problem solving. Psychol. Monogr., 76, No. 529, 1962.

40. Merrifield, P. R.; Guilford, J. P.; and Gershon, A. The differentiation of divergent-production abilities at the sixth-grade level. Rep. Psychol. Lab., Univ. Southern California, No. 27, 1963.

41. Miles, Josephine. The use of reason. Teachers Coll. Rec., 63, 540-547, 1962.

42. Murphy, Gardner. Creativeness. Menninger Quart., 11, 1-6, 1957.

43. Riesman, D. The Lonely Crowd. New Haven: Yale University Press, 1950.

44. Roe, Anne. A psychological study of physical scientists. Genet. Psychol. Monogr., 43, 121-235, 1951.

45. Roe, Anne. A psychological study of eminent psychologists and anthropologists, and a comparison with biological and physical scientists. Psychol. Monogr., 67 (2), #352, 1953.

46. Schweitzer, Albert. The Teaching of Reverence for Life. (Translated from the German by Richard and Clara Winston.) New York: Holt, Rinehart and Winston, 1965.

47. Sperling, Otto E. Thought control and creativity. J. Hillside Hosp., 8, 149-161, 1959.

48. Symonds, P. The Dynamics of Human Adjustment. New York: Appleton-Century-Crofts, 1946, p. 495.

49. Taylor, C. W.; and Ellison, R. L. Biographical predictors of scientific performance. Science, 155, 1075-1080, 1967.

50. Terman, Lewis M. The discovery and encouragement of exceptional talent. Amer. Psychologist, 9, 221-230, 1954.

51. Terman, Lewis M.; and Oden, Melita H. Genetic Studies of Genius. Vol. V, The Gifted Group at Mid-Life. Stanford, Calif.: Stanford Univ. Press, 1959.

52. Voss, James F. (Ed.) Approaches to Thought. Columbus, Ohio: Charles E. Merrill Publishing Co., 1969.

53. Wells, H. G. Babes in the Darkling Wood. New York: Alliance Book Corporation, 1940, pp. 196-197.

54. Whitman, W. Leaves of Grass. New York: Doubleday & Co., Inc., 1924.

55. Wilson, R. C.; Guilford, J. P.; Christensen, P. R.; and Lewis, D. J. A factor-analytic study of creative-thinking abilities. Psychometrika, 19, 297-311, 1954.

chapter 2

Behavior which leads to becoming an educated person and also to making high grades

A. Introduction and a Preliminary Caution

"Most of us feel as if we live habitually with a sort of cloud weighing on us, below our highest notch of clearness in discernment, sureness in reasoning, or firmness in deciding. Compared with what we ought to be, we are only half awake. Our fires are damped, our drafts are checked, we are making use of only a small part of our possible mental and physical resources."[137]

To utilize more fully our inner resources, to have our fires leap high — these are major objectives. But how can we achieve them? How can we more nearly live up to our capacities? How can we even raise our grades?

Psychologists and educators have studied these problems from several approaches. They have examined the procedures used by successful students and neglected by unsuccessful ones. They have investigated the pronounced changes which occurred when the "unsuccessful" students started practicing some of these techniques and procedures and developed new study habits. Results from that research and also from the extensive experimental work in learning are offered here for your consideration.

These are ways in which you can make fuller use of your resources, develop your present abilities, and ultimately become more nearly the person you long to be. They are ways of profiting more richly from college—both in terms of becoming a more educated person and in terms of making higher grades.

Let us forewarn you: The suggestions itemized below cannot be applied simply by resolving to do so. This disheartens many a student. When his resolutions do not lead to immediate success, he often concludes (erroneously) that he is "stupid," incapable of doing what he resolved, or else that the suggested methods are worthless. Then he gives up. We hope you avoid those pitfalls.

Being partially unsuccessful in your first several attempts does not mean you are stupid. It means only this: To learn to study effectively, one must develop complicated skills; and to develop any new skill requires considerable practice—in addition to firm resolutions.

To help you start on this project, we have listed in the headings various ways of studying more effectively. Then, under each heading, are suggestions on how you can develop the habit stated in the heading. All of these suggested techniques, remember, are ways of becoming better educated and also of making high grades.

B. *Knowing Your Goals*

1. REACHING ANY GOAL IS FACILITATED BY KNOWING
   CLEARLY WHAT YOU ARE TRYING TO DO.

This was discussed in the introduction to Chapter I. We merely mention it here as a reminder that this is the place to start. The first step in studying more effectively is to formulate your goals.

2. DO NOT BLINDLY ADOPT OTHER PEOPLE'S OBJECTIVES.

People differ greatly in what sort of life they regard as worth living. They differ in what sort of persons they want to become. Even your closest friends have value systems somewhat different from yours. Therefore, what is best to them and right for them will not always be what is best to you and right for you. This means you cannot blindly adopt their objectives as your own, nor satisfactorily pattern your life wholly after theirs.

3. FORMULATE YOUR OWN OBJECTIVES, IN DETAIL, AND
   REMEMBER THEM.

Work out for yourself what *you* are trying to achieve through studying and attending classes. In addition to outlining your goals for college in general, formulate also some of the sub-goals for each of your courses. Jot down these goals, add to them, and save them for reference. Whenever you start wondering why you are studying, what you are trying to achieve through study and other activities, refer to your list of goals. See if those goals do still matter to you and are worth much effort. If they are, live accordingly – giving to them the efforts, devotion, and skills they merit.

4. NOT ALL GOALS CAN BE BEST ATTAINED BY ATTENDING COLLEGE OR THE UNIVERSITY.

Colleges and universities have much to offer. Nonetheless, to expect them or any other set of institutions or procedures to be all things to all people is unreasonable. There are other lives that are also worth living, lives not particularly facilitated by attending college. Tap dancing is a wonderful thing; so is painting pictures. However, to give everyone tap-dancing lessons or art lessons would be a foolish squandering of resources and inappropriate to the nature of the individual.

Neither should everyone attend a college or university. Many circumstances exist which make it wise to withdraw from college, or never start, a few of which have been indicated (See page 6.) If you find yourself exceedingly discontented with college or the university, perhaps college and university life is an inappropriate undertaking for you and dropping college would be your most rational course of action. Your goals may be best met through some other kind of endeavor, not involving college and university work.

Another possibility exists: If you are deeply discontented with college or the university, perhaps you are approaching your college and university work in an inappropriate way and should modify your ways of studying, listening, writing.

These are the matters on which the present book is offered as an aid.

C. *Choosing a Place to Study*

1. START WITH ONE SPECIAL PLACE FOR STUDY.

Trying to study in many different places increases the difficulty of learning to study efficiently.

When you are first developing skill in studying, try to do all your home study in the same room, at the same desk, in the same chair. If practicable, use them only for studying.

These suggestions sound a bit trivial, don't they? Their results, however, are far from trivial. When you follow them, fairly soon just sitting down at that desk will make you feel like studying; you will need far less time for warming up.

You need not go on forever studying in one place only. After you have become skillful in studying in one place, you readily can learn to study in another place, and another and another. Finally you will be able to study easily and well almost anywhere, under almost any circumstances.

Under some circumstances, shifting your study room can be a distinct help. When one has a great deal of the same sort of thing to do, one's performance is apt to progressively deteriorate;[66, 152] changing rooms can reduce this deterioration and facilitate learning and retention.[66]

2. A QUIET ROOM IS NOT ESSENTIAL FOR
   CONCENTRATION.

For eliminating distractions, *where* you study makes little difference. *How* you study and how you approach studying are crucial. In Chapters 4 and 5 the elimination of distraction is considered in detail. For now you might note merely this: *Any* room will be free of distractions when you develop enthusiasm for learning and break up emotional habits such as fear and resentment. Otherwise, *no* room (regardless of how quiet it may be) will be free of distractions.

3. KEEP PICTURES OF FAVORITE PEOPLE AWAY FROM YOUR DESK.

When such pictures are present, either they distract you or else you become negatively adapted to them. That is, you learn to ignore them.

Negative adaptation is fairly simple to acquire. But do you want to, in this case? Do you want to become indifferent to even the pictured sight of your favorite person? Probably you do not. Yet neither do you want such pictures to catch your attention and arouse thoughts unrelated to what you are studying. The solution is obvious: Simply do not have those pictures around your study desk.

4. HAVE THE TOOLS OF YOUR PROFESSION HANDY.

Just as a doctor has an office equipped with the tools of his profession, so also you will find it convenient to have an "office" equipped with the tools of yours. Some of the most useful tools to have within reach are these: dictionary, pen, ink, pencils, eraser, notebooks, pad for miscellaneous notes, and textbooks.

When getting your supplies, do not omit that last item — textbooks. Many of us are in narrow financial straits. However, in view of the immense amounts of time, money and energy we invest in going to college, failure to buy the texts is an unwise economy. Purchase of texts is an investment that pays large dividends — both in terms of getting educated and in terms of getting grades.

At the end of the term, consider keeping your textbooks rather than turning them in for a rebate. They make extremely handy reference books during the years to come. Of all the books in that field, the one you used as a text is probably the one you know best — and therefore one of the ones you can use most effectively. To a remarkable degree

you know what is in it and what is not; you know where
various facts and charts are to be found in it; you are familiar with and at home with the style of writing; you are
peculiarly adept in using it. When subsequent questions
arise, you can use your old textbooks quickly and effectively
as an aid in answering the questions. In addition, when you
save your textbook, you save your marginal notes. Marginal
notes are valuable (at least to the writer). Even when you do
not save your texts, your notes aid learning and reviewing.
However, when you know you are going to keep your books,
you can make marginal notes such that the book becomes of
yet greater use to you—both at the time and in later years:
notes such as "but in contrast see page 22," or "examples
given on page 14," notes indicating cross-references or
making tie-ins with other courses, notes of questions you
have, indications of things you wish to check upon, passages
marked which you especially wish to be able to find again,
ideas of your own extending what is written. Such notes can
be invaluable.

5. Use sufficient and even lighting.

For maintaining clear vision, daylight is best. Almost its
equal is indirect lighting from an I.E.S. lamp. Light which
shines directly from the bulb onto your books is an extremely
poor substitute.[91, 280] After working two hours under a direct light, the loss in clear vision is almost four times as great
as with indirect light. After three hours, the loss is about
nine times as great. In fact, three hours of work under a
direct light has brought an average loss of 81% in clear
vision.[91]

Have ample light. A minimum intensity for studying is
three foot-candles. (That is the amount of light about four

feet below a 50-watt bulb in an ordinary lamp.) Light intensities greater than this are better. Intensities even up to 15 or 20 foot-candles are fine. They significantly increase visual acuity[239, 255, 257, 259] and decrease the tension and fatigue developed during reading.[18, 91] Avoid, however, having the light excessively bright (e.g., 200 foot-candles), as this too can cause decrements in speed of reading.[258]

You can further reduce eyestrain and increase visual acuity by lighting the page evenly, so no shadows are cast on it by your hand or by any other object. Also, arrange the light so it does not glare on your paper nor shine in your eyes. The situation is similar to that in night driving. Headlights from oncoming cars cast far more light on the road than do your lights alone, but often you see less well. When headlights shine into your eyes, you may be unable to see the road at all—despite the additional light now falling on the road. Lights glaring on your paper or shining in your eyes while reading have a similar effect, decreasing greatly your visual acuity.

For similar reasons, try to light the entire room as evenly as possible, with no marked differences between the desk area and other parts of the room. *Even* illumination and freedom from glare are as important as lighting of proper intensity.[253, 254]

A new kind of bulb remarkably free from glare is the tungsten "soft-white." It gives an even, diffuse light which reduces eyestrain and general physiological stress.

Fluorescent lighting is a delight to some people, cool and effective.[173] However, fluorescent lights have a flicker some people detect and find exhausting.[280] In fact some people detect flicker of a rate far faster than that from fluorescent lights.[167] If you tire quickly when working under fluorescents,[280] try shifting to daylight or lamps with incandescent bulbs. This may reduce the burdens on you to an amazing degree.

Eyestrain also can be eased by wearing glasses, when needed. Not always does one realize when he needs glasses, so a check on one's eyes by an oculist or ophthalmologist is worthwhile if the eyes often become strained or weary from even small amounts of reading.

6. AVOID CONSIDERABLE MUSCULAR RELAXATION.

Most people should study at a desk using a chair not of the lounging type. Experimenters have demonstrated repeatedly that slight amounts of muscular tension generally lead to increased efficiency and accuracy in mental work.

For example, when people gently but firmly squeezed a hand dynamometer (an instrument designed to measure strength of grip), they learned lists of nonsense syllables in fewer trials. They also had better recall after three hours than people who had learned the lists without this slight added muscular tension.[28] Similar results have been found for solving simple arithmetic problems,[28, 29] and learning to recognize various visual forms.[242]

Do not conclude that the greater the tension the better. You probably have observed that one can be too "keyed up" and too tense for effective learning. This observation is borne out by the experimental literature: It is small amounts of tension which facilitate learning.[1, 28, 29, 62] Note also that it is tension of the skeletal muscles which is beneficial, not tensions of the anxiety or fear type.[27, 57]

7. UNDER MOST CIRCUMSTANCES, STUDY ALONE; UNDER SOME CONDITIONS, STUDY WITH SOMEONE ELSE.

Studying independently is generally more effective than studying with a companion.[279]

However, in four special circumstances, another person may be helpful. (1) If both of you have already mastered the material very well, quizzing each other may be more effective than self-quizzing only. (2) If the material is so difficult you cannot figure it out alone, collaboration with some other student may be profitable. (3) Similarly, for review and final polish, a small study group of four to eight persons meeting on the days before examinations can be mutually helpful. Syntheses one person has made, another may not have been able to make. Examples and implications one person has worked out may have caused another to stumble. Questions troubling you, some other student in your group may be able to answer; and you may be able to help him on matters clear to you but troublesome to him. Here again, for this to work well, you each must have studied in advance and have gained respectable mastery of the subject. (4) If you feel isolated and desolate when alone, having a partner who works quietly and without interruptions (if you can find such a person) can reduce anxiety and conflict.

D. Deciding When to Study

1. MATERIALS REVIEWED JUST BEFORE SLEEP ARE REMEMBERED BETTER.

Material learned just before going to sleep often is remembered better than material learned at other times — if it is learned.[138, 177, 207, 266, 267] The "if" complicates matters, since many people learn more slowly just before going to bed than they do earlier in the day.[177] This poses a dilemma.

You can, however, take advantage of both facts: *Learn*

the material early in the day, when acquiring new information and the execution of complex skills are done more efficiently. Then *review* it just before going to bed.

Reviewing just before you go to sleep seems most efficacious for retaining details not previously integrated well. An enlightening study by Newman illustrates and clarifies the point.[207] The subjects of this study read three stories and reported them eight hours later. In some cases, the eight hours were spent asleep; in other cases, they were spent awake. The average amounts of retention after eight hours sleeping vs. eight hours waking were practically the same for those parts of the stories essential to the broad outlines of the plot. (For those parts, 87% was retained after eight hours asleep compared to 86% after eight hours waking.) Very different results were obtained, however, for the details which few students would be apt to integrate either with the rest of the story or with anything else. For such fragmentary material, more than twice as much was retained on an average after eight hours asleep than after eight hours awake (47% and 23% respectively).

The superiority of retention during sleep may be even more pronounced for nonsense syllables than for details of stories.[138, 177] In one experiment the students recalled about six times as many syllables after eight hours of sleep as after eight hours awake (56% and 9% respectively).[138] Incidentally, almost all of the forgetting that occurred during sleep took place in the first two hours.*

---

*In this last study, only two subjects were used (both seniors in college). However, the study is worth our attention, since the results for the two subjects are nearly identical and the differences are very large in the amount of retention after time spent in sleep compared to time spent awake.

2. REVIEWING IMMEDIATELY AFTER CLASS HELPS CONSOLIDATE LEARNING.

In Sones' suggestive investigation,[243] one group of students had no immediate review after the class meeting; another group had a five-minute review test at the end of the session. This difference in procedure seems minor, but six weeks later the "immediate test review" group recalled one and a half times as much material as the non-review group— a significant difference in retention.

Other data likewise suggest the efficacy of reviewing class notes either just after or just before the class meeting. If you have a class break and a free hour, you can use it effectively. But even the ten minutes between classes affords excellent opportunity for review or preview.

3. PROPER SPACING OF STUDY PERIODS FACILITATES EFFECTIVE WORK.

In any learning situation you can bunch together your practice or learning trials. This procedure is called massed or undistributed practice. Or you can make each practice period shorter and spread the same total amount of study over a relatively longer period of time. This procedure is called spaced or distributed practice. Although the problems of massed vs. distributed practice are extremely complex, a study of some of the experimental literature will clarify the pertinent considerations.

a) *For rote memorizing and for the acquisition of many motor skills, spaced practice is distinctly superior to massed practice.*

For example, various individuals each were given two hours in which to learn a code.[249] They had the time distributed differently: The first group had twelve 10-minute periods; the second group, three 40-minute periods; and the third group, one 2-hour period. The efficiency with which they mastered the code varied greatly depending upon the way in which the study time was distributed: the longer the study period, the slower the learning of the code. Figure 1 clarifies this point and others as well.

In other experiments too, distributed practice has facilitated learning code substitutions,[101, 121, 175] as well as learning mazes,[53] mirror-drawing and mirror-reading,[103, 175] some other tasks involving new hand-eye coordinations,[2, 175] and lists of numbers and nonsense syllables.[128, 129, 175, 181, 262] This advantage of distributed trials over massed practice is

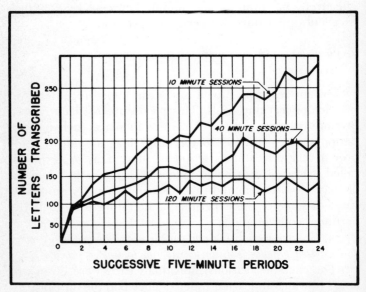

Figure 1. Advantage of relatively short practice periods in learning to transcribe a code. (From data presented by D. Starch, J. Educ. Psychol., *3*:212, 1912.)

greater for longer lists of material than for shorter lists.[130, 180]

Although study periods as short as ten minutes can be extremely effective and can be even more effective than longer study periods, it is possible to make learning periods too short. This is what you would expect on logical grounds and this is what has been found experimentally. For example, ten minutes of practice once a day was superior to five minutes twice a day, for mastering problems similar to code-learning.[68]

So far we have examined the relative facility with which learning is achieved by distributed practice as contrasted with massed practice. Let us look now at the degree of retention achieved.

b) *For lists of numbers, words, and nonsense syllables, for codes, mazes, and some manual skills, distributed practice generally results in higher retention than does massed practice.*[47, 94, 195, 210]

For example,[210] four groups of students tried to learn and remember a list of seven pairs of nonsense syllables. They were given 1, 2, 4, or 8 presentations of the list per practice period, until each student had been given a total of 16 presentations. Two weeks later they were tested for recall of the syllables. The greater the number of times the list was presented per practice period, the poorer was average retention.

Evidence of the same phenomenon from another experiment[47] is shown in Figure 2. Distributing the same amount of practice over more study periods resulted in better retention of nonsense lists.

Some of your studying is probably much like memorizing lists of nonsense syllables. You have a bunch of nearly meaningless, isolated globs of information which you need to remember. For such work especially, do not drive

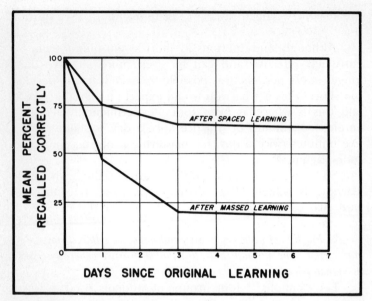

Figure 2. Retention of nonsense syllables memorized by spaced trials and by massed trials. Retention tests were given 1, 3, and 7 days after the original learning. (After L. F. Cain and R. Willey, J. Exper. Psychol., 25:211, 1939; courtesy of the American Psychological Association.)

yourself to study for long periods. Instead, study such material intensively for 10 or 15 minutes. You probably will be pleasantly surprised to discover how much you can learn when you use a lot of short study periods rather than one long unbroken period for such assignments.

Let us summarize two implications of the above data: (1) Extremely short periods of time can be utilized effectively in study—e.g., the ten minutes between classes. (2) For rote memorization and for some other activities, these short study periods actually are superior to long unbroken stretches—both in terms of speed of learning and extent of retention.

None of the foregoing means that short study periods are the only effective way to study. When school work is to you not like memorizing nonsense syllables, when you enjoy the studying and are doing it because you want to and not as a slave who "has to," you can study extremely well for even very long times. Nothing in the experimental literature suggests that short study periods are superior to long study periods for such a person.

c) *In some situations, massed practice is superior to distributed practice.*

A considerable massing of trials is desirable, for example, in writing a term paper, outlining a talk, deriving the implications of sets of data, or working out basic principles implicit in readings. In short: Massed practice is preferable when the learner is deriving and organizing relationships for himself.[60, 61, 101] After the main insights and understanding of relationships are attained, the superiority of massed trials tends to disappear.[60, 61, 64] Even here you can have too much massing; you need time to rest and periods of incubation in creative work.[95]

4. STOP STUDYING WHEN YOUR ATTENTION PERSISTENTLY WANDERS.

People differ greatly in how long they can work without getting bored or inattentive. This must be considered when determining the proper distribution of one's study time.

Regardless of how long you have or have not been studying, if you *repeatedly* come to the bottom of a page with little notion of what it said, you would be wise to stop studying.

Whenever you do not stop at those times, you are not merely *failing to learn* the information and habits you value;

you actually are learning an inability to concentrate. While you are daydreaming at your desk, the sight of your textbook, the stimuli from sitting at your desk, all the other stimuli present at that time, are becoming cues not for study but for daydreaming.

Suppose you persist in "studying" when what you actually are doing is merely daydreaming or feeling bored. Soon you will not need to study for an hour or two, nor become fatigued, in order for those responses to be evoked. The stimuli from merely sitting down with a textbook (even though you now are refreshed) will elicit feelings of boredom and thoughts of other action. You may even reach the point where merely entering your study room evokes those responses. Some of you probably have had this happen to you — much to your consternation and despair.

In general,[3, 113, 114, 142, 153, 196, 236, 268-270] whatever patterns of stimuli are present while some response is underway become cues for that response. Later, any of these stimuli will tend to elicit that response. The phenomena sketched above illustrate, rather poignantly, that highly important principle. You actually can learn to be unable to study! Sitting with a textbook before you while daydreaming or half-asleep is a fine way to learn that inability; and learned it will be under those circumstances — albeit you heartily dislike the habit.

Here is a system whereby you can avoid learning that habit. (1) When not concentrating, stop studying. (2) Review the sort of person you are trying to become, the particular habits and skills you are trying to learn. (3) Review also the various ways for better achieving your ends. (4) Select a few of them to practice during your next study session. (5) Then do something else for a few minutes — listen to a record, wash a pair of stockings, rearrange some furniture, do anything which requires five minutes or so and is different from the activities involved in studying. (6) Then return to your studies, and start out practicing a few of the suggestions you just reviewed. Throw yourself into the studying. Begin, at least, with all the enthusiasm and fire at your disposal.

No matter how low you rate your abilities to concentrate, even you believe you can concentrate for five minutes. Do so. If you cannot concentrate longer than that, stop at the end of five minutes—for a few minutes. Repeat the process sketched in the paragraph above, stopping whenever you find yourself daydreaming. Before long, if you are free from the disrupting emotional habits discussed later, you will be studying for 15 minutes (really studying); then 20, then 30. Eventually you will join the happy group who can study for several hours with verve and profit. And you will love it. Studying will become one of the most exhilarating and exciting games you ever discovered. You may even wonder why concentration once was so difficult. The system is worth trying, don't you think?

5. STUDYING THE NIGHT BEFORE A TEST HAS GRAVE DISADVANTAGES.

Of all the times for study, the night before a test is one of the least efficient. If that is the time you do most of your studying, it is probably *the* least efficient time for you.

Several factors make this practice undesirable.

a) Studying the night before a test results in a massing of "trials" which is highly inefficient. (See pages 43-47.)

b) During marked anxiety or rage, complex mental processes such as thinking and reasoning are impaired.[21, 120, 162, 185, 194, 224, 228, 229, 235, 245, 276]

As you and I both know, many students are terribly anxious the night before a test, far more anxious than usual. This means that on that particular night, those students will think less clearly than usual. And yet at just that inauspicious time, they attempt to study. This is pathetically inefficient.

During anxiety-ridden states it is practically futile to try to ascertain fundamental principles, or acquire an ability to see the implications of various facts, or get new integrated pictures, or build skill in seeing what leads to what, or do anything else toward becoming an educated person. All of those activities demand a feeling of leisure, a sense of security, and an intellectual playfulness wholly incompatible with pre-examination haste and semi-panic. If learned at all, they must be learned at times other than the night before a test.

Even your ability to memorize is impaired by marked anxiety. Studying the night before a big exam (if you are seriously unprepared before beginning that session) costs far more time for poorer results than can be accomplished during other hours.

Anxiety is particularly great, of course, when you have done but little studying previous to the eleventh hour. This means that the less you have done before the night preceding the test, the less you can accomplish on that evening. Nonetheless, we sometimes try to do the bulk of our studying at those unfavorable times. Small wonder we become discouraged and distrustful of our capabilities.

c) The skills of studying wholeheartedly and with concentration tend to be broken up by last-minute cramming, for worry is a potent distractor and is incompatible with enthusiastic enjoyment. After the test, therefore, you will have suffered a setback in developing the skills of effective study.

d) For some people, the mere *sight* of a textbook arouses anxiety. Have you wondered how this came about? Worried cramming is one way the habit is learned. Whenever you study with anxiety, all aspects of that study situation tend to become cues for anxiety. If you do most of your studying during pre-examination apprehensive states, you will reach the point where test *or no test,* just picking up a text, just the sight of a text, even the thoughts of studying, will send you off into a state of apprehension or a sort of gloom.

e) Doing most of your studying the night before a test has another grave drawback: It precludes learning to study independently of threats. It also precludes learning to study for intrinsic rewards such as the joy of discovering more about the nature of the world. Those delightsome habits can be developed only if you study in situations relatively devoid of threats.

f) In short, frantic last-minute cramming is ineffectual: It affords almost no opportunities for becoming educated. It furnishes relatively poor preparation for tests. It seriously impairs your skill in studying at other times. And ultimately it ruins what could have become an exciting, satisfying endeavor.

The foregoing does not mean that you should do no reviewing, or that you should never review the night before a test. *If* you have studied well previously, and if you are free of undue emotional stress (which you may well be when you already have pretty thoroughly mastered the material), no harm inheres in studying the night before a test. Under those circumstances, it can be a benefit. Reviewing, when it is calm re-viewing, is known to be helpful.[80]

E. Starting Study—Some Ways to Avoid Long Warming-Up Periods

Many students take a long time to get "warmed up." They may even spend the major part of their study period simply trying to get started. This is not due to some innate characteristic. Though you may be like that now, nothing compels you to remain that way. You need not go on wasting half your time getting into the swing. You can learn how to sit down, immediately become engrossed in what you are doing, and study effectively. Here are some hints to help you develop those skills.

1. BEFORE SITTING DOWN AT YOUR DESK, DECIDE WHETHER OR NOT YOU ARE GOING TO STUDY.

Attempting two tasks at once can impair performance.[16, 35, 37, 172] Most of us know this; yet we are prone to ignore it. For example, we neglect to decide whether or not we are going to study, what we are going to study and for how long, and whether we are going to continue under various circumstances; we then undertake making these decisions simultaneously with endeavoring to study. This introduces needless wear and tear.

Before trying to study, ideally before even getting out your books, decide whether you are going to study or do something else. Ask yourself: Am I going to telephone someone? If anyone suggests going somewhere during the next hour, am I going to accept the invitation? Or am I going to study? Really decide these matters. Failing to do this causes much difficulty in studying and prevents concentration.

Do you ever sit down at your desk and find something like this happening? "I wonder if I should go to the movies tonight with Charlie? No, I'd better study. . . . But Charlie sure is a swell guy. . . . It's an awfully long time since I saw him. . . . Need to study. . . . Maybe I ought to go and pick him up and catch that show. . . . No, I'd better not. . . . Gosh! I haven't got my clothes pressed for tomorrow. . . . Guess I'd better do that now. . . . No, I'll finish this first. . . . Might forget them again, though. Better do it now, No! I *have* to study and I'm not getting anything done. . . . But still. . . ." And so it goes. During the time represented by the dots, you try to study. Simultaneously you try to decide *whether* to study. Those attempted responses are wholly incompatible.

Clearly one must make these decisions—or have them continue to hound one. Clearly too, it is simpler, and more efficient, to make these decisions *before* rather than *during* the studying.

In deciding whether to study, the crucial point is this: What do *you* prefer doing at this time—everything considered? Whether you study or not is up to you. To no one else does it matter nearly as much as to you. Studying is not an imposed task, but a privilege—a privilege you may or may not want to exercise at some particular time. There is a choice, and the choice is yours.

2. BEFORE BEGINNING STUDY, DECIDE WHAT YOU ARE
   GOING TO STUDY AND FOR HOW LONG.

Your decision of how long to study may be made either in terms of time (e.g., studying mathematics one hour) or in terms of activities to be completed (e.g., solving twelve problems). The second system frees you from having to watch a clock and generally results in less time being needed to accomplish the same amount of work.

Too often we neglect to make these decisions. We say in

an off-hand fashion, "Guess I'll do some math now," and then keep wondering if maybe we ought to be studying something else instead. This is one reason we become so tired studying. We are in an almost constant state of conflict and indecision, tearing against ourself.

Weariness and inefficiency can be reduced if you take a bit more time before beginning study to make the necessary decisions. Weigh at that time the various relevant considerations; reach a clear-cut decision as to what you are going to do; then make it a habit to adhere to your decision.

Postponing decisions does not reduce their number; it simply increases their difficulty. The number of decisions can be reduced, of course, by setting definite hours for study and by devising an order for studying subjects, studying them always in that same order except when unusual considerations make changes advisable.

3. AFTER DECIDING WHAT YOU INTEND TO DO, SIT DOWN
   AND THROW YOURSELF INTO THE PROJECT
   ENERGETICALLY.

When you truly decide to study, sit down at your desk as if you meant business; open your books and begin. Throw yourself into studying heart and soul. If you cannot begin with genuine enthusiasm and wholehearted endeavor, begin anyway with as much earnestness and intentness as you can muster. To the best of your ability, act *as though* you felt wholeheartedly enthusiastic. Paradoxical though this sounds, simply going through the motions of intently studying facilitates intently studying.

4. ARRANGE YOUR STUDYING SO YOU START WITH SOME
   PARTICULARLY EASY OR INTERESTING ASPECT.

For example, if you are working on a term paper, start with correcting spelling. If you are studying a text, start with a self-quiz over the earlier sections. You can learn to start studying with less dread, if you customarily stop where the task is particularly easy and seldom stop at an especially difficult stage. Then begin with that easy part the next time you study. You need not keep this up forever. When you become skilled at studying, you can start effectively with anything.

5. PREPARE FOR THE NEXT STUDY PERIOD AS YOU FINISH
   STUDYING EACH SUBJECT.

As you finish studying each subject, write yourself a note of what you plan to do next on that subject. This note will enable you to begin more smoothly when you later return to the subject. For best results, your note should be very definite. It should be more definite than "Start with page such and such," though that is better than nothing.

Try notes such as these: "Chapter 21 — See if remember underscored parts with section headings as clues." "Term paper — check spelling, punctuation, and grammar of parts completed; fill in outline for next parts to be written." Or for a text assignment, formulate the main questions you hope to partially answer from the next sections and make a written note of these questions.

Such analyses can be made in a few minutes, or even seconds, at the end of studying; whereas they may take half an hour or more at the beginning of the next study period. That half hour is squandered needlessly.

Such notes help get you off to a fine start when you return to your study; you know exactly what you are going to do and can start doing it immediately. When you combine this technique with the others presented in this section, you will have virtually eliminated the "warming up" period.

F. The Use of Books for Becoming Educated

1. READING BOOKS AS MOST PEOPLE READ NEWSPAPERS RESULTS IN LITTLE GAIN.

Do you read texts in much the same casual way you read newspapers? If you have read the newspaper today, this little experiment might be enlightening. Ask yourself what was in the paper; then notice closely what happens. Do you start to tell of some event, but slip over almost all of the facts?

"Someone said something about some senator who did something wrong." That is what one person remembered from the morning newspaper. What had the senator reputedly done? Who was the senator? Are you reasonably sure it was a senator? Who said he had done "it"? Under what conditions was the accusation made? These questions drew blanks. "I'm not much good at details," my informant said, "only at remembering the general idea." But did he have the "general idea" even? Or did he have merely vague impressions and remnants of an emotional tone? To have an accurate "general idea," we must remember precisely at least some of the pertinent details. Details give the idea meaning.

If we read texts and newspapers in similar ways, we should expect similar results. If anything, our impressions from the textbook will be even more incomplete and inaccurate than from the newspaper, for textbooks present many more complicated relationships. How can the results of our reading be any more useful than the "somebody said some senator did something wrong" memory?

2. HOW OFTEN YOU READ SOMETHING IS IMMATERIAL; HOW YOU READ IT IS CRUCIAL.

Often we just plow through pages, over and over again. Sometimes we combine this re-reading with desultory (or else frantic) attempts to memorize certain scattered details. We mark a few sentences and read them ten or twenty additional times. When quite clever at this, we sometimes can spot on a test certain sentences which look like something we have seen before and can spot other sentences which do not. At best we can answer a few true-false items correctly, provided the items are of the superficial recognition type. Is *this* something you care about tremendously?

It is quite possible for us to re-re-read a text in these ways and still fail to learn anything we value. We even can fail to learn anything that helps on an examination. How many times have you heard this bewildered cry? "I read the book four times! And I flunked the test! It's not fair." Often to this anguished accusation is appended: "And Doug only read it *once,* but *he* got an A!"

Some such reports undoubtedly are correct. How often one reads something makes little difference in the outcome. A person *could* walk through the Louvre one hundred times and still learn almost nothing about the pictures there — he could have gained little understanding of various uses of color, or combinations of forms, or placement of figures to achieve various effects; he could have negligibly increased his appreciation of beauty and his awareness of it. You can imagine circumstances under which this would happen. How many times the person walks through the museum is relatively insignificant. The crucial matter is this: What did he do while there?

As with art exhibits, so it is with books. *Not how often* you read a book, *but how* you read it is the major determinant of the outcome.

How can you read with greater retention and other satisfying results? The secret is this: Practice the habits you wish to make skills. In reading, as in all of life, do what you want to learn. Dewey made this suggestion and it is a wise one, for whatever you actually do, you learn. Moreover, you learn *only* what you actually do. These propositions afford basic clues on how to read effectively. More specific suggestions are presented below.

3. READ IN THE WAY YOU CONVERSE WITH AN ESTEEMED FRIEND.

Some people approach books with a bored lethargy verging on contempt. Instead of doing that, start with an intent to make the very most you can from whatever you read. Treat the author as you do your friends.

When talking with a friend, you listen attentively and eagerly. You watch for contributions of value and are sensitive to them. You actively respond to his ideas with ones of your own. Together you build new syntheses.

You can read with similar expectations and results. Expect the author to present facts you had not known before, to offer ideas of which you had not thought, to give new slants on old problems and to formulate new problems. When alert to these things, you will see them. Reading then becomes refreshing fun, and stimulating.

As with your friend, supplement what the author presents with your own ideas and facts. Ask questions of him, and look for clues to the answers.[216] Make as many tie-ins as you can among the parts of what you are learning, and between what you already know and what you are learning.[82, 105, 170, 199, 213, 263, 264] Try to reconcile differences and build new syntheses.[50, 133] In short, each time you study, practice collaborating with the author.

See authors as your friends, joyful and eager to share with you their thinking and observations. They worked long hours to make this sharing possible, so that you could know worlds you otherwise might not meet. When you regard authors in this light, reading is transformed. Books become fascinating. All reading becomes an occasion of new growth and learning.

4. READ WITH A ZEST TO FIND OUT MORE ABOUT THE
   WORLD IN WHICH YOU LIVE AND TO FIND PARTIAL
   ANSWERS TO YOUR QUESTIONS.[7, 50, 133, 140, 168]

In the preceding section, a new way of reading was offered to you. This section presents one special application of those principles.

Have you ever asked a colleague studying, what he was doing? If you have, he probably made some such reply as this: "I'm doing psych." Another student, also studying a psychology text, might say: I'm discovering how we see colors." Or, "I'm getting new information on what happens when we use ridicule to try to improve behavior." Perhaps your colleague is "doing anthropology." He could have replied, "I'm finding various conditions which lead the Zuni Indians to become marvelously cooperative and the conditions which lead some other groups to be fiercely aggressive and competitive." Or, "I'm being introduced to a new culture — and learning how radically different 'human nature' is when the individual lives in a different social context." Instead of "doing philosophy," one could be "finding out what two rather brilliant thinkers conceive to be the ideal state."

The differences in these words are small. The differences in the reflected activities are large. Does the "studying" of the first person have anything in common with the "studying" of the second? Not much, we surmise, beyond such insignificant resemblances as sitting at a desk, looking at a book, turning pages.

Will there be much similarity in what these two persons *become* as a consequence of studying? Since what they are actually doing differs greatly, the results also will differ greatly. The habits they learn, the skills they develop, the information they acquire, will be scarcely comparable.

Try studying with the second outlook and organization — that of an explorer seeking to learn and understand. If you try out this new system of studying, you probably will find yourself learning much more while expending less time. You may even discover that studying can be a joy.

5. THINK — DO NOT MERELY MEMORIZE OR
   REHEARSE.[38, 50, 133, 140, 226]

What is meant by thinking? In large part, thinking is comprised of these skills: adroitly finding implications of facts and principles, seeing the concepts and principles which underlie and are implicit in various materials, discovering for yourself new relationships.

You can develop those skills while reading. Here are some ways you can do that, and thus read with more retention and greater edification.

a) Before reading the body of the text, read the pertinent parts of the table of contents or the main headings of the chapter. From these, build a framework within which to place the facts and ideas presented in that chapter.

b) As you read, make some sort of written or mental outline. Written outlines have the merit of getting the main framework on a page or two where you can see it as a whole. However, any kind of outline will help bring out the nature of the total picture as well as clarify how the details fit together. Incidentally, your outline need not follow the author's organization, if some other organization is more meaningful to you.

c) While reading, establish logical connections between

all facts or ideas presented in the text and the facts and ideas already at your command from previous courses or observations in your daily world.

Formulate underlying principles — generalizations which can be inferred from and which integrate various facts presented in the text and elsewhere. Apply these principles to diverse problems which occur to you.

Whenever you meet a new concept or principle, note with care any examples given, what they have in common with each other and what about them is different from each other and irrelevant to the categorization. Find also your own examples. Forming new concepts is greatly aided by the study of instances illustrating the concept.[48, 70, 75, 118, 232]

Make abstractions more concrete and meaningful.[105, 219] Look for new examples, illustrations, tie-ins, supporting data, and possibly refuting evidence. Look for them in stories, articles, news reports, anything you read or hear, in drawings and movies, and in your life in general.

Re-interpret your current impressions in terms of the new information and ideas you meet in college. If you are learning anything really worthwhile in school, the world outside should look different to you as a result.

In every way you can devise, apply the results of your study. Tie in what you are studying with the rest of your life. Tie the rest of your life in with what you are studying. These possibilities are, really, the whole point of going to the university and college: to get the knack of living adult life with more skill and grace and wisdom, to become more thoroughly the human being you most want to be.

d) Develop the art of asking yourself questions; then answer them! Do you know how to ask yourself questions? An excellent question is your favorite: "So what?" Be sure, however, not to stop after asking the question; answer it too.

Other questions you can profitably ask are these: If this material is true, then what follows? What can I infer from those facts? To what problems is this information or concept pertinent? How does this accord, or fail to accord, with my current beliefs? If this were the case, how would I behave differently? What ideas would I reformulate? What opinions would I revise? What difference would there be in the way I view various situations? (Pick out specific situations about which to ask this question.) What does this fact or idea mean for a specific point of view? Does it fit? If not, how can the point of view be revised so that the facts and principles do fit? What is the evidence for and against some idea?

Take time to answer each of your questions. Try to answer them yourself before calling upon your friends, or teachers, or others to answer them.

e) In everything you read, try to anticipate what is coming next. When you can repeatedly forecast parts to come, you have become highly skilled in seeing the implications of what you are reading.

Whenever you come to something you did not forecast, see if you now can infer that fact or principle from something else you know. If you cannot do so, be certain to make a visible note of that point, for apparently it is a fundamentally new one to you.

f) After meeting several new facts and concepts, stop reading and draw your own conclusions. Then check on how well these conclusions fit with information presented later.

g) Watch for apparent inconsistencies in the material you study, mark them, and in your leisure try to reconcile these discrepancies.

All of these are ways to understand and remember far better the things you read. They also are ways of learning to think more quickly and more clearly.

6. PRACTICE MAKING INTELLIGENT AND INTELLIGIBLE
   STATEMENTS.

   a) From your reading, make notes in your own words.
If ever you are to be able to talk, or write, or even think
about the matters you now are studying, if you are to use
them in any way different from that of a parakeet, you must
be able to express that material in your own words. It is
logical, therefore, to practice that skill from the start.

   b) Summarize and recite the material to yourself. Make
lists of related facts and rehearse them, silently or
aloud.[46, 142, 190] After each paragraph you read, ask yourself,
"Now what was that all about?" And answer the question as
best you can. If you fail to recall some fact, mark it (e.g., by a
check in the margin) and try to tie it in better with other
material. As you become increasingly skillful in this, you can
read longer and longer sections, finally reading several
pages or even a chapter, before stopping and rehearsing.

   Retention can be facilitated by spending the major part
of your study time rehearsing (as contrasted with straight
reading). In a classic experiment by Gates,[102] the value of
rehearsal is demonstrated vividly. The amount the students
learned (in the same length of time) increased progressively
as the amount of rehearsal increased from zero percent of
the total study time, to 20%, to 40%, to 60%, and even to
80%. As you can see from Figure 3, the gains from frequent
rehearsal *vs.* frequent reading are much greater for
memorizing nonsense syllables than for learning facts in
short biographies. For both kinds of material, however, learning and retention are at least somewhat facilitated by
spending a rather large proportion of time in active
rehearsal.

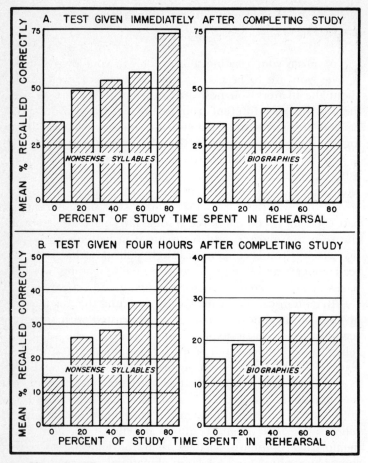

Figure 3. Effects on retention of spending various proportions of study time in rehearsal rather than in silent reading. These data are for eighth-grade children. Substantially the same trends were found for somewhat younger children and for college students. (From data of A. I. Gates, Arch. Psychol., 6, No. 40, 1917.)

7. DEVELOP A MORE ADEQUATE VOCABULARY.[23, 100, 261]

Rare words are used by some people merely to gain prestige; but this is not their only use. When a skilled thinker and careful writer uses some rare word, he usually is attempting to communicate a meaning not expressed adequately by a common word. You miss these meanings whenever you fail to familiarize yourself with the words used.

With any word, knowing its meaning increases your understanding of sentences in which it occurs. With technical words, knowing their meaning is imperative for even a rough understanding of the material presented. You must know these words in order to develop accurate ideas.

A new, enlarged vocabulary can clarify your thinking in other ways also.[139] Less often, for example, will you be obliged to use the same word for different concepts, and thus muddy or even forget differences you at one time saw clearly. You can tack down the differences you perceive, and thus make neater, more precise distinctions in your thinking.[119]

The purpose of words is to enable us to infer from them the meaning of sentences. We know this, of course. Still, we sometimes forget it and go at our job backwards: We try to infer the meaning of words from the "guessed meaning" of the sentence. This is no way to grasp the ideas of any author. Further, that system, and the limited vocabulary which results, virtually preclude being able to read rapidly.

Whenever an unfamiliar word appears, you are stopped abruptly—though you may not be conscious of this. Your eyes jump back to take another look at the strange thing you just met. Obviously, stopping and backtracking slow down reading. If new-to-you words occur often, stopping and backtracking can become a habit. You will automatically go back and re-read phrases even when they do not include unfamiliar words. Thus you lose all chance of becoming a very rapid reader.

Consulting a dictionary takes time. However, you can look up many words in the time wasted in repeated encounters with unfamiliar words. Also, you soon will need to look up fewer and fewer words, and with your new enlarged vocabulary, you will have a new speed in reading and a new comprehension.[4, 67, 116, 117, 134, 161]

Limited in your expression by your limited vocabulary, you say what you can. With a more complete vocabulary, you can communicate your own ideas more adequately. You can say what you mean — not some discouragingly rough and misunderstood approximation. This is a boon in writing term papers, taking examinations, listening to lectures, and in conversation.

One of our modern poets and novelists (Rumer Godden) noted:[26] "If books were Persian carpets, to assess their value one would not look only at the outer side, the pattern and colourings, one would turn them over and examine the stitch, because it is the stitch that makes a carpet wear, gives it its life and bloom. The stitch of a book is its words." A person who has "never explored words, never searched, sifted through his knowledge and memory, his dictionaries, the thesaurus . . . to find the right word, is like someone owning a gold mine who has never mined it, someone living near a mountain who never walks to the top of it to see the view, someone putting his gift into a cage when it might fly free."[26]

8. READ ALL THE HEADINGS.

Students sometimes skip headings, believing them to be extraneous material or intended merely as a guide for locating material. Headings, however, are an integral part of the text. They give one an idea of what is coming next, serving as an orientation and making the meanings of the author easier to follow. With some books, skipping the headings will cause one wholly to lose the thread and become utterly unable to comprehend the text. Material which would have been simple becomes enormously difficult.

If you customarily skip headings and cannot break this habit all at once, be sure to try reading the headings first. You may warmly welcome this preview and over-view of the material to be presented, giving a framework into which you can fit the details.

9. Use the graphs, tables, and pictures.

Most of us skip such materials, after noting gleefully that there are fewer pages to read than we had first thought. This is a pity, for graphs and tables can be a great help. They can clarify enormously what some fact means; they can bring out new implications of the fact; they can present clearly some facts difficult or even impossible to state simply in words. When you give them a chance, graphs and tables do remarkable things.

10. Read selectively, varying your speed with the nature of the material.

For most effective use of your time, do not read all materials at the same rate.[34, 51, 133, 165] When reading a novel to get the outline of its plot, you need not dwell long on any sentence. You can learn to skip right along. On the other hand, when reading highly technical work, go more slowly. That kind of material often is highly condensed and you need more time per page to catch the author's meanings. Similarly, practice covering the familiar rapidly, the unfamiliar more slowly.

Bracket, or in some other way note, the important sentences. By "important" sentences we do not mean merely those you believe will be covered on a test. We mean all principles, facts, and concepts which are new to you. Anything you did not infer from other material at your command is new to you and is important.

Subtle dangers lurk here. Caution: Some extremely important matters take only a few words to express. A short sentence, a mere sub-point within the particular framework used, may present a concept enlightening and revolutionary when understood.

Also, the fact that a passage sounds eminently reasonable to you does not mean you already knew what it is presenting. Many students believe that whenever they are saying, "Obviously," "Quite so," or the like, in response to some passage, its contents must be common facts and ideas which they understand thoroughly and can recall easily. This is a mistake. Plausibility does not mean commonness nor does it mean familiarity with the facts or ideas.

Similarly, suppose all of the words look familiar, and the sentences are graceful, easy to read. Do these mean you understand the passage and probably can recall that material accurately? Not at all. What all of these phenomena really mean is this: The author is a skilled writer.

Watch for this. Confusion on these matters can slip up on one and cause havoc.

11. WHEN SOME PASSAGE IS INCOMPREHENSIBLE, RE-READ
     IT IN A NEW WAY.

Sometimes a paragraph makes no sense at all when we first read it. Then we re-read it, in much the same way we read it the first time, and with much the same results. We may read the paragraph over and over, a dozen times or more, and still not understand it. We begin to feel mildly feebleminded. Sometimes we feel like a fool for having tried to understand such difficult material. We may even get so wrought up that the rest of the chapter too is almost wholly incomprehensible.

Instead of that, try this system: When some passage is incomprehensible, re-read it, but not in the same way you first read it. This time stop after each sentence and ask yourself what that sentence means. Usually you will be able to translate the first sentence into something you understand. Then go on to the next sentence. Read it and ask yourself what it means. Often the whole passage becomes clear when tackled in this way, sentence by sentence.

However, if the passage still is unclear, mark it and temporarily skip it. Simply go on to the rest of the chapter, and come back later to the unclear part. Usually when you return with new information at your disposal and a new internal organization, the points no longer are obscure. You may even wonder why they seemed so difficult before. (Incidentally, this same technique works delightfully well with mathematics problems which at first seem impossible to solve.)

Although exceedingly effective, every now and then this system does not help to any appreciable extent—or at least, not sufficiently. If it does not, you might see the professor during an office hour or bring the question up in class. The chances are high that if you had this difficulty after seriously trying to fathom the meaning of the passage, others will have run into similar difficulties. By active participation, and the answer from a classmate or the professor, the likelihood is heightened that this new information will be grasped and retained.

12. DEVELOP SKILL IN THE MECHANICS OF READING.

Not always,[187] but often,[110, 182] scholastic achievement is related to skill in reading. Some people can read 500 words per minute; that is one or two pages in a single minute. Some people can read much faster than that and with high comprehension. How do they do it? In part their ability consists in having developed considerable skill along the lines sketched above; and in part it consists in having developed skill in the mechanics of reading.[107, 168, 274] In contrast to more average readers,[252] the more skillful read by phrases,[107, 117, 169] their eyes progressing along the line in quick even jerks with only a few brief fixation points[157, 169, 256] and virtually no backtracking.[107, 169] They make few if any lip movements.[279]

If you can read 500 words per minute, with high comprehension, probably you already have developed those habits or ones equally effective. If, however, you read slowly, probably you are weak in some or all of them. Some people for example read one letter at a time. When they come to "cat," they sound out c-a-t. Probably you do not do this. You can read a whole word at a time. But perhaps you can read *only* one word at a time.[252] Just as you learned to read a word as a whole, instead of letter by letter, so also you can learn to read a phrase as a whole instead of word by word. This enormously increases reading speed and can increase your comprehension too.

Many universities and colleges have reading laboratories, free to anyone enrolled at the school. The members of these laboratories are outstandingly adept in helping people develop new skills in reading. In a few months, many students have doubled or even tripled their speed of reading, with little or no loss in comprehension.[58, 201, 233, 274]

So also have other adults.[200] For some people, the increase in speed of reading is accompanied by a significant increase in vocabulary and comprehension[197, 241] as well as grade point average.[241] These gains not only were maintained, but in at least one study they had increased after a lapse of 60 weeks with no further formal training.[241] You too can take advantage of these opportunities. No college student need continue to spend ten or fifteen minutes, nor even five minutes, merely reading an ordinary page.

13. CHECK ON POSSIBLE STRUCTURAL DEFECTS IN YOUR EYES.

Difficulties in reading and chronic eyestrain can stem from various defects, such as muscular imbalance, astigmatism, myopia, or hypermetropia.[19, 83, 123, 144]

If your head aches and your eyes ache while you are at the movies or reading love stories, as well as while studying, possibly something is wrong with your eyes. If you have trouble reading for long periods, becoming exhausted or nauseated after a few hours or even less, perhaps you need glasses.

One's eyes change from year to year: Glasses may not be needed at one stage of life and badly needed at another; lenses appropriate one year may not be most appropriate a few years later. Even astigmatism can change from year to year. You can be free of astigmatism and then develop one, or have an astigmatism and then grow free of it. Astigmatisms and other difficulties sometimes go undetected for years. An optometrist or ophthalmologist can tell you whether you are so afflicted and can prescribe corrective lenses.

14. IF READING DIFFICULTIES PERSIST, A CLINICAL
    PSYCHOLOGIST OR OTHER SPECIALIST MAY BE
    OF HELP.

Despite patiently practicing all these suggestions, some
students still cannot read with speed or high comprehension.
Persistent troubles with reading often reflect deep emotional
distress.* Severe emotional distress is extremely difficult to
remedy without assistance. Fortunately you do not need to,
for expert assistance is available. Psychologists and other
specialists in this field can help you resolve these problems
and build new, more satisfying habits.

G. *Profiting More Fully from Lectures*

One way to swiftly communicate patterns of facts, ideas,
and viewpoints is through lectures. During your college
years and subsequent years, you will have the opportunity
to hear experts on many topics; with great good fortune,
on hundreds of topics. Many of these lectures will be wasted.
They will, that is, unless you recognize this danger and strive
to avert it.

How could you make lectures worthwhile? Let us put
the question differently: How could you be changed by a
person's talking to you for an hour? Suppose you already
knew all the facts he presented. Even then you could be
changed: You could be seeing new relationships from the
particular contexts in which he introduces those facts. You
could be getting leads on sources of information. You could
be exploring ideas which had not occurred to you before he
spoke. You could be developing a somewhat different and

*The relationships between various emotions and ability to read have
been studied extensively. Some of the most enlightening of these studies are
listed in the bibliography: Numbers[14, 15, 22, 31, 32, 78, 88, 92, 131, 154, 164, 198, 217, 237, 250]

more comprehensive picture of the world. All of these and more too you could be doing. Sometimes, though, we do none of them and leave the classroom almost unchanged.

Whenever we leave a class-meeting unchanged, we have squandered a bit of life. This section points a way to living that part of your life more fully.

1. LISTENING IS A COMPLEX SKILL.

Listening comprehendingly and retentively is not an innate ability some lucky people have and some do not. As with much else, it does not inevitably materialize merely because we have a capacity for it.[72, 85, 90, 126, 178, 179, 203] Effective listening is a set of intricate skills[72, 151, 271] which, to possess, we must learn and practice and polish. This can be facilitated by various arrangeable conditions.

2. SIT AS NEAR THE FRONT OF THE CLASSROOM AS IS COMFORTABLE FOR YOU.

Ease in concentrating and understanding can be greatly influenced by your position in the classroom. If currently your attention wanders, shift to a different part of the room.

Try sitting near the front. The many inevitable noises are not as distracting there nor do they blur as many words and phrases. You understand the words better and therefore can understand the ideas better.

For many students, sitting near the center of a room has resulted in better learning (as measured by high grades) than sitting near the back of a room or on the aisles.[112] Perhaps the majority feel more secure when surrounded by their colleagues than when on the fringes. However, avoid crowding, if possible. With somewhat scattered seating, rather than shoulder to shoulder seating, listeners can better focus attention on the speaker.[96]

3. BEFORE CLASS BEGINS, GET SET FOR THAT SORT OF
   CLASS.

You do not have to lose the first ten minutes of each class while trying to get organized. You can become oriented toward that class before the hour begins. For example, you can go over your notes from the previous day's meeting just before the class begins. Or you can review the reading assigned for that day. Both of these help you "get in the mood" for that class.

Classes taken at 1:00 or immediately after lunch seem to cause trouble. One is apt to be distracted, particularly disoriented, and sluggish. The blood and oxygen are not zipping to the brain in optimum quantities but going instead to the digestive tract in larger-than-usual proportions.[99] This is fine for digesting lunch, but not much help to thinking. With some students this phenomenon is so pronounced they tend to go to sleep—more so in one o'clocks than usual.

If you are such a student, try eating early in the period available for lunch, eat a light snack, and then eat again after classes are finished. And take special care to spend the last few minutes before class getting prepared for that class. If the course is a difficult one or particularly important to you, postpone lunch.

4. SHOULD YOU TAKE NOTES?

Much needless confusion has resulted from assuming this question has one best answer equally applicable to all lectures. That simply is not the case.

As you know, things classified under the same heading may differ greatly. Golf and bowling are both sports—but not all the activities necessary for skill in one are desirable in the other. Keeping your eye on the ball is fine for golf, but it does not improve bowling. So it is with studies. *You must modify your procedure in accord with the particular course you are taking and the particular skills you are trying to acquire.*

In some courses, taking many notes is virtually imperative; in others, a few notes suffice. When the lecturer repeats the textbook, probably no notes are necessary. That material already is accessible. At the other extreme, when the lecturer presents a host of new facts and ideas, many notes may be necessary in order to deeply understand the material — or even to understand it at all.

In lectures, as in reading, do not be lured by a plausible, graceful presentation into believing you already know and understand the material and so need no notes. "Understanding" the ideas while a skillful lecturer is presenting them is one thing; understanding them when alone is something quite different.

5. To PROFIT FULLY FROM SOME COURSES, MANY NOTES
   ARE ESSENTIAL.

Anything important which is clearly expressed can be remembered by attentively listening to it once — or at least so we seem to believe. The belief is encouraged by some conversations which contain little we had not previously known. The belief is further fortified by radio advertisements, and speeches filled with over-simplifications and repetitions. Such material we can remember, of course, without notes. But not all lectures are like those conversations, advertisements, and speeches.

Would you remember most of the material from a complex book, after reading it once as fast as you could? Such a feat you might deem miraculous. Yet that is what many of us attempt with lectures! We feel strangely disappointed when we do not understand and recall in detail a lecture heard but once. Why do we try to do with lectures what we know cannot be done with books?

There is nothing magical about converting words from visual stimuli into auditory ones. When new-to-you, complex ideas and a wealth of condensed information are presented in a lecture, do not expect to recall the material, far less understand its implications, from hearing it once. Such accomplishments require reviewing and reflective study. In order to have the materials you need for this reviewing and study, take notes on such lectures.

6. MAKE WRITTEN NOTES OF EVERYTHING WHICH STRIKES YOU AS RIDICULOUS, OR WHICH CONFLICTS WITH YOUR PRESENT DESIRES AND BELIEFS.

Material which conflicts with your desires or beliefs is particularly apt to be overlooked, misconstrued, or forgotten. Many experimental data demonstrate that phenomenon.[86, 115, 166, 184, 186, 214, 215]

For example, a large number of college students listened to a 10-minute speech containing facts favorable and other facts unfavorable to a well-known political position.[86] Immediately thereafter, they took an objective test on that material. A questionnaire had shown that some of these students favored the position discussed, and that others were opposed. Both groups remembered best the parts of the speech which fit their own views. The pro-position students answered correctly significantly more questions based on the favorable facts than those based on the antagonistic facts. The anti-position students correctly answered significantly more of the questions based upon the unfavorable portions than upon the favorable portions. Three weeks later the students were given a second test on the speech. By then, their tendency to remember accurately only those facts harmonizing with their beliefs was even more pronounced than it had been immediately after the speech. The implications are obvious.

Deviant ideas or facts (and they may be facts, not opinions) are not only diffcult to remember. They are difficult to understand without thinking about them. Clearly, you cannot think about something unless you can remember it. This behooves us to make careful, detailed notes of anything we do not believe.

7. RECORD AT LEAST SOME OF THE DETAILS OF THE
   LECTURE, AS WELL AS THE "GENERAL IDEA."[136]

The basic ideas are meaningless (even when remembered!) and lack significance except in terms of the details they imply. Jotting down some of the illustrations, for instance, clarifies the main idea and helps fix it in your memory by showing a few of its implications.

Record the details of any experiments given. Again this increases the meaningfulness of the "main" points. Such notes are valuable too if later you wish to pursue the subject further, or get to wondering what sorts of evidence exist for some viewpoint.

8. TRY TO GET THE FRAMEWORK OF THE LECTURE, AS
   WELL AS WHAT YOU CONSTRUE TO BE THE MAIN AND
   MINOR POINTS.

Oftentimes some of the main points are not statements, but are implicit in the particular ways in which the materials are integrated. In other words, the framework itself constitutes, tacitly, many ideas.

This does not mean there is only one way to organize facts. It means more nearly the opposite: There are many ways to organize facts and the organizations themselves have meanings. After class, try integrating the material in new frameworks of your own creation.

9. BE ACCURATE.

In taking condensed notes, do not omit such words as "usually," "sometimes," "very," or "somewhat." Omitting such words changes the basic meaning of the sentence. Avoid also substituting "is" for "tends to be." Such a substitution radically changes the whole sentence and its implications.

Avoid the common mistake of writing the converse in place of the statement actually made. The converse is an interchange of the subject and predicate. For example, suppose the lecturer says: All hostile aggression stems from frustration. Do not write: Frustration always results in hostile aggression. That could be false, while the original statement was true.

When several conditions are listed as being necessary for some specified outcome, be certain to record them all. If the lecturer states that $2 + 5 + 8 = 15$, getting down in one's notes that $2 + 5$ gives 15 is not merely incomplete; it is downright wrong and highly misleading.

Accuracy and completeness are facilitated by using some system of shorthand. You can devise your own system. Use symbols and abbreviations you already know, supplemented by ones of your own creation. For example, abbreviate common words by the first few letters, use contractions, and leave out unnecessary vowels. Use the same abbreviation for the same word each time. Do not bother about writing complete sentences. In taking notes, the trick is to do as little writing as possible while still getting down as many of the facts and principles as possible.

10. JOT DOWN REMINDERS OF QUESTIONS WHICH OCCUR TO YOU DURING CLASS.

Jot down reminders also of any disagreements you may have. During the lecture is not ŏpportune for following up these questions, for almost certainly you would miss hearing some subsequent ideas. But after class, try to answer your questions.

11. WHEN FIRST LEARNING TO TAKE NOTES, MOST PEOPLE HAVE DIFFICULTY IN WRITING AND LISTENING AT THE SAME TIME.

This difficulty does not last forever. With practice of the two skills (note-taking and attentive listening), you can easily do them simultaneously. You can learn this even as many people, after much practice, have learned to knit and converse well at the same time. First practice the two skills separately; then practice them combined.

12. AFTER TAKING NOTES, WHAT SHOULD WE DO WITH THEM?

Rote copying of notes is almost pointless. Reworking notes has great value. Rewrite parts that are legible the next hour, but will be illegible the next day. Fill in gaps. Add points you still remember but did not have time to record during the lecture. These things can best be done shortly after the lecture.

Then, answer the questions you have noted in the margin of your notes. Find examples of the facts and principles presented. Ideally, use your notes in the ways suggested in connection with studying books.

Suppose, after taking notes, you never looked at them. Taking them still would not have been a waste of time. For one thing, you would have started building skill in note-taking, and that skill is indispensable in some situations for fully utilizing the opportunities afforded for becoming educated. In addition, the mere act of writing something enables many people to remember it better—even though they do not look at their notes again.

13. DURING CLASS, BE ACTIVE.

Learning is facilitated immensely by active participation of the learner.[17, 25, 46, 190, 191, 275, 278] Rather than passively sitting, waiting to become educated, be as responsive and attentive as you can be. Listen with the intent to understand and remember the material presented.[25, 238] Do you recall the study by Sones?[243] The heartening results for one group in that study may have been due largely to the students' listening with a greater "intent to remember."

In numerous other ways too, you can be active and growing. You can be developing skill in seeing the meanings of material by looking for examples or other applications of the material presented, by answering aloud or to yourself the questions raised by your teacher or classmates, by comparing other people's answers with your own, by trying to anticipate how the lecturer will develop a point. You can be re-examining old beliefs and looking at your world through new eyes. You can be following the ideas as well as the words of the lecturer. There is much you can do and learn during lectures.

14. BEFORE DEVISING COUNTER-ARGUMENTS, BE CERTAIN YOU UNDERSTAND THE IDEAS BEING PRESENTED— ESPECIALLY IF THEY DIFFER FROM YOUR OWN.

It is these strange, new viewpoints and facts which furnish you with bases for new actions . . . for new interests . . .

for new ways of looking at old problems ... for new conceptions of the world. And these, in turn, are the bases for growth.

You did not enter college hoping to end the same as you began. You hoped to change. So when someone presents a fact or opinion very different from what you believe, note it with care. After class think about it, discuss it with your friends, try to understand it and see in what senses it is true.

When you are sure you understand the material, try to think of counter-arguments. Then see if you can devise some way to make the apparently disparate data fit.

H. *Profiting from Televised Courses*

Many universities and colleges are offering courses through television. Difficulties in obtaining sufficient numbers of professors to keep pace with expanding enrollments make it likely that an increasing number of televised courses will be introduced in the future.

1. TV INSTRUCTION CAN BE HIGHLY EFFECTIVE.

Extensive research has been devoted to the impact of TV instruction. Tests have been made at a variety of colleges and universities throughout the United States, for a variety of students, and with a variety of subject matter.

Tests for grasp of subject matter in psychology, chemistry, economics, composition, physics, literature, mathematics, and various social sciences show that in general the students with TV instruction learn an appreciable amount, doing as well on the average as students with more familiar instructional procedures.[24, 41, 52, 77, 132, 135, 156, 189, 231, 234, 251] Retention also is high—for short-range measures and for long-range.[24, 52, 132, 145, 209, 277] Televised instruction, even when students have had little or no previous opportunity to learn how to profit from such instruction, appears to be as effective for communicating subject matter as the other modes of instruction used for comparison in these studies.

The impacts on attitude and interest are chaotic at the college and university level. Sometimes the students like the TV instruction as well as other instructional procedures,[52, 111, 244] sometimes better,[156, 244] sometimes less well[77, 89, 206]—no clear trend being discernible. For some students, interest in that particular course or even interest in that whole area is heightened during the term with TV; with other students it is impaired relative to the interest engendered through other techniques of instruction. Individual differences are large.

2. Televised courses have special advantages.

The TV lecturer can be one of the most skilled and most informed on campus and, through TV, come in contact with many more students than otherwise would be possible. When TV presentations are taped, guest lecturers can be brought in who otherwise would not be able to address this class. Special film strips can be smoothly incorporated, which otherwise could not be presented at all or presented only clumsily. Displays can be constructed and filmed which would be too unwieldy or too expensive to present to one "live" class only. Various other audio-visual aids can be employed effectively.

Whether these advantages are utilized depends upon the imagination and care of the instructor and also upon the imagination and responsiveness of the students.

3. TELEVISED COURSES ALSO POSE DIFFICULTIES.

The main difficulty from the students' point of view seems to be keeping attention focused upon the lecturer and the subject. What is going on up there on the screen seems terribly remote sometimes and far removed from one's own world. One waits to be "entertained," in accord with habits practiced throughout childhood. One daydreams. One becomes listless and bored.

The techniques suggested for more profitable listening to lectures can all be used to advantage here. (See Section G.) Since with televised instruction there often is no professor to check on how you are doing, or what you are doing, you need to take even more initiative and more responsibility for your education and behavior than is true in more conventional situations. Notable opportunities for growth are afforded if you meet the challenge.

4. THE IMPERSONALITY OF TV CAN BE ALLEVIATED.

With televised instruction especially, students seem to feel that the TV instructor is on another planet, a world removed from theirs with no point of contact. They cannot see and talk with him; he cannot see and really talk with them. They feel isolated.

The sense of isolation is mitigated by remembering that though the TV professor cannot see you, he does know you exist and is talking to you. He has met many hundreds of students, usually, and is addressing all those sorts of individuals. If you resemble any of them, the lecturer will be presenting his lectures partly in terms of you—though he cannot see you. Even if you are rare in your major interests and attributes, he probably will have met someone sometime resembling you. He will be remembering this, trying to slant his lectures in terms of you and your presumed existence. He will be trying to answer at least some of the questions he suspects you have . . . exploring some of the paths he has reason to believe will be new and interesting to you . . . showing you phenomena, and introducing concepts, and communicating facts not likely to be readily available to you elsewhere. He may never have an opportunity to meet you face to face, but he will nonetheless be addressing you and hoping the You he thinks is there really is there.

A large part of the success of this endeavor rests upon your keeping faith in his existence as he keeps faith in yours.

I. Using Special Learning Aids

Various special aids are available for the student having difficulty or the student simply desiring a supplement to the more usual materials and methods of learning. Most notable are teaching machines and programmed texts, the effective development of which was pioneered largely by A. A. Lumsdaine and his associates.

1. TEACHING MACHINES CAN EFFECTIVELY SUPPLEMENT LECTURES.

Teaching machines are special devices which present a series of statements and questions, usually in some special order to facilitate understanding of the material. The student reads the statements and the questions, answers them sequentially (either mentally or more overtly), and then manipulates the machine to reveal the answer and the next question.

These devices have some special assets.[33, 122, 222, 240, 260] Teaching machines respect individual differences in learning rates, the student being able to go through the material at his own preferred pace, rapidly when things are going well, more slowly when matters are obscure or difficult. The machine stops when the student wants to stop and ponder; it proceeds when he wants to proceed. The machine provides also an immediate check on knowledge and understanding; it keeps the learner active and lets him learn by trying his own answers first. Students seem to enjoy using these machines and can employ them effectively to obtain relatively large amounts of information in relatively short amounts of time, with good retention.[54, 56, 97, 148, 158, 222]

However these devices have drawbacks, particularly when used as the sole or primary mode of instruction and study. Some students find them stultifying and frustrating and profit little from their use.[40] The information gained may be very fragmentary, with a loss of integration of ideas, little opportunity or tendency to see relationships between facts, and little transfer of the acquired information or skill to new situations.[98, 208, 248]

2. PROGRAMMED TEXTS ARE AVAILABLE AND USEFUL.

These are similar to teaching machines, except that the material is in book form. These too can be effective aids to learning,[160, 171, 222, 223, 247] but not always.[5, 40, 81, 205] For some people, programmed texts heighten habits only of rote memorizing, discourage thinking, and require more time than ordinary texts for acquiring the same amount of knowledge.[81, 171, 205] If you are looking for some addition to your textbook, either for a review or for a preview introducing you to the material, you might find these a helpful and refreshing supplement.

Here again the questions are presented sequentially, and you can write your answer, think it to yourself, or simply read the answers. All of these methods can work, but writing your answer seems best for difficult material, whereas for relatively easy or already well-understood material, the latter two methods can be used efficiently.[109, 158] When learning new material, answer the question yourself before checking the answer; this is far more effective than simply reading the answer.[20]

3. Tutors are available too.

We often solicit help from our friends. The assistance which tutors offer is similar, but usually more extensive and sometimes more expert.

If you are having especial difficulty with some particular course, or some particular phase of some course, remember skilled assistance is available. One need not, of course, hire a tutor for the entire term, if at all, but only for those aspects elected.

4. Typing is a valuable aid in study, review, and elsewhere.

Many professors require that term papers and various reports be typed. Even when not required, you would be wise to type any report being turned in to a professor. No person's handwriting is as easy to read as neat typing. The added ease in reading enhances communication, and may well enhance also the perceived quality of the work. Things which look messy are apt to be perceived as inferior in other ways too.

Entirely apart from such considerations, typing is handy for your own private purposes. You can take notes on your texts more rapidly and read them more readily. This can save hours. You can make your lecture notes more useful:

Typing up lecture notes affords excellent review and in other ways facilitates learning. For example, with typed material you see more facts at a glance, thus making the material easier to comprehend and easier to remember.

Typed notes are easier to review. In fact, typed notes sometimes are the only kind which can be reviewed. Every student probably has discovered that cold, untyped notes are at least part of the time just barely decipherable, and sometimes are wholly indecipherable. The discovery is jarring when made the night before a test.

Typing preliminary drafts of reports and papers enables you to better evaluate your own work and improve its quality. When material is typed, you more easily can pick up ambiguities, repetitions, incomplete sentences, undeveloped thoughts; you see easily more appropriate organizations, smoother transitions, and other features of importance to your paper's overall worth. Instead of merely having the feeling that something somewhere is radically wrong, you can see precisely what is wrong and fix it. You also can see better what is right and leave it alone.

5. SPECIAL RECORDINGS AND OTHER AIDS ARE AVAILABLE FOR THE BLIND.

An organization called Recordings for the Blind had compiled by 1969 a circulating library of 77,000 books in 16 different languages. These include the book you are reading and textbooks in many diversified fields. The books, taped by expert readers, are circulated free of charge to blind students. Further, the organization will specially record books not already on tape for any blind student at no charge to the student.

The American Foundation for the Blind also provides many materials to blind people without charge.

Another aid is typing. Some blind students do know how to type. An asset for any college student, typing for blind students has special boons. Knowing how to type, you can listen to taped recordings of your textbooks and take your own notes, organized in your own way, while listening to the tape. When reviewing, your notes (rather than the text) can be read to you. This saves time: Having only certain portions of a text re-read obviously is swifter than re-playing the entire tape. But in addition, even if you are only moderately skilled at typing, typing is faster than punching Braille.

J. *Learning Another Language*

1. OTHER LANGUAGES ARE USED, AND SOMETIMES REQUIRED.

Three hundred and twenty million of the people of the world speak English.[63] Seventy-seven million speak French; 120 million speak German; 194 million speak Russian; 580 million speak Mandarin; 240 million, Hindustani; 183 million, Spanish; 5 million, Afrikaans; and one million Esperanto,[63] an interlanguage constructed as an auxiliary language on the roots of words from all the Greco-Latin languages, thus facilitating its learnability. Many many educated persons (and even many millions not educated, by your standards) speak two or more languages. English is a lovely language, but it may well not be enough for your purposes either.

Being able to talk with persons of varying experiences enriches both participants. Being able to read what they have taken the trouble to write makes one more of a human being. Comprehending what they are saying opens the way to better comprehension of the world and more complete understanding. We know too that an increased skill with one language can facilitate learning another language and increase our skill with another language.[6, 146, 218]

Should you desire to learn another language, the task is not as difficult as you might fancy. Especially if you are a good student in other areas, learning a foreign language should go well.[6, 30, 54, 225, 246]

2. A VARIETY OF TECHNIQUES FACILITATE THE PROCESS.

a) Practice labeling the objects around you in the new language.[71] As you sit in your home, glance around the room labeling everything you can. As you walk down the street, list the things you see. Describe them as best you can. Summarize in whatever sentences you can construct, the events you observe.

b) If the language has genders, label objects using the article as well as the noun — taking care to practice this correctly. One sometimes strongly tends to repeat old errors (rather than correct them) as well as to make new errors on successive rehearsals if one does not check his accuracy with the original list.[202]

c) When first starting a new language, you will be helped by making your own vocabulary lists — grouping together similar entities.[49, 76, 155, 191–193, 273] For example, make separate lists for nouns, verbs, adjectives, phrases, idioms, putting the new words in one column and the English "equivalent" in a second column. Visualize the object denoted (or the activity, person, or quality) and label it aloud with your new word.[13, 93, 163] Tie it in with your major interests.[174]

Cover one column and try to reproduce the English; cover the English and try to reproduce the other column.

Going from language 1 to language 2 is a different process from starting with language 2 and going to language 1. If you wish to be skillful in both, practice both.

d) Construct simple sentences depicting some action (e.g., I pick up the book; he sits in the chair). Building sentences helps you remember the component parts.[106, 108] In addition, go through the action depicted by the sentence, or imagine it, while you say the sentence. Such activities while first learning a new language enhance both learning and retention.[10-13, 159] Using this system, adults far exceed children in rapidity of acquiring a language.[13]

e) Whenever you become proficient with some new word or phrase, omit translating it. You not only can but should omit translating word by word as soon as you are able; you thereby save time, learn to think in the new language, and lay the groundwork for swifter, more complete communication in your new language.

When proficient with the entire language, you will not need to translate at all but will simply read and speak and listen to it as you do the language you learned first. In the meantime, though, while you are first learning, it is wise to think the nearest English equivalent as you are reading the new language.

f) If you make little lists of words in your new language and their English equivalents (and vice versa: lists of English and new language equivalents), you can carry these around with you and practice them in moments apt to be lost while waiting — waiting for a friend to turn up, waiting for a lecture to begin, waiting for a subway or trolley or bus, waiting for a dentist or doctor. As mentioned in a prior section, an amazing amount can be learned during these stray moments, and learned delightfully easily and well.

Similarly, you can prop a list near where you do washing

or comb your hair, keep one on the dresser where you can glance at it and practice while dressing, tape one over the sink to practice while doing dishes or fixing meals. The possibilities here are endless.

This is a highly effective way to learn, since spaced practice on this kind of material is far more effective than massed practice. It also is relatively painless—freeing you from spending so many hours at a desk.

g) Your lists should be short for best results. Six or seven words, or even less, work fine and indeed work better than longer lists. This is one of the places in the history of psychology where concordant data are available from the time of the first experiments published on learning (the astounding work of Ebbinghaus),[84] through the many intervening years,[180, 181, 183, 221] to the present time:[55, 108, 191–193] the data show that one learns more items per unit time when the learning is done with short lists than when learning is done with long lists. However, the first-acquired items of a list may be acquired at the same rate, a rate independent of length of list.[55] This suggests an additional technique: When you have all but two or three items learned from a list, begin a new list and add these recalcitrant items to it.

h) A foreign language is the kind of material apt to be retained better when learned just prior to sleep rather than at other times of day.[138, 207, 220, 266, 267] Hence, another handy place to keep some of your lists is by your bed. By reading a list just before retiring, you can practice the vocabulary while falling asleep and learn large parts of it.

You need not limit yourself to vocabulary. Your lists may be of irregular verbs, or conjugations, or infinitives falling into the same conjugation, and so on. Here again, possibilities are wide for a student with ingenuity.

i) Straightening out differences in words (or objects) is easier when they are sitting near each other and are stripped of irrelevancies.[272] When a language has several words all of which look or sound much alike to you but have different meanings, or when the language has one or more words which look or sound like an English word but mean something different from it, make a list of them. Study them so you see clearly exactly wherein they differ.[147] Practice these words with especial care.

j) Notice parallels with your own language, as well as differences.[204] As a starter, note words which are similar to yours and words which are very different, and note exactly what the similarities are and what the differences are.

Note the sounds of your language which do not occur in the new language, and note exceedingly carefully the sounds of the new language which do not occur in yours. These new sounds you will need to practice with special care.

Note similarities of grammar and differences; note similarities of word-order and differences. The meanings of language do not rest solely on vocabulary, but depend heavily on structure too. The importance of structure to meaning is at least dimly apparent to anyone who knows that school music is different from music school, and that the professors of education are not the same as the education of professors. The importance of structure is dismally clear to one who has found the meaning of every word in a sentence of a new language and still not known the meaning of the sentence—a phenomenon disconcertingly common when one fails to understand the structure of the language.

k) Practice conversing with a friend. This is fun, and profitable. If by some lucky chance you know someone from another country who speaks the language you are learning, converse with him in your new language—as best you can.

He will be pleased, quite probably, to hear even a mangled version of his beloved first-learned language. And you, of course, will learn a great deal more than the language.

l) Be active. Especially when first learning an additional language, being active is superior to passivity. The above data imply this, as do others. For example, incidental learning is increased when you make a guess at the meaning of a new-language word, rather than merely read its English equivalent,[25] though when one is intent upon learning, seeing the equivalent and pronouncing it aloud is as good or better.[25] Similarly, practicing the more active art of speaking a new language before being trained in listening exceeds the reverse order, both for acquiring skills in speaking and for acquiring skills in listening comprehension.[149, 150]

m) A general principle runs through the above: Make as many associations as you can between the new label and your old label. The more associations we have to a word or to a nonsense syllable (and most new languages are close to being nonsense syllables), the better our chances of recalling that word or nonsense syllable.[42, 69, 141, 174, 265]

n) Learning a language adapts itself beautifully to spaced practice. While mending your clothes, or brushing your teeth, or waiting for a friend, or walking to classes, or dropping off to sleep, you can practice the new vocabulary and practice building sentences with your new language. The few minutes before dinner is served, the few minutes of ironing, all the stray moments too short to do much of anything else, are long enough to gain added skill in your new language. An astounding skill is attainable this way.

o) For many languages, records are available which aid understanding the spoken language and aid perfecting finer pronunciation. Heightened skill in discriminating sounds helps one produce those sounds.[6, 43]

p) Some universities and colleges have facilities enabling you to record what you say. Studying playbacks of what you yourself have said speeds development of skillfully speaking the new language and more fully understanding it when it is spoken to you.[176]

q) Very recently,[188] an analysis was made of French, setting forth the words most useful in that language. Words were assessed on several bases, including their frequency in everyday speech and writing, the range and number of contexts in which they appeared, and their coverage—i.e., their capacity to replace other words. A list was compiled of the 3,626 words having highest usefulness by these criteria. This could be handy for a person with little time to learn a language.

r) Books are available in both English and another language. Reading in the new language a sentence or paragraph or page, depending upon your skill, and then reading the English translation gives you a mode of checking on your accuracy and progress. It also affords practice with the language in a sensible context, and is far more delightful than many of the more conventional modes of studying. Some translations, as you will discover if you try this technique, are hilarious—even when done by a professional.

s) Reading, speaking, and writing a language are related[9, 79, 124] but somewhat different skills.[6, 8, 36, 39, 59, 74, 79, 125, 127, 149, 225, 230] Practice them all if you wish to attain them all. Being able to read a language, unfortunately does not enable you to write or speak it with grace or precision. Nor will being able to speak a language guarantee your being able to read it. You need experience with each to master each.

t) In what order should these various skills be practiced? No easy answer is available to this question because the individual differences are immense.[9, 212] For some people,[211, 230] and in particular those with low aptitude,[9, 212] hearing the words pronounced and receiving training in the audio skills of listening and speaking before studying printed words is an efficacious way to begin a new language—especially if what one is interested in is acquiring skill in speaking.[230] This should not be continued too long, as the advantage appears to hold primarily or only in the early stages of learning.[9, 212]

For other students,[8, 9, 212, 230] practicing visual learning first and then relearning aurally works better than the reverse procedure. That is, learning the word or phrase first by seeing it, then by hearing it, works out better than learning it first by hearing it only. This is no surprise when one remembers how many years go by of hearing a language daily before a child has a vocabulary of more than a few hundred words and grammar even faintly acceptable to educated adults. For the good student especially, this procedure of seeing the new word and its meaning, then hearing it, is superior.[9, 212] It appears superior also for low ability students who are beyond the initial stages of learning.[212]

The advantage is marked for the reading-writing skills[230] and when the word is not pronounced in the way expected.[212] Greater positive transfer occurs from the visual to the audio skills and also from the audio skills to the visual when one uses visual-then-audio training than occurs with audio-then-visual training.[9]

The most effective system of all, however, may be simultaneously seeing and hearing the new word,[59, 227] rather than having many repeated trials of first one and then the other.

K. *Learning While Not Studying Formally*

1. WHILE NOT AT A DESK NOR IN A CLASSROOM, YOU CAN
    GO FAR TOWARD MASTERING THE SUBJECT MATTER OF
    VARIOUS COURSES.

In a recent experiment, a university course was conducted via telephone. Lectures, panel discussion, questions
and answers, even role playing, all were conducted over a
multiple hook-up telephone. Students have attempted
something along these lines often before; what made this
experiment extraordinary was that this time it was instigated
by professors and was an eminent success. The students
learned a great deal—despite the absence of sight of the
professor and absence of the usual classroom setting.[65]

But it is not only in that type of setting, still rather
formal and structured, that you can learn. You can learn
anywhere.

While waiting for buses or for others to keep appoint-
ments, you can gnash your teeth or bite your nails. Or you
can mull over what you discovered that day in college. You
can integrate what you observe in daily living with what you
learned in the classroom. You can study and rehearse previously prepared lists of facts or vocabularies. As you roam the
world, you can be alert for reflections of the principles you
met in college. You can observe current events and not stop
with the mere observation, but interpret the events in terms
of what you have learned about economics, political science,
history, sociology, anthropology, psychology. Time between
classes, time walking to and from school, other stray moments, all can be used for similar purposes. When you do,
scattered minutes become highly effective times for learning
and reviewing.

Some students have done much of their studying at such times, and with beautiful results. Courses became more interesting because of the many relevancies they found with their life in general. Their grades were high. And years after the final examination was over, they still remembered much of what they learned in school. Further, they had added to that knowledge. What they learned in classes became an integral part of their living.

2. WHILE CARRYING ON DAILY ACTIVITIES, YOU CAN
   PRACTICE AND DEVELOP THE SKILLS WHICH
   COMPRISE BEING EDUCATED.

This begins to be made clear by the above examples. Because of the importance of the matter, however, let us look into it further.

Consider bull sessions. In some you idly chatter; in others you practice the skills of critical thinking.

Critical thinking consists partly in seeing what is wrong about certain arguments. This is the part usually recognized, but it is a small part. Far more important, skill in critical thinking consists also in seeing what is "right" about the argument, in seeing the logical consistencies, the valid implications which can be drawn from the ideas presented, the new syntheses which can be made with the ideas, the new clues afforded for solving various problems. Skilled "critical thinking" is a highly constructive, creative enterprise. You can greatly increase those skills by practicing them during conversations and discussions.

Practice maintaining a tentative attitude with regard to the validity of other people's conclusions, and your own! Be alert for new ideas and new ways of looking at things. Explore the meanings of beliefs, ideas, and hypotheses of all kinds. These activities are the sorts of activities which are a part of and contribute toward skillful thinking and creativity.[104] Conversing in such ways is wonderful fun and also wondrously effective for becoming more nearly an educated person.

In all your interactions with other human beings, you can be developing deeper understanding and sympathy, a new compassion. Every complex skill requires practice; none can be developed *in vacuo.* To gain greater understanding of people, you must practice reacting to people in new ways: You must learn not only that different people have different goals, different value systems, but also learn to recognize clues to these value systems. You must learn what expressions and behavior patterns reflect various emotional states. You must practice responding to more dimensions of the external world, in order to develop habits of being more perceptive. All these you can practice during any of your social interactions, becoming thereby more truly sympathetic.

Understanding is diluted by misconceptions. One of the most pathetic is a notion that people agree with each other primarily to win favor or save face. Even university students are prone to accept this fallacy and seriously overestimate the degree to which verbal agreement stems from a fear of disagreeing.[73, 143] In conversation, reading, public forums, you will come across much new information which can obliterate varied misconceptions. You will be presented thousands of new facts which, if reflected upon and acted upon, greatly enhance understanding of your world and its people.

During concerts, you can practice being alert to the various musical forms, hearing more keenly the contrapuntal themes, appreciating more acutely the development of the piece. Through using what you have learned in your music courses and elsewhere, you can learn to respond with fresh appreciations, and music will gain new richness.

In everything you do, you can practice the habits which comprise being educated. Thus, through the way you meet daily experiences, you will become increasingly educated.

As you recall, being highly educated does not consist merely in possessing great masses of information. It also consists in acting in certain ways and developing certain skills. Being educated is a way of responding to the world.

This means we can become more educated while not formally studying. It means further, we can become more educated *only* if we live in some such ways as those just presented. No one can become educated through classroom activities and formal study periods alone—even when he manages those parts of life with consummate skill. He also must live outside classes and study rooms in ways consonant with the habits he is striving to make part of himself. Being educated is not the result solely of studying. Being educated is a way of living, and the result of living in certain ways.

Bibliography for Chapter 2

1. Adams, J. A. Effect of experimentally induced muscular tension on psychomotor performance. J. Exper. Psychol., 48, 127-130, 1954.
2. Adams, J. A. Psychomotor performance as a function of intertrial rest interval. J. Exper. Psychol., 48, 131-133, 1954.
3. Allen, Max M. Cueing and retrieval in free recall. J. Exper. Psychol., 81, 29-35, 1969.
4. Anderson, C. C. A factorial analysis of reading. Brit. J. Educ. Psychol., 19, 220-221, 1949.
5. Anderson, Richard C.; Faust, Gerald W.; and Roderick, Marianne C. "Overprompting" in programmed instruction. J. Educ. Psychol., 59, 88-93, 1968.

6. Arendt, Jermaine D. Predicting success in foreign language study: A study made in selected Minneapolis schools from 1963 to 1964. Diss. Abstr., 28 (12A), 4869-4870, 1968.

7. Artley, A. Sterl. But—skills are not enough. Education, 70, 542-546, 1959.

8. Asher, J. J. Sensory interrelationships in the automated teaching of foreign languages. Percept. Mot. Skills, 14, 38, 1962.

9. Asher, James J. Vision and audition in language learning. Percept. Mot. Skills, 19, 255-300, 1964.

10. Asher, James J. Toward a neo-field theory of behavior. J. Humanistic Psychol., 4, 85-94, 1964.

11. Asher, James J. The strategy of the total physical response: An application to learning Russian. International Rev. Appl. Linguistics, 3, 291-300, 1965.

12. Asher, James J. The learning strategy of the total physical response: A review. Mod. Lang. J., 50, 79-84, 1966.

13. Asher, James J.; and Price, Ben S. The learning strategy of the total physical response: Some age differences. Child Dev., 38, 1219-1227, 1967.

14. Austin, Mary C. Personal characteristics that retard progress in reading. Suppl. Educ. Monogr., No. 72, 112-117, 1950.

15. Austin, Mary C.; Jones, Daisy M.; Crossen, Helen; and De Vere, Eona. How to develop a classroom environment and climate that insures maximum progress in and through reading. Suppl. Educ. Monogr., No. 72, 92-111, 1950.

16. Baddeley, A. D.; Scott, Denise; Drynan, Rosemary; and Smith, Janet C. Short-term memory and the limited capacity hypothesis. Brit. J. Psychol., 60, 51-55, 1969.

17. Bahrick, Harry P. Discriminative and associative aspects of pictorial paired-associate learning: Acquisition and retention. J. Exper. Psychol., 80, 113-119, 1969.

18. Bálint, Istvan; and Hodos, Tibor. A munkatevekenyseg es a munka-korulmenyek pszichologiai vizsgalata fonouzemben. (Psychological examination of working operations and working conditions in a spinning mill.) Pszichologiai Tanulmanyok, 9, 345-363, 1966.

19. Ball, R. J. Visual functioning in reading disability. Education, 82, 175-178, 1961.

20. Barlow, John A. Note: Student cheating in studying programmed material. Psychol. Rec., 17, 515-516, 1967.

21. Beier, E. G. The effect of induced anxiety on the flexibility of intellectual functioning. Psychol. Monogr., 65, No. 365, v + 26 pp., 1951.

22. Bell, J. E. Emotional factors in the treatment of reading difficulties. J. Consult. Psychol., 9, 125-131, 1945.
23. Bendig, A. W. Comparison of the validity of two temperament scales in predicting college achievement. J. Educ. Res., 51, 605-609, 1958.
24. Benschoter, Reba Patterson; and Charles, Don C. Retention of classroom and television learning. J. Appl. Psychol., 41, 253-256, 1957.
25. Berlyne, D. E.; Carey, S. T.; Lazare, S. A.; Parlow, J.; and Tiberius, R. Effects of prior guessing on intentional and incidental paired-associate learning. J. Verbal Learning Verbal Behav., 7, 750-759, 1968.
26. Best, M. A. Rumer Godden. Book-of-the-Month Club News, page 5, September, 1969.
27. Bevan, William; and Maier, Richard A. Emotional tension and the generality of its effects upon intellectual performance. J. Personality, 26, 330-336, 1958.
28. Bills, A. G. The influence of muscular tension on the efficiency of mental work. Amer. J. Psychol., 38, 227-251, 1927.
29. Bills, A. G.; and Stauffacher, J. C. The influence of voluntarily induced tension on rational problem solving. J. Psychol., 4, 261-271, 1937.
30. Birkmaier, Emma; and Lange, Dale. Foreign language instruction. Rev. Educ. Res., 37, 186-199, 1967.
31. Bixler, R. H. Treatment of a reading problem through non-directive play therapy. J. Consult. Psychol., 9, 105-118, 1945.
32. Blanchard, P. Psychoanalytic contributions to the problems of reading disabilities. Psychoanal. Stud. Child., 2, 163-187, 1946.
33. Blank, Stanley S. Teaching machines: What have studies in the classroom shown? Calif. J. Educ. Res., 12, 99-115, 1961.
34. Blommers, P.; and Lindquist, E. F. Rate of comprehension and reading: Its measurement and its relation to comprehension. J. Educ. Psychol., 35, 449-473, 1944.
35. Boggs, David H.; and Simon, J. Richard. Differential effect of noise on tasks of varying complexity. J. Appl. Psychol., 52, 148-153, 1968.
36. Brilhart, Barbara L. The relationship between some aspects of communicative speaking and communicative listening. J. Communication, 15, 35-46, 1965.
37. Broadbent, D. E. S-R compatibility and the processing of information. Acta Psychologica, 23, 325-327, 1964.
38. Bruner, Jerome S. Learning and thinking. Harv. Educ. Rev., 29, 184-192, 1959.

39. Bryan, Miriam. Tests with a new look and a new purpose. DFL Bull., 6, 6-8, 1966.

40. Bryan, Quentin R. Experimental use of the University of Michigan Audio-lingual Self-instructional Course in Spoken Spanish. Inglewood, Calif.: Inglewood Unified School District, 1965.

41. Buckler, William E. A college English teacher looks at television: Composition. J. Educ. Sociol., 31, 346-352, 1958.

42. Bugelski, B. R. Presentation time, total time, and mediation in paired-associate learning. J. Exper. Psychol., 63, 409-412, 1962.

43. Buiten, Roger; and Lane, Harlan. A self-instructional device for conditioning accurate prosody. International Rev. Appl. Ling. in Lang. Teaching, 3, 205-219, 1965.

44. Buschke, Herman. Encoding for short-term storage. Psychonomic Bull., 1, 14, 1967.

45. Buschke, Herman. Verbal noise and linguistic constraints. Psychonomic Science, 12, 391-392, 1968.

46. Buschke, Herman; and Hinrichs, James V. Controlled rehearsal and recall order in serial list retention. J. Exper. Psychol., 78, 502-509, 1968.

47. Cain, L. F.; and Willey, R. The effect of spaced learning on the curve of retention. J. Exper. Psychol., 25, 209-214, 1939.

48. Calfee, Robert C. Recall and recognition memory in concept identification. J. Exper. Psychol., 81, 436-440, 1969.

49. Calfee, Robert C.; and Peterson, Richard E. Effect of list organization on short-term probe recall. J. Exper. Psychol., 78, 468-474, 1968.

50. Capretta, Patrick J.; Jones, Reginald L.; Siegel, Laurence; and Siegel, Lila C. Some noncognitive characteristics of Honors Program candidates. J. Educ. Psychol., 54, 268-276, 1963.

51. Carlson, T. R. The relationship between speed and accuracy of comprehension. J. Educ. Res., 42, 500-512, 1949.

52. Carpenter, C. R.; and Greenhill, L. P. Instructional television research: I and II. An investigation of closed-circuit television for teaching university courses. University Park, Pa.: Penn. State Univ., 1955 and 1958.

53. Carr, H. A. Distribution of effort. Psychol. Bull., 16, 26-28, 1919.

54. Carroll, John B. A primer of programmed instruction in foreign language teaching. International Rev. Appl. Ling. in Lang. Teaching, 1, 115-141, 1963.

55. Carroll, John B.; and Burke, Mary Long. Parameters of paired-associate verbal learning: Length of list, meaningfulness, rate of presentation, and ability. J. Exper. Psychol., 69, 543-553, 1965.

56. Cassel, R. N.; and Ullom, W. L. A preliminary evaluation of programmed instruction with students of high ability. Psychol. Rep., 10, 223-228, 1962.

57. Chansky, Norman M. Threat, anxiety, and reading behavior. J. Educ. Res., 51, 333-340, 1958.

58. Chansky, Norman M.; and Bregman, Martin. Improvement of reading in college. J. Educ. Res., 51, 313-317, 1957.

59. Chastain, Kenneth D. A comparison of the audio-lingual habit theory and the cognitive code-learning theory to the teaching of Introductory College Spanish. Diss. Abstr., 29 (3A), 830-831, 1968.

60. Clark, B. E. The effect upon retention of varying lengths of study periods and rest intervals in distributed learning time. J. Educ. Psychol., 19, 552-559, 1928.

61. Cook, T. W. Massed and distributed practice in puzzle solving. Psychol. Rev., 41, 330-355, 1934.

62. Courts, F. A. Relations between experimentally induced muscular tension and memorization. J. Exper. Psychol., 25, 235-256, 1939.

63. Culbert, Sidney S. The principal languages of the world. In Long, Luman H. (Ed.) The 1970 World Almanac and Book of Facts, page 349. New York: Newspaper Enterprise Assoc., 1969.

64. Cummins, R. A. Improvement and the distribution of practice. Teachers Coll., Columbia Univ., Contr. Educ., No. 1, pp. vi + 72, 1919.

65. Cutler, R. L.; McKeachie, W. J.; and McNeil, E. B. Teaching psychology by telephone. Amer. Psychologist, 13, 551-552, 1958.

66. Dallet, Ken; and Wilcox, Sandra G. Contextual stimuli and proactive inhibition. J. Exper. Psychol. 78, 475-480, 1968.

67. Davis, F. B. Fundamental factors of comprehension in reading. Doctoral dissertation. Cambridge, Mass.: Harvard Univ., 1941.

68. Dearborn, W. F. Experiments in learning. J. Educ. Psychol., 1, 373-388, 1910.

69. Deese, James. Associative structure and the serial reproduction experiment. J. Abnorm. Soc. Psychol., 63, 95-100, 1961.

70. Denny, J. Peter; and Benjafield, John G. Concept identification strategies used for positive and negative instances. Psychonomic Sci., 14, 277-278, 1969.

71. Deno, Stanley L. Effects of words and pictures as stimuli in learning language equivalents. J. Educ. Psychol., 59, 202-206, 1968.

72. De Sousa, Albert M. The effect of training on the listening ability of seventh grade students. Diss. Abstr., 28 (5-A), 1729, 1967.

73. Deutsch, M. The pathetic fallacy: An observer error in social perception. J. Personality, 28, 317-333, 1960.

74. Dizney, Henry F.; and Gromen, Lauren. Predictive validity and differential achievement on three MLA-Cooperative Foreign Language Tests. Educ. and Psychol. Meas., 27, 1127-1130, 1967.

75. Dominowski, R. L. Role of memory in concept learning. Psychol. Bull., 4, 271-280, 1965.

76. Dong, Tim; and Kintsch, Walter. Subjective retrieval cues in free recall. J. Verbal Learning Verbal Behav., 7, 813-816, 1968.
77. Dreher, Robert E.; and Beatty, Walcott H. Instructional television research: I. An experimental study of college instruction using broadcast television. San Francisco: San Francisco State Coll., 1958.
78. Dreikurs, R. Emotional predispositions to reading difficulties. Arch. Pediat., 71, 339-353, 1954.
79. Duker, Sam. Listening and reading. Elem. Sch. J., 65, 321-329, 1965.
80. Duncan, C. P.; Bell, G.; Bradt, K.; and Newman, S. E. How the poorer student studies: A research report. J. Educ. Res., 45, 287-292, 1951.
81. Dwyer, Francis M., Jr. The effectiveness of visual illustrations used to complement programed instruction. J. Psychol., 70, 157-162, 1968.
82. Eagle, Morris N. The effect of learning strategies upon free recall. Amer. J. Psychol., 80, 421-425, 1967.
83. Eames, T. H. The influence of hypermetropia and myopia on reading achievement. Amer. J. Ophthal., 39, 375-377, 1955.
84. Ebbinghaus, Hermann. Über das Gedächtnis: Untersuchungen zur experimentellen Psychologie. Leipzig: Duncker and Humblot, 1885. (Translated by Ruger, Henry A.; and Bussenius, Clara E., as Memory: A Contribution to Experimental Psychology, with a new introduction by E. R. Hilgard. New York: Dover Publications, 1964.)
85. Edinger, Lois Virginia. The effectiveness of television teaching in developing pupil skills of listening comprehension and critical thinking. Diss. Abstr., 26 (3), 1509, 1965.
86. Edwards, A. L. Political frames of reference as a factor influencing recognition. J. Abnorm. Soc. Psychol., 36, 34-50, 1941.
87. Edwards, A. S. Effects of the loss of one hundred hours of sleep. Amer. J. Psychol., 54, 80-91, 1941.
88. Ellis, A. Results of a mental hygiene approach to reading disability problems. J. Consult. Psychol., 13, 56-61, 1949.
89. Erickson, C. G.; and Chausow, H. M. Chicago's TV College—Final Report of a Three-Year Experiment. Chicago, Ill.: Chicago City Junior College, 1960.
90. Fawcett, Annabel Elizabeth. The effect of training in listening upon the listening skills of intermediate grade children. Diss. Abstr., 25 (12), 7108-7109, 1965.
91. Ferree, C. E.; and Rand, G. Good working conditions for the eyes. Personnel J., 15, 333-340, 1937.
92. Fisher, B. Group therapy with retarded leaders. J. Educ. Psychol., 44, 354-360, 1953.

93. Frincke, Gerald. Word characteristics, associative-relatedness, and the free-recall of nouns. J. Verbal Learning Verbal Behav., 7, 366-372, 1968.

94. Frost, Robert R.; and Jahnke, John C. Proactive effects in short-term memory. J. Verbal Learning Verbal Behav., 7, 785-789, 1968.

95. Fulgosi, A.; and Guilford, J. P. Short-term incubation in divergent production. Amer. J. Psychol., 81, 241-246, 1968.

96. Furbay, Albert L. The influence of scattered versus compact seating on audience response. Speech Monogr., 32, 144-148, 1965.

97. Gagné, R. M.; and Dick, W. Learning measures in a self-instructional program in solving equations. Psychol. Rep., 10, 131-146, 1962.

98. Gagné, R. M.; and Dick, W. Learning measures in a self-instructional program in solving equations. Psychol. Rep., 10, 131-146, 1962.

99. Gardner, E. Fundamentals of Neurology. Philadelphia: W. B. Saunders Co., 1963.

100. Garms, Joe D. Predicting scholastic achievement with nonintellectual variables. Diss. Abstr., 28 (8-B), 3460, 1968.

101. Garrett, H. E. Variability in learning under massed and spaced practice. J. Exper. Psychol., 26, 547-567, 1940.

102. Gates, A. I. Recitation as a factor in memorizing. Arch. Psychol., 6, No. 40, 104 pp., 1917.

103. Gentry, J. R. Immediate effects of interpolated rest periods on learning performance. Teachers Coll., Columbia Univ., Contr. Educ., No. 799, pp. vi + 57, 1940.

104. Gibson, James W.; Kibler, Robert J.; and Barker, Larry L. Some relationships between selected creativity and critical thinking measures. Psychol. Rep., 23, 707-714, 1968.

105. Giorgi, Amedeo. Learning as a function of meaning levels with American and German Ss. Psychol. Rep., 23, 27-39, 1968.

106. Gladis, Michael; and Abbey, Osborne. Relationship between whole and part methods of learning and degree of meaningfulness of serial lists. J. Exper. Psychol., 81, 194-196, 1969.

107. Glock, M. D. The effect upon eye-movements and reading rate at the college level of three methods of training. J. Educ. Psychol., 40, 93-106, 1949.

108. Goggin, Judith; and Stokes, Charles. Whole and part learning as a function of approximation to English. J. Exper. Psychol., 81, 67-71, 1969.

109. Goldbeck, R. A.; and Campbell, V. N. The effects of response mode and response difficulty on programmed learning. J. Educ. Psychol., 53, 110-118, 1962.

110. Gowan, J. C. Intelligence, interests, and reading ability in relation to scholastic achievement. Psychol. Newsltr., N.Y.U., 8, 85-87, 1957.

111. Greenhill, L. P.; Carpenter, C. R.; and Ray, W. S. Further studies of the use of television for university teaching. Audio-Visual Comm. Rev., 4, 200-215, 1956.

112. Griffith, C. R. A comment upon the psychology of the audience. In Bentley, M. (Ed.) Critical and Experimental Studies in Psychology. Psychol. Monogr., 30, No. 136, 36-47, 1921.

113. Guthrie, E. R. The Psychology of Human Conflict. New York: Harper & Brothers, 1938.

114. Guthrie, E. R. The Psychology of Learning. New York: Harper & Brothers, 1935 and 1952.

115. Haigh, G. V.; and Fiske, D. W. Corroboration of personal values as selective factors in perception. J. Abnorm. Soc. Psychol., 47, 394-398, 1952.

116. Hall, W. E.; and Robinson, F. P. An analytical approach to the study of reading skills. J. Educ. Psychol., 36, 429-442, 1945.

117. Hatch, S.; and Sheldon, W. D. Strengths and weaknesses in reading of a group of fourth-grade children. Elem. Engl., 27, 254-260, 1950.

118. Haygood, Robert C.; Sandlin, J.; Yoder, D. J.; and Dodd, D. H. Instance contiguity in disjunctive concept learning. J. Exper. Psychol., 81, 605-607, 1969.

119. Henle, Paul. (Ed.) Language, Thought, and Culture. Ann Arbor, Mich.: Univ. Michigan Press, 1958.

120. Henn, T. R. The causes of failure in examinations. Brit. Med. J., No. 4729, 461-464, 1951.

121. Henry, L. K.; and Wasson, R. The repetition of classical experiments: I. Starch's distribution of practice. J. Appl. Psychol., 23, 503-507, 1939.

122. Hilgard, E. R. Teaching machines and learning theory. In Sutherland, R. L.; Holtzman, W. H.; Koile, E. A.; and Smith, B. K. (Eds.) Personality Factors on the College Campus: Review of a Symposium. Austin, Texas: Hogg Foundation for Mental Health, 1962.

123. Hirsch, M. J. The relationship of school achievement and visual anomalies. Amer. J. Optom., 32, 262-270, 1955.

124. Hollingsworth, Paul M. Can training in listening improve reading? Reading Teacher, 18, 121-123, 1964.

125. Hollingsworth, Paul M. So they listened: The effects of a listening program. J. Communication, 15, 14-16, 1965.

126. Hollingsworth, P. M. Effectiveness of a course in listening improvement for adults. J. Communication, 16, 189-191, 1966.

127. Horowitz, Milton W.; and Berkowitz, Alan. Listening and reading, speaking and writing: An experimental investigation of differential acquisition and reproduction of memory. Percept. Mot. Skills, 24, 207-215, 1967.

128. Hovland, C. I. Experimental studies in rote-learning theory. III. Distribution of practice with varying speeds of syllable presentation. J. Exper. Psychol., 23, 172-190, 1938.

129. Hovland, C. I. Experimental studies in rote-learning theory. V. Comparison of distribution of practice in serial and paired-associate learning. J. Exper. Psychol., 25, 622-633, 1939.

130. Hovland, C. I. Experimental studies in rote-learning theory. VII. Distribution of practice with varying lengths of list. J. Exper. Psychol., 27, 271-284, 1940.

131. Hrastnik, Marjory. Making detailed clinical studies of unusually handicapped readers. Suppl. Educ. Monogr., No. 72, 143-147, 1950.

132. Husband, R. W. Television vs. classroom for learning general psychology. Amer. Psychologist, 9, 181-183, 1954.

133. Husbands, K. L.; and Shores, J. H. Measurement of reading for problem solving: A critical review of the literature. J. Educ. Res., 43, 453-465, 1950.

134. Irion, T. W. H. Comprehension difficulties of ninth-grade students in the study of literature. Teachers Coll., Columbia Univ., Contr. Educ., No. 189, pp. v + 116, 1925.

135. Irwin, John V.; and Aronson, Arnold E. A comparison of the effectiveness of a live conventional lecture versus a highly visualized film presentation in television teaching at the college level as measured by an objective verbal examination and by a film examination. Madison, Wis.: Univ. Wisconsin Television Laboratory, 1958.

136. Jain, Sharat K.; and Jain, Surendra K. Study of habits and academic attainments. Psychol. Res., 2, 13-20, 1967.

137. James, William. Principles of Psychology. New York: Henry Holt & Co., 1890. Re-issued by Dover Publications, Inc., 1950 ($1.65).

138. Jenkins, J. G.; and Dallenbach, K. M. Oblivescence during sleep and waking. Amer. J. Psychol., 35, 605-612, 1924.

139. Jenkins, James J. Language and thought. In Voss, James F. (Ed.) Approaches to Thought. Columbus, Ohio: Charles E. Merrill Publ. Co., 211-237, 1969.

140. Johnson, Marjorie Seddon. Factors in reading comprehension. Educ. Admin. & Superv., 35, 385-406, 1949.

141. Johnson, Ronald C.; and Watson, Nancy. Individual meaning production as related to amount of verbal learning. J. Gen. Psychol., 67, 117-120, 1962.

142. Johnson, Ronald E. Rehearsal effectiveness as a function of similarity of rehearsal activities to a paired-associate task. J. Verbal Learning Verbal Behav., 7, 439-445, 1968.

143. Jones, E. E.; Jones, R. G.; and Gergen, K. J. Some conditions affecting the evaluation of a conformist. J. Personality, 31, 270-288, 1963.

144. Joslin, E. S. Physical factors in reading. The Columbia Optometrist, 23, 6-7, 1949; and 24, 5-6, 1950.

145. Kanner, J. H.; Runyon, R. P.; and Desiderato, O. Television in Army training: Evaluation of television in Army basic training. Washington, D.C.: George Washington University, Human Resources Research Office, 1954.

146. Kaufman, Maurice. The effect of instruction in reading Spanish on reading ability in English of Spanish-speaking retarded readers. Diss. Abstr., 28 (4-A), 1299, 1967.

147. Kausler, Donald H.; and Olson, Richard D. Homonyms as items in verbal discrimination learning and transfer. J. Exper. Psychol., 82, 136-142, 1969.

148. Keislar, E. R.; and McNeil, J. D. A comparison of two response modes in an auto-instructional program with children in the primary grades. J. Educ. Psychol., 53, 127-131, 1962.

149. Keislar, Evan R.; and Mace, Larry L. Sequence of speaking and listening training in Beginning French. In Krumboltz, John D. (Ed.) Learning and the Educational Process. Chicago: Rand McNally and Co., 163-191, 1965.

150. Keislar, Evan R.; Stern, Carolyn; and Mace, L. Sequence of speaking and listening training in Beginning French: A replication experiment. Amer. Educ. Res. J., 3, 169-178, 1966.

151. Kelly, Charles M. Listening: Complex of activities—and a unitary skill? Speech Monogr., 34, 455-466, 1967.

152. Keppel, Geoffrey; Postman, Leo; and Zavortink, Bonnie. Studies of learning to learn: VIII. The influence of massive amounts of training upon the learning and retention of paired-associate lists. J. Verbal Learning Verbal Behav., 7, 790-796, 1968.

153. Kimble, G. A.; and Kendall, J. W., Jr. A comparison of two methods of producing experimental extinction. J. Exper. Psychol., 45, 87-90, 1953 (white rats).

154. King, M. L. Factors in the school and classroom environment that influence progress in reading. Suppl. Educ. Monogr., No. 72, 87-91, 1950.

155. Kintsch, Walter. Recognition and free recall of organized lists. J. Exper. Psychol., 78, 481-487, 1968.

156. Klapper, Hope Lunin. Does lack of contact with the lecturer handicap televised instruction? J. Educ. Sociol., 31, 353-359, 1958.

157. Klare, George R.; Shuford, Emir H.; and Nichols, William H. The relationship of style difficulty, practice, and ability to efficiency of reading and to retention. J. Appl. Psychol., 41, 222-226, 1957.

158. Krumboltz, J. D.; and Weisman, R. G. The effect of overt versus covert responding to programmed instruction on immediate and delayed retention. J. Educ. Psychol., 53, 89-92, 1962.

159. Kunihira, S.; and Asher, J. J. The strategy of the total physical response: An application to learning Japanese. International Rev. Appl. Ling. 3, 277-289, 1965.

160. La Gaipa, John J. Programmed instruction, teacher ability, and subject matter difficulty. J. Psychol., 68, 257-260, 1968.

161. Langsam, R. S. A factorial analysis of reading ability. J. Exper. Educ., 10, 57-63, 1941.

162. Lantz, B. Some dynamic aspects of success and failure. Psychol. Monogr., 59, No. 1, pp. vi + 40, 1945.

163. Lappin, Joseph S.; and Lowe, Charles A. Meaningfulness and pronounceability in the coding of visually presented verbal materials. J. Exper. Psychol., 81, 22-28, 1969.

164. Letson, Charles T. Speed and comprehension in reading. J. Educ. Res., 52, 49-53, 1958.

165. Letson, Charles T. The relative influence of material and purpose on reading rates. J. Educ. Res., 52, 238-240, 1959.

166. Levinger, G.; and Clark, J. Emotional factors in the forgetting of word associations. J. Abnorm. Soc. Psychol., 62, 99-105, 1961.

167. Levinson, John Z. Flicker fusion phenomena. Science, 160, 21-28, 1968.

168. Lewis, N. An investigation into comparable results obtained from two methods of increasing reading speed among adults. Coll. Engl., 11, 152-156, 1949.

169. Lewis, N. How to Read Better and Faster. (Rev. Ed.) New York: Thomas Y. Crowell, 1951.

170. Liftik, Joseph; and Leicht, Kenneth L. Effect of number and relatedness of stimulus-term components on paired-associate learning. Psychonomic Sci., 13, 315-316, 1968.

171. Lindell, Ebbe. (Ed.) An experiment with self-instructing material in the language laboratory and in written programs. Pedagogisk-Psykologiska Problem, #53, 26 pages, 1967.

172. Lindsay, Peter H.; and Norman, Donald A. Short-term memory loss with divided attention. Psychonomic Bull. 1, 14, 1967.

173. Lion, Judith S.; Richardson, E.; and Browne, R. C. A study of the performance of industrial inspectors under two kinds of lighting. Ergonomics, 11, 23-34, 1968.

174. Loginova, E. A. Ovliyanii interesa na zapominanie novykh slov pri izuchenii inostrannogo yazyka. [On the influence of interest on remembering new words during the study of a foreign language.] Vop. Psikhol., No. 1, 61-64, 1962.

175. Lorge, I. Influence of regularly interpolated time intervals upon subsequent learning. Teachers Coll., Columbia Univ., Contr. Educ., No. 438, 57 pp., 1930.

176. Lorge, Sarah W. Language laboratory research studies in New York City high schools: A discussion of the program and the findings. Mod. Lang. J., 48, 409-419, 1964.

177. Lovatt, D. J.; and Warr, P. B. Recall after sleep. Amer. J. Psychol. 81, 253-257, 1968.

178. Lundsteen, Sara W. R. Teaching abilities in critical listening in the fifth and sixth grades. Diss. Abstr., 24, No. 12, 5247-5248, 1964.

179. Lundsteen, Sara W. R. Critical listening-permanency and transfer of gains made during an experiment in the fifth and sixth grades. Calif. J. Educ. Res., 16, 210-216, 1965.

180. Lyon, D. O. The relation of length of material to time taken for learning, and the optimum distribution of time. Part II. J. Educ. Psychol., 5, 85-91, 1914.

181. Lyon, D. O. The relation of length of material to time taken for learning, and the optimum distribution of time. Part III. J. Educ. Psychol., 5, 155-163, 1914.

182. McDonald, Arthur S. Influence of a college reading improvement program on academic performance. J. Educ. Psychol., 48, 171-181, 1957.

183. McGeoch, John A.; and Irion, A. L. The Psychology of Human Learning. New York: Longmans, Green, 1952.

184. McGinnies, E.; and Adornetto, J. Perceptual defense in normal and in schizophrenic observers. J. Abnorm. Soc. Psychol., 47, 833-837, 1952.

185. McKeachie, W. J. Anxiety in the college classroom. J. Educ. Res., 45, 153-160, 1951.

186. McKillop, Anne S. The relationship between the reader's attitude and certain types of reading response. Teachers Coll., Columbia Univ., Contr. Educ., 101 pp., 1952.

187. McQueen, R. Diagnostic reading scores and college achievement. Psychol. Rep., 3, 627-629, 1957.

188. Mackey, W. F.; and Savard, J. G. The indices of coverage: A new dimension in lexicometrics. IRAL: International Rev. Appl. Ling. Lang. Teaching, 5, 71-122, 1967.

189. Macomber, F. G.; and Siegel, L. Final report of the experimental study in instructional procedures. Oxford, Ohio: Miami University, 1960.

190. Mager, Robert F.; and McCann, J. Learner-controlled Instruction. Palo Alto, Calif.: Varian Associates, 1961.

191. Mandler, George. Organization and memory. In Spence, Kenneth W.; and Spence, Janet T. (Eds.) Psychology of Learning and Motivation. Vol. 1. New York: Academic Press, 1967.

192. Mandler, George. Organized recall: Individual functions. Psychonomic Sci., 13, 235-236, 1968.

193. Mandler, George. Association and organization: Facts, fancies, and theories. In Dixon, Theodore R.; and Horton, D. L. (Eds.) Verbal Behavior and General Behavior Theory. Englewood Cliffs, N. J.: Prentice Hall, 1968.

194. Marquart, D. I. The pattern of punishment and its relation to abnormal fixation in adult human subjects. J. Gen. Psychol., 39, 107-144, 1948.

195. Melton, Arthur W.; and Shulman, Harvey G. Further studies of a distributed practice effect on probability of recall in free recall. Psychonomic Bull., 1, 13-14, 1967.

196. Miller, J. The rate of conditioning of human subjects to single and multiple conditioned stimuli. J. Gen. Psychol., 20, 399-408, 1939.

197. Miller, J. O., Jr. A comparison of a self-improvement and teacher-oriented approach to reading improvement at the college and university level. Diss. Abstr., 28 (12-A), 4955-4956, 1968.

198. Missildine, W. H. The emotional background of thirty children with reading disabilities with emphasis on its coercive elements. Nerv. Child, 5, 263-272, 1946.

199. Montague, William E.; and Wearing, Alexander J. The retention of responses to individual stimuli and stimulus classes. Psychonomic Sci., 9, 81-82, 1967.

200. Morton, J. An investigation into the effects of an adult reading efficiency course. Occup. Psychol., 33, 222-237, 1959.

201. Mullins, C. J. Reading improvement course aimed to increase speed. Personnel J., 33, 172-174, 1954.

202. Murray, D. J. Repeated recall in short-term memory. J. Verbal Learning Verbal Behav., 7, 358-365, 1968.

203. Myers, Ruth L.; and Gates, Louise W. Effective Listening and Cognitive Learning at the College Level. Muncie, Ind.: Ball State Univ., 1966.

204. Nakazima, S.; and Saheki, O. A study on an English teaching method in Japan based on a comparative study of Japanese and English. Jap. J. Educ. Psychol., 15, 39-54, 1967.

205. Neale, J. G.; Toye, M. H.; and Belbin, E. Adult training: The use of programmed instruction. Occupational Psychol., 42, 23-31, 1968.

206. Neidt, Charles O.; and French, Joseph L. Reaction of high school students to television teachers. J. Genet. Psychol., 100, 337-344, 1962.

207. Newman, E. B. Forgetting of meaningful material during sleep and waking. Amer. J. Psychol., 52, 65-71, 1939.

208. Norberg, Robert B. Teaching machines—six dangers and one advantage. In Roucek, Joseph S. (Ed.) Programmed Teaching. New York: Philosophical Library, 1965.

209. Paul, J.; and Ogilvie, J. C. Mass media and retention. Explorations, 4, 120-123, 1955.
210. Perkins, N. L. The value of distributed repetitions in rote learning. Brit. J. Psychol., 7, 253-261, 1914.
211. Pimsleur, Paul; and Bonkowski, R. J. Transfer of verbal material across sense modalities. J. Educ. Psychol., 52, 104-107, 1961.
212. Pimsleur, Paul; Sundland, D. M.; Bonkowski, R. J.; and Mosberg, L. Further study of the transfer of verbal materials across sense modalities. J. Educ. Psychol., 55, 96-102, 1964.
213. Pollio, Howard R.; and Gerow, Joshua R. The role of rules in recall. Amer. J. Psychol., 81, 303-313, 1968.
214. Postman, L.; Bruner, J. S.; and McGinnies, E. Personal values as selective factors in perception. J. Abnorm. Soc. Psychol., 43, 142-154, 1948.
215. Postman, L.; and Schneider, B. H. Personal values, visual recognition, and recall. Psychol. Rev., 58, 271-284, 1951.
216. Pyper, John Romney. Attentional factors in learning from written texts. Diss. Abstr., 29 (2-A), 486-487, 1968.
217. Redmount, R. S. Description and evaluation of a corrective program for reading disability. J. Educ. Psychol., 39, 347-358, 1948.
218. Reeber, Arthur S. Transfer of syntactic structure in synthetic languages. J. Exper. Psychol., 81, 115-119, 1969.
219. Reed, Homer B.; and Dick, R. Dale. The learning and generalization of abstract and concrete concepts. J. Verbal Learning Verbal Behav., 7, 486-490, 1968.
220. Repin, V.; and Orlov, R. S. The use of sleep and relaxation in the study of foreign languages. Australian J. Psychol., 19, 203-207, 1967.
221. Robinson, E. S.; and Heron, W. T. Results of variations in length of memorized material. J. Exper. Psychol., 5, 428-448, 1922.
222. Roe, A. Automated teaching methods using linear programs. J. Appl. Psychol., 46, 198-201, 1962.
223. Roe, K. V.; Case, H. W.; and Roe, A. Scrambled versus ordered sequence in autoinstructional programs. J. Educ. Psychol., 53, 101-104, 1962.
224. Russell, R. W.; and Steinberg, H. Effects of nitrous oxide on reactions to "stress." Quart. J. Exper. Psychol., 7, 67-73, 1955.
225. Ryberg, D. C. Review. J. Couns. Psychol., 15, 299-300, 1968.
226. Salisbury, Rachael A. A study of the effects of training in logical organization as a method of improving skill in study. Doctoral dissertation. Madison, Wis.: Univ. of Wisconsin, 1934.
227. Saltzman, Irving J. Programmed self-instruction and second-language learning. International Rev. Appl. Ling. Lang. Teaching., 1, 104-114, 1963.

228. Sarason, Irwin G. Test anxiety and the intellectual performance of college students. J. Educ. Psychol., 52, 201-206, 1961.

229. Sarason, Irwin G.; and Palola, Ernest G. The relationships of test and general anxiety, difficulty of task, and experimental instructions to performance. J. Exper. Psychol., 59, 185-191, 1960.

230. Scherer, George A. C.; and Wertheimer, Michael. A Psycholinguistic Experiment in Foreign-Language Teaching. New York: McGraw-Hill Book Co., 1964.

231. Schramm, Wilbur. What we know about learning from instructional television. In Stanford Institute for Communication Research. Educational Television the Next Ten Years. Stanford, Calif.: Stanford University, 1962.

232. Schulz, R. W.; Miller, R. L.; and Radtke, R. C. The role of instance contiguity and dominance in concept attainment. J. Verbal Learning Verbal Behav., 1, 432-435, 1963.

233. Schwartz, Marvin. An evaluation of the effectiveness of the reading training given in the U.S. Naval school, pre-flight. USN Sch. Aviat. Med. Res. Rep., Proj. No. NM 14 02 11, Sub. 12, No. I, ii + 8 pp., 1957.

234. Seibert, W. F. An evaluation of televised instruction in college freshman mathematics. Television Project Report 6. West Lafayette, Indiana: Purdue University, 1958.

235. Serra, Mary C. Study of fourth grade children's comprehension of certain verbal abstractions. J. Exper. Educ., 22, 103-118, 1953.

236. Sheffield, F. D. Avoidance training and the contiguity principle. J. Comp. Physiol. Psychol., 41, 165-177, 1948.

237. Shulman, P. F. The vision specialist in a remedial reading program. Optom. Wkly., 43, 1941-1945, 1951.

238. Silverstein, Albert; and Marshall, Alice. Incidental vs. intentional paired associate learning. Amer. J. Psychol., 81, 415-424, 1968.

239. Simonson, E.; and Brozek, J. Effects of illumination level on visual performance and fatigue. J. Opt. Soc. Amer., 38, 384-397, 1948.

240. Skinner, B. F. Teaching machines. Science, 128, 969-977, 1958.

241. Smith, D. E. P.; and Wood, R. L. Reading improvement and college grades: A follow-up. J. Educ. Psychol., 46, 151-159, 1955.

242. Smock, C. D.; and Small, V. H. Efficiency of utilization of visual information as a function of induced muscular tension. Percept. Mot. Skills, 14, 39-44, 1962.

243. Sones, A. M. A study in memory, with special reference to temporal distribution of reviews. Univ. of Iowa Studies, Aims & Progress in Research, No. 72, 65-72, 1943.

244. Southwestern Indiana Educational Television Council. Second Year Report, 1959-1960. Evansville, Indiana, 1960.

245. Spache, G. D. Personality characteristics of retarded readers as measured by the picture-frustration study. Educ. & Psychol. Measurement, 14, 186-192, 1954.

246. Srivastava, S. S. Study in relationship between vocabulary and academic achievements. Indian J. Psychol., 41, 35-38, 1966.

247. Stabler, John R.; and Perry, Oliver B. Learning and retention as a function of instructional method and race. J. Psychol., 67, 271-276, 1967.

248. Stafford, K. R.; and Combs, C. F. Radical reductionism: A possible source of inadequacy in autoinstructional techniques. Amer. Psychologist, 22, 667-669, 1967.

249. Starch, D. Periods of work in learning. J. Educ. Psychol., 3, 209-213, 1912.

250. Strang, Ruth. Reading and personality formation. Personality, 1, 131-140, 1951.

251. Stuit, D. B.; Harshbarger, H. C.; Becker, S. L.; Bechtoldt, H. P.; and Hall, A. E. An Experiment in Teaching. Iowa City: State University of Iowa, 1956.

252. Taylor, Earl A. The spans: Perception, apprehension and recognition: As related to reading and speed reading. Amer. J. Ophthal., 44, 501-507, 1957.

253. Tinker, M. A. Cautions concerning illumination intensities used for reading. Amer. J. Optom., 12, 43-51, 1935.

254. Tinker, M. A. Trends in illumination standards. Illum. Engr., 43, 866-881, 1948.

255. Tinker, M. A. Cumulative effect of marginal conditions upon rate of perception in reading. J. Appl. Psychol., 32, 537-540, 1948.

256. Tinker, M. A. Fixation pause duration in reading. J. Educ. Res., 44, 471-479, 1951.

257. Tinker, M. A. The effect of intensity of illumination upon speed of reading six-point italic print. Amer. J. Psychol., 65, 600-602, 1952.

258. Tinker, M. A. Length of work periods in visual research. J. Appl. Psychol., 42, 343-345, 1958.

259. Tinker, M. A. Brightness contrast, illumination intensity and visual efficiency. Amer. J. Optom., 36, 221-235, 1959.

260. Traxler, A. E. (Ed.) Improving the Efficiency and Quality of Learning. Washington, D.C.: American Council on Education, 1962.

261. Trembly, Dean. Laws of learning general and specialized vocabularies. Proceedings 74th Annual Conv. APA, 229-230, 1966.

262. Tsao, J. C. An analysis of the achievements in spaced and massed practice: A study of the inhibition theory. J. Gen. Psychol., 44, 189-197, 1951.

263. Tulving, E.; and Osler, Shirley. When is recall higher than recognition? Psychonomic Bull., 1, 15, 1967.

264. Tulving, E.; and Pearlstone, Z. Availability versus accessibility of information in memory for words. J. Verbal Learning Verbal Behav., 4, 381-391, 1966.

265. Van Krevelen, Alice. The relationship between recall and meaningfulness of motive-related words. J. Gen. Psychol., 65, 229-233, 1961.

266. Van Ormer, E. B. Retention after intervals of sleep and of waking. Arch. Psychol., 21, No. 137, 49 pp., 1932.

267. Van Ormer, E. B. Sleep and retention. Psychol. Bull., 30, 415-439, 1933.

268. Voeks, V. W. Postremity, recency and frequency as bases for prediction in the maze situation. J. Exper. Psychol., 38, 495-510, 1948.

269. Voeks, V. W. Acquisition of S-R connections: A test of Hull's and Guthrie's theories. J. Exper. Psychol., 47, 137-147, 1954.

270. Voeks, V. W. Gradual strengthening of S-R connections or increasing number of S-R connections? J. Psychol., 39, 289-299, 1955.

271. Wachtel, P. L. Anxiety, attention, and coping with threat. J. Abnorm. Psychol., 73, 137-143, 1968.

272. Walker, Clinton M.; and Bourne, Lyle. The identifications of concepts as a function of amount of relevant and irrelevant information. Amer. J. Psychol., 74, 410-417, 1961.

273. Watts, Graeme H.; and Anderson, Richard C. Retroactive inhibition in free recall as a function of first- and second-list organization. J. Exper. Psychol., 81, 595-597, 1969.

274. Wedeen, Shirley U. Mechanical versus non-mechanical reading techniques for college freshmen. Sch. & Soc., 79, 121-123, 1954.

275. Weir, Morton W.; and Helgoe, Robert S. Vocalization during discrimination: Effects of a mixture of two types of verbalization patterns. J. Verbal Learning Verbal Behav., 7, 842-844, 1968.

276. Weisskopf, Edith A. Intellectual malfunctioning and personality. J. Abnorm. Soc. Psychol., 46, 410-423, 1951.

277. Williams, D. C. Mass media and learning—an experiment. Explorations, 3, 75-82, 1954.

278. Wood, Gordon; and Terborg, Robert H. Learning strategy, list abstractness, and free-recall learning. Psychonomic Sci., 13, 113-114, 1968.

279. Wrenn, C. G.; and Larsen, R. P. Studying Effectively. Stanford Univ., Calif.: Stanford Univ. Press, 1943, pp. 1-3.

280. Zaccaria, A.; and Bitterman, M. E. The effect of fluorescent flicker on visual efficiency. J. Appl. Psychol., 36, 413-416, 1952.

chapter 3

Taking examinations expertly: becoming educated and making high grades

A. Introduction — the Pervasiveness of Tests

Throughout much of life we are confronted by examinations: aptitude tests, intelligence tests, achievement tests, tests of knowledge, of vocabulary, or of our skills, examinations for entering college, for continuing college, for getting various jobs in industry, business, the civil service, tests for the Army, Navy, or Marine Corps, tests for entering the practice of law or medicine or other professions, tests for licensing, promotion, or reclassification, tests for driving. . . . These are some of the obvious ones. In addition, we take many many tests not so obvious — try-outs for plays, or symphonies, or teams; interviews for new jobs, transfers, or promotions; on-job ratings; reviews by critics; casual-appearing conversations which nonetheless are evaluative of us and influential of trends for our future life. The list is far longer than this. As is apparent on reflection, we take tests of one kind or another throughout our lives — no matter what line of work we undertake.

Much of our life hinges upon how we do on various tests. And the tests go on for as long as we live.

We need, therefore, to develop skill in facing and taking examinations — both because they themselves are a sizable portion of our life and because they influence other aspects of our present and future. College is as good a time as ever for developing the skills and healthy outlooks which will enable one to do more gracefully and effectively those portions of human life. Certainly one has a lot of opportunities to practice. No day goes by, probably, that you are not taking *some* kind of test.

Practice can make perfect. Practice also can make one a mess. The latter happens if one practices sloppy ways, and errors, and disruptive patterns. One gets more and more habits of an adverse sort, and can reach the point where any examination (even a physical examination by an M.D.) sends one into an apprehensive, poorly functioning state. The thought of an examination, the mere word "examination," can cue disorganizing thoughts and behavior.

We can practice, on the other hand, ways of responding which make us increasingly adroit and cheerful. We can practice the techniques, approaches, attitudes, and feelings which build into habits comprising amazingly skillful handling of examinations. Grade school would have been a fine time to begin, but your years at the university are convenient times too.

B. Formal Review and Other Preparations

1. PRACTICE SKILLFUL PREPARATION AND EXECUTION ON TRIVIAL TESTS.

One advantage to university and college work is that one usually takes a considerable number of rather unimportant tests. Compared with many tests one meets later in life, relatively little rides on some college quizzes. This furnishes an almost perfect chance to practice more sensible habits of preparing for and taking tests. When you study for an unimportant test, it is easier to stay collected and serene. If you study for a small quiz with calmness and alertness, you thereby have a start on studying for other tests with calmness and alertness. Habits do generalize. If you do this a lot, the chances are high that these healthy emotional habits will generalize even to quite important tests, and from them to very important tests.

The same point holds for the intellectual skills of studying and taking examinations, and also for the mechanics of studying and taking examinations. If you practice these on unimportant matters, you can practice more serenely and thereby facilitate the acquisition of complex skills and increase the likelihood of transfer to exceedingly important tasks. Building up new skills in thinking, studying, writing, and other complex chains, discriminations, and organizations, is easier when you are calm than when it is critically important that you establish new habits and get the hang of the new skills with alacrity and almost no errors.

2. STUDYING IN THE WAYS PREVIOUSLY SKETCHED IS
   EXCELLENT PREPARATION FOR TESTS.

If you have studied in the ways sketched so far, you will be well-prepared for any test. When an examination is announced, you need do little more, except tie together a few loose odds and ends, and perhaps do some further reviewing.

Reviewing means, of course, re-viewing. It should not be restricted to your formal study periods. Rather, re-viewing should be a continuous process, a part of your daily living. That type of reviewing we already have considered. Let us look now at more formal types.

Some students do their original studying and also their formal reviewing of the material at the same session, often with disastrous results. Other students study in advance, but then review by merely re-reading everything, one or more times. This too can have miserable results, and at best is a flagrant waste of time. Little merit exists in devoting equal amounts of time to all aspects of the material. More profitable uses of time are available. Let us consider some of them.

3. IN FORMAL REVIEWING, ATTEMPT FIRST TO RECALL THE
   CHAPTER SUB-HEADINGS OR THE MAIN HEADINGS OF
   YOUR OUTLINE.

Do this before looking at that material. Then check the accuracy of your memory, visibly marking any omissions or errors.

4. NEXT TRY TO RECITE THE DETAILS UNDER EACH
   HEADING.

After doing that, read the section rapidly, marking
anything you omitted in your rehearsal. The parts you
remember correctly at this time probably need no further
attention. The parts you forget are a different matter.

5. TIE THE FORGOTTEN PARTS IN MORE ADEQUATELY
   WITH OTHER FACTS.

Integrate these elusive data and concepts with other
parts of your world, so you do not again forget them. Various ways of making such integrations were presented in
Section F of Chapter 2 (The Use of Books, pages 58-63
especially).

6. GROUP TOGETHER SIMILAR OR RELATED FACTS AND
   LABEL THE CATEGORIES.

Grouping similar things together helps greatly in
remembering them. Even lists of words are remembered
better by organizing the words in some way, almost any way
which occurs to the learner.[13, 14, 21, 53, 62-65, 72, 107, 109] So are
facts and concepts and other materials.[3, 12, 13, 20, 30, 38, 60, 75,
77, 91] Labeling the categories increases the efficacy of organizing.[14, 72, 105]

In your study, when you have a great array of facts to
remember, try arranging them so that similar facts are
together. For example, sort out important dates and make a
list of them and the events occurring on each of them —
preferably arranging the dates in order;[12] list together
animals or plants or other phenomena having certain
characteristics in common; compile a glossary of technical
terms and basic concepts (with their definitions), grouping

together those which are related and labeling the categories; collect the names of key persons and what they did, putting persons with similar achievements together.

This is a way of re-working your notes (rather than merely copying them over or re-reading them, which is tedious at best) and it is a way of enhancing memory. A precise memory for details is helpful on any type of examination, but especially helpful on essay tests[21, 51] where one needs to re-capture facts, not simply recognize them.

7. ASK YOURSELF QUESTIONS AND PRACTICE ANSWERING THEM.

The basic idea, here again, is to practice doing what you want to learn. If you want to learn to use what you have been studying to answer questions, then practice doing that. Ask yourself questions and answer them, checking the answers against your notes and textbooks.

This method has an added merit: With practice, the questions which you ask yourself will often resemble the test items. There is, after all, only a limited number of questions one can sensibly ask on any specified material.

When you are preparing for a true-false examination, be sure to write yourself some false items. As long as we are in lecture or studying in ordinary ways, we are confronted with "trues" only—or at least what someone deems true. On the test, we suddenly are in a morass of trues and falses and partial truths—a jungle. This sudden change can be highly disconcerting and even terrifying. We are apt to be disrupted by this strange world, and become worried lest we learn the falses and forget the trues and get all mixed up. The confusion and anxiety can be reduced by familiarizing yourself in advance with tangles of trues, half-trues, quarter-trues, trues except for one word, and outright falses. In the civilized quiet of your study, familiarize yourself with these messes and practice sorting trues from falses. You can become very adroit at such sorting. It is, of course, a handy skill to have in real life.

8. STUDY AS IF THE TEST WERE TO BE AN ESSAY EXAMINATION.

An experiment by Meyer is illuminating.[70] In this experiment, some students were told to study for an objective test and they did. Then they were given an essay test. You will not be astonished that their performance was inferior to that of students who had studied for an essay test.

However, you may be somewhat astonished that the reverse was not true. Students who had prepared for an essay test and then were given a conventional objective test, did just as well as those who had studied for the objective test. This has been found repeatedly.[35, 36, 70]

As you know, many of us study quite differently when preparing for objective tests than when preparing for essay tests.[71] In studying for essay tests, we practice presenting in an orderly fashion as many facts and ideas as we can with only a few cues being furnished. We look for implications and tie-ins; we practice applying the material; and in other ways too, we try to make the material meaningful. In studying for objective tests, on the other hand, we often merely reread the chapters and memorize some isolated facts. This is poor preparation for making the logical analyses, reconstructions, and integrations requisite for fine performance on essay tests.[35, 36, 70] It even is poor preparation for some kinds of objective tests.

Some true-false, short-answer, and multiple-choice tests measure substantially the same skills as do essay tests: e.g., the ability to reconstruct material, the ability to remember information with few cues, the ability to draw logical inferences from facts and principles, and the ability to see the pertinence of these facts to new problems. In taking such objective tests, people who studied in the usual way for an objective test would be handicapped gravely compared to ones who studied for an essay examination. And even when the objective test is of the recognition type, such persons have no advantage (you recall) over people who studied for an essay test.

These facts suggest that even in terms of grades a wise policy is this: Always study as if an essay test were scheduled, regardless of whether the test will be essay or objective. In terms of becoming educated, the policy also is wise, for the activities you engage in during that kind of study are far more similar to the habits you wish to make part of yourself and to the skills you need in the rest of life. With this approach to reviewing, you can prepare for any type of test and simultaneously prepare for living.

9. REVIEW, AND THEN GO TO SLEEP.

Almost nothing is forgotten during sleep for material that is well-integrated or meaningful. This you know (see pages 41-42). Further, even material that is lightly learned is apt to be remembered almost as well as much-practiced material, if the time between learning and testing is spent in sleep. For example, college students learned pairs of adjectives; some they learned to the point of one correct anticipation, some to two, some to three, four, five, six, or seven, and some to eight or more correct anticipations. The amount remembered after nine hours spent mainly in sleep was almost identical, regardless of the amount of correct practice (viz., 92, 87, 89, 92, 95, 90, 97, and 98%).[55]

10. ON THE NIGHT BEFORE THE TEST, GET YOUR USUAL
    AMOUNT OF SLEEP.

Review well in advance of the examination; sleep the
night before the test. This is far superior to the more common practice of sleeping well in advance of the test and then
reviewing madly on the last night.

During last-night cramming, you may pick up some
miscellaneous bits of information. However, the odds are
slim that the value of those facts will offset the losses in
concentration, clear thinking, and perceptual organization
which occur when you are badly fatigued.[4, 8, 9, 22, 56] Certainly these last-minute gains in information will not counter-
balance other losses incurred by cramming (see pages 49-51
and 141).

Perhaps you are afraid to review well in advance of tests,
lest you forget before the test many important facts and
principles. Retention curves for some materials do drop
rapidly for the first few hours and then level off; but this is
true mainly for nonsense syllables. We hope what you are
learning bears little resemblance to nonsense syllables. We
hope it is not a bunch of memorized, nearly meaningless
globs. But even if it is, you cannot get the jump on this drop
in retention. The sharp drop (for nonsense material) occurs
too rapidly and ends too soon. To take the examination
before that retention drop occurs would require that the test
be given only a few hours after your original learning and
reviewing. You simply cannot do much learning nor efficient
reviewing in that period of time.

Further, and this is worth noting well, material you have
tied in with your life and made meaningful has no sharp
quick drop in retention. For such material, very little is
forgotten in a few days or even weeks. Using the methods of
study we have been considering, you can finish your formal

review long before the test and run no danger of forgetting much between then and the time of the test. A great deal of it you will remember for years. Rarely will you forget what you use.

C. Taking Examinations with Skill and Freedom from Terror

Skill in the mechanics of taking examinations has rather little to do with becoming educated, but it has much to do with grades. Since high grades probably are one of your objectives too, here are some ways whereby you can more skillfully take tests.

1. HOW SHOULD ONE TAKE ESSAY EXAMINATIONS?

a) Read the entire set of questions before starting to write.

b) Start with the question on which you feel most qualified to write. Cogent arguments favor this approach, even when items have unequal weight: (1) That is the question for which you need least time to ponder. (2) You avoid the danger of losing your best ideas while struggling with the questions which are harder for you. (3) While writing on it, ideas concerning the other questions will occur to you. (4) Also, while answering the question directed most along the lines of your previous thinking, you become calmer and more self-possessed. This calmness, in turn, facilitates clearer thinking on the other questions. You get in the "set" of thinking coherently, and the set carries over to other problems. It is pleasant to discover that "hard" questions look far easier when you return to them after doing the ones simplest for you.

This set of coherently thinking cannot be created well

when you start out with the questions most difficult for you. When you begin with them, the set you create is apt to be distraught apprehension and anxiety. This too can carry over and seriously impair your performance even on questions you understand thoroughly.

c) For full credit, you must answer the question asked, and not one of your own creation. Therefore, before beginning to write, re-read the question carefully. Make certain you understand exactly what is being asked.

d) Make at least a sketchy outline of your answer, before starting to write your full answer.

e) Be as specific *and also as complete* in your answer as you can in the time available. Give all general points which are relevant, but do not stop there. Also give some examples, substantiating facts, and correlated details. (You need not give *all* that occur to you, nor would there be time.) Always write to the point.

f) While writing on one question, you will get ideas pertinent to other questions. Jot down some clue to these ideas on a separate sheet, in order that you neither forget them nor have to remember them while writing on another topic. This procedure increases the coherency and completeness of your answers. It also helps reduce your tension and anxiety.

g) Leave space for additions to your answers. One practicable method is to write on only one side of bluebook pages. Then you can draw arrows from any sentence to the back of the preceding page, and there make any additions which later occur to you.

h) Budget your time, checking frequently. When you first receive the test, figure out how much time to allow for each question. Save some time to go over the test, checking and filling in parts, or to take care of emergencies (such as some part requiring longer than you had thought, or for going blank for a while). An incomplete answer to all items is better than no answer to some questions and a too long answer to some others, so be certain to keep track of the time. If you fail to check on your time, or fail to budget it, you may find yourself in the unhappy predicament of knowing an answer but not having time to write it down. Few things are more disheartening than to know the answer to a question, or to several questions, and to get a zero on that section simply because of poor planning of your time.

i) Use the terminology of the lecturer and of the subject under consideration. In spite of our lament that we said the same thing as someone given more credit, but said it in different words, the tacit accusation often is unjustified. Different words do not have the same meaning; therefore, they may not be "just as good."

j) Unconventional spelling and grammar, poor handwriting, sloppy punctuation, and clumsy sentence construction are serious impediments to communication. At best, they distract the reader. At worst, they cause him to completely lose the thread of your ideas while attempting to decode the misspelled words, translate the misused terms, cipher some peculiar script, and straighten out garbled phrases and sentences.

During a test it is difficult to write well, but use as lucid and graceful a style of composition as you can under those rather trying circumstances. Be concise and precise in your wording. Write legibly, using accurate spelling, grammar, and punctuation. Attending to these details can enormously enhance communication and greatly enhance also the perceived quality of your answer.

If your spelling and punctuation are standing in your way, a little book by Anderson, Straub and Gibson could help you considerably.[2] The book gives a very clear, and short, set of rules for spelling and for effective punctuation. It includes notations of words commonly interchanged by college students and briefly defines them.

Trying to achieve proper, clear spelling is a bugaboo to some students; but English is not the horrendous mess you might fancy. Approximately 90% of its syllables are phonetic, enabling one thereby to spell correctly a great many words. Of 17,000 words analyzed,[34, 42–44, 46] almost half could be perfectly spelled phonetically, and more than two-thirds of the remaining words could be spelled with one error only. That leaves only 14% which are rather tricky.

In trying to achieve greater accuracy in spelling, watch for words which sound alike but are spelled differently and for misspellings where the letters have the same sound as the correct spelling but are not appropriate (e.g., "work" spelled as "werk"). Such errors are easy to overlook.[57]

k) Allow time to re-read your answer and to make any changes necessary for clarity and completeness. This practice always is sound; for some people, it is indispensable for achieving a truly coherent answer.

l) Suppose you have no clear ideas on any of the questions. Then what? Fold your tent and silently steal away? You can find wiser procedures. One is to start writing anyway.

On a separate piece of paper (not to be turned in), jot down any scattered, fragmentary thoughts which occur to you in connection with various questions. If you can get a few general headings for an outline, fine. Write them—even if you cannot recall immediately any of the facts necessary to support the points, nor many of the main points. Some of these additional facts will occur to you later.

If worst comes to worst, and absolutely no sensible, partial answers occur to you, start writing anyway. Write anything which is even remotely relevant to any of the questions. Never mind how remote the relevancy is. Start writing. Gradually your thoughts will become more germane to the topics involved. Although this approach sounds a bit idiotic, it does work.

This procedure helps rescue you from the near trance-like state, or panic, into which you otherwise tend to subside. Using it, you gradually recall more nearly relevant facts; then, wholly relevant ones. (Do not turn in those first preliminary notes, of course. They served their purpose in getting you started.)

m) Try all questions. On *every* question, turn in the best answer you can devise—even though you feel your best is miserable. Never wholly omit a question, unless you are certain any answer would be faking. Seldom is there a question about which you know absolutely nothing. Although you can give only a fragmentary, poorly developed answer, write that! Then develop it the best you can. "Never decline a challenge" is a motto with much in its favor.

2. How should one take objective examinations?

a) Do not read into the question. For example, do not add an "always," "all," or "every" that is not there, and then say the item is false. This happens with dismal frequency. Suppose an item states: "A great deal of bickering occurs among brothers and sisters." This is true. Some students will miss it, however, by adding "all." Their mental item reads: "A great deal of bickering occurs among all brothers and sisters." The revised item is false (a few brothers and sisters fight very little), but it is *not* the same item as the one on the test.

Similarly, refrain from adding some qualifying phrase and then saying "true" to this new item you just composed. For example, suppose an item is this: "Hunger generally leads to decreased activity and increased apathy." This is false. Suppose we add a phrase: *Extremely intense and prolonged* hunger generally leads to decreased activity and increased apathy. This new item is true. Some students will add that italicized phrase, unwittingly, and thus put down the wrong answer.

Likewise, if the question says, "If X, then Y," do not change it mentally to "If and only if X, then Y." That is a different question from the one asked and may well have a different answer. "If a person boasts a lot, he probably has intense feelings of inadequacy." "Only if a person boasts a lot, does he probably have intense feelings of inadequacy." The first statement is true; the second is false.

Perhaps we should warn you: Many students are utterly unaware that they do these things. This complicates their problem. However, if you watch closely for such tendencies in yourself, you will become better able to detect them and thus better able to avoid them.

b) Guard against reading out of the question — e.g., dropping qualifying phrases which are in the statement, ignoring a "generally" or a "to some extent." Answer the question asked, not some alternative question you make up during the test. One way to guard against this danger is by underlining "generally," "not," "sometimes," "in part," and other similar modifying words or phrases. For example, suppose an item on a true-false test is this: "Hostile aggression is caused in part by frustration." That statement is true.

However, some students will mark it false because they will forget the "in part" and will remember that frustration is not the entire cause. If you underline "in part," this will help you avoid making that mistake.

c) Watch carefully the meaning of double negatives. "No one is always incorrect" does not mean "someone is always correct."

d) Of all occasions for attempting to educate your professor, during an objective test is least propitious. On an objective test, you have no opportunity to develop your view. You have no opportunity to state why you think your answer is more sound than the one you suspect the professor deems "right." You have no chance, even, to show that you know which answer he considers right — unless you put that answer down.

If you value being a free spirit, a test is no time to declare your independence. Far better times are an office hour, class-time, or over a cup of coffee, for then you can present your ideas more adequately and discuss with your professor the evidence you think is inconsistent with his views.

e) Watch for systematic errors. By a systematic error we mean making the same kind of mistake over and over, and making that kind of mistake much more often than other kinds. For example, some students make the majority of their errors by marking false items "true"; some others make the majority of *their* errors by marking true items "false." Some students, when they change their answers, consistently change more correct answers to incorrect than they change incorrect answers to correct. Not all students, however, change more correct answers to incorrect than fix incorrect answers to be correct. Check for yourself to ascertain what your own tendencies are and what, if any, kinds of systematic errors you make. Look for such systematic errors in yourself.

f) Do not assume that because a proposition looks unfamiliar, it probably is false. Although a proposition may not have been in the textbook or lectures, quite possibly it can be derived logically from that material and therefore is "true."

g) If at first the answer to some question is obscure, take a few minutes to try to figure out the answer. Use your store of relevant facts and principles, and see if you can deduce from them an answer.

If the answer still is not clear, mark the item and skip it temporarily. You can learn during tests, gaining new insights and new understandings. You also can get free of the set with which you first viewed the question. Quite often, therefore, when you return to these items, you will find the answer is now clear in light of your new information and new internal organization.

h) Under no circumstances stay on some question until you become anxious and apprehensive. Doing so merely impairs your ability to answer other questions which would have been easy for you.

i) When you receive the test, glance over the test to ascertain whether all parts are about the same. Then plan your time (see Section H, pages 126-127).

j) Know before you begin the test whether guessing will be penalized, whether wrong items will be subtracted from right, etc. Procedures vary from professor to professor, and also from test to test. If the answers to these questions are known before the test begins, full attention can be devoted to the test without needlessly cluttering your mind with such simple, but important, questions.

3. ANXIETY CAN BE REDUCED BY STUDYING AND TAKING
   TESTS IN THE WAYS OUTLINED ABOVE.

How one has studied throughout the term is a large part
of skill in taking examinations. This takes only a sentence to
say, but probably it is the most important single pointer you
can be given.

The techniques of study and preparing for examinations discussed in the preceding sections not only help one
do a more creditable job on a test; they also help one stay
calm. Let us now look into some of the other, deeper aspects
of test-panic.

4. ARE WE NERVOUS BECAUSE THE QUESTIONS MAY BE
   UNFAIR?

Often we say we are nervous because the test may be
unfair. Sometimes we really are. More usually, however,
when we say we fear the test will not be fair, we fear the
opposite even more: We are deeply afraid the test will be
fair, all too fair. We are terrified lest our real or imagined
weaknesses be displayed. When unprepared or when deeply
unsure of ourself, no prospect is more terrible than that of a
fair test. Only rarely is the possibility of illegitimate questions
a major cause of anxiety.

5. OFTEN WE WORRY AND DO POORLY BECAUSE WE FEEL
   WE DESERVE TO FAIL.

Bizarre though this idea at first appears, it is true. Often
we feel incompetent, inadequate, and as though we simply
do not deserve to succeed. We feel unworthy of high success.
As a common consequence, we become panic-stricken and
do poorly. (You will find vivid, penetrating analyses of such

instances in articles by Sperry[96] and Sutherland[100] and in books by Freud.[26, 27])

Guilt feelings, as they technically are called, often are rooted deeply and stem from basic conflicts or from imagined sins. Experts can help you alleviate such difficulties. Other times, guilt feelings arise from relatively superficial causes. For example, we may have feelings of guilt because we studied only a little when we feel we were morally obliged to study more.

6. STUDYING A TREMENDOUS AMOUNT ALSO CAN CAUSE ANXIETY, WHEN THIS STUDYING IS DONE PRIMARILY FOR GRADES.

With such a procedure, too much is at stake during the test. Too much depends upon "success" on the test to be able to stay calm. *If* you feel you have made heavy sacrifices in order to study, and *if* the main point of that studying was to make a high grade, then you feel you *must* make a high grade in order to justify the expenses already occurred. You simply must do well on the test, in order to keep your sacrifices from having been in vain. The possibility that all those sacrifices may have been for nought can lead to real terror.

So we see that studying very little can lead to anxiety and also studying a great deal can lead to anxiety (under the particular circumstances specified above).

This dilemma can be resolved neatly: Instead of studying for grades primarily, study for intrinsic values. For example, if you value becoming more skilled in thinking, practice thinking while studying; then the study process itself is valuable to you. If you care about having a wide fund of information, be increasing your store of facts while studying. In short, study in such a way that the studying itself is worthwhile, and is worthwhile *regardless* of grades or any other extrinsic reward which may or may not accrue subsequently. That method can greatly reduce your anxiety on examinations. You can take tests with new nonchalance, for no matter how the test goes, you cannot possibly lose everything. You *know* that not all can be lost—no matter what the grade you get, for your studying will already have been profoundly worth doing.

In life in general, much anxiety, many disappointments, considerable bitterness can be avoided by following this policy: In all your activities, do them in ways such that the "doing" itself is of worth. In other words, strive largely for intrinsic values rather than extrinsic rewards (such as grades, higher pay, or people's applause). This approach to life can free you from many deep, unverbalized fears, and give you new peace, new exuberance in living.

The feeling that "all will be lost unless I do well on this test" can be alleviated in other ways too. One is this: Ask yourself, "If I should fail to do well on this test, just what will be lost?" Then determine whether that is everything to you. Is it even what you value most in life?

To face these questions requires courage. Much courage always is needed for looking at ourselves, or for looking at anything else—when we fear what we may discover. If, however, you can bring yourself to face these matters, you often will discover that not as much rests solely on the outcome of the test or other dreaded event as you originally felt. In a few rare instances, your fundamental values actually will be at stake. Even then, you often can create alternative ways of achieving those same values. A high grade on some examination or in some course is not, for example, the only conceivable route to your most fundamental goals.

7. Loss of anonymity is a source of near-terror to some students.

We spend much of our lives immersed in groups. We sit in large lectures, a part of a sea of persons. We shop in supermarts, anonymously. We belong to committees and are one of several names at the bottom of the report. We go to concerts, talks, mass meetings, and are one of the many—unidentified, not sorted out. We speak of "our group." We may think of ourselves primarily in terms of our membership in some group—as a Gamma Delta, a hippie, a Young Republican, a teen-ager, a. . . . We are accustomed to living as part of a group, acting as a part of a team, working as a part of committees, a part of a choir, a part of some other group.

Probably no one thinks of himself only as a part of some group. Nor are anyone's actions ever wholly anonymous. And yet this is a large part of our accustomed life.

Examinations are quite different. Examinations can become very personal. One can feel that one is being scrutinized, sorted out, no longer just one of an amorphous class. This can be frightening. On examinations we are expected to act separately and independently, and are held responsible for whatever answers we put down. These are highly desirable skills to possess but they are not ones with which many students begin their college career, and this poses problems hard to handle.

Knowing what the problem is can help you some in coping with it. Some other aids are these: Know that rarely or never is your worth being judged; seldom are you yourself being evaluated, but only one fragment of you. (By the way, in some courses you will be as anonymous as ever on examinations.) Realize that very rarely are you on display, being singled out. Use examinations as a place to practice being an independent, self-reliant, self-contained unit of action. Take test situations as an opportunity to grow and to extend your skills and abilities to handle various situations.

In the last chapter of this book, suggestions are offered on ways to handle problems of dependency, self-debasement, fear of failure and ridicule. These can aid you here too.

8. FEAR ON EXAMINATIONS CAN STEM FROM FEAR OF
   LOSING FRIENDS.

Sometimes we hardly dare do well on an examination lest people no longer like us. Almost anyone, of course, is apt to dislike us if we belittle his efforts, make adverse remarks about his intelligence, or in other ways demean him.

But suppose you are not a braggart nor a bully, and do not flaunt your achievements nor debase those of others. There is no evidence, then, that high grades place you in jeopardy. In fact, there are many data suggesting the opposite (see pages 232-236).

High grades do not jeopardize friendship. This is what one would expect if one were thinking about the matter quietly. Friends, by definition, want you to develop your potentialities the very best you can—especially those potentialities you care most about (whether or not *they* value developing those same assets in themselves). If you do not ridicule their interests and talents, they are not apt to ridicule yours nor lament your successes.

9. SET REASONABLE GOALS FOR YOURSELF.

Demanding the nearly impossible as a prerequisite for self-respect is another major cause of anxiety on examinations. For that matter, it causes much of the deep anxiety which plagues our lives. We should, therefore, try to eliminate habits of perfectionism.

A procedure opposite to perfectionism that is hit upon by some of the very young, and some not so young, will not do either for civilized human living: viz., jettisoning all goals, junking all values. We cannot build any of the things which take time; we cannot pool resources; we cannot count on others, nor upon ourselves, without clear and definite standards. But we need not be perfectionists. Another way is open.

Make your self-respect rest upon *approaching* your ideals with increasing closeness, rather than upon *reaching* those ideals. Ideals should be something to steer by and work toward, not something to attain instantly or else to abandon.

10. SKIP SCARING YOURSELF.

Some students try to motivate themselves on examinations by impassioned pep-talks on the importance of remembering everything. We have considerable reason to believe that being-motivated-to-remember while learning is a facilitator to learning,[6, 39, 58] but being-motivated-to-remember only while taking a test is no help at all.[39, 111] In other words, if you are going to make speeches to yourself stressing how important it is to remember a great deal—do it while you are studying, not while taking tests. During tests, such injunctions are apt merely to frighten you and impair your chances of doing well.

11. TO REDUCE TEST PANIC, DO NOT STUDY THE NIGHT
      BEFORE A TEST — UNLESS YOU CAN STUDY
      SERENELY AT THAT TIME.

This proposition follows directly from our previous consideration of the effects of anxious cramming on anxious test-taking. (See pages 49-51.)

Note too that fatigue increases anxiety. With inadequate amounts of sleep, one worries more and is more apprehensive and anxiety-ridden. A part of the very intense anxiety students suffer during final examinations may well arise from the serious deficiencies in sleep they incur at that time. This again suggests that whether you do or do not study the night before a test, arrange life so you get sufficient sleep. Especially if you are prone to high anxiety, arrange your time to get adequate rest.

12. ALLOW TIME TO GET TO THE TEST LEISURELY.

We have watched our friends rushing about the house and campus, madly collecting things, frantically finishing last-minute details, dashing to class at something approaching a wild gallop, arriving with pounding heart as the bell rang and the papers were being passed out. Yet they wonder why they are tense when the test begins, and why they need half an hour to get calm enough to think. This is no occasion for wonder, really. Those students had made themselves appallingly tense and anxious before ever getting to the test.

13. SIT WHERE YOU USUALLY SIT.

The chair you have used during lectures and discussions has decided advantages over other spots. In that spot you have done some clear thinking, have considered in detail the subject matter of this course, have answered aloud or to yourself some questions, and have been relatively calm. You also feel at home there. This means that when you sit there, you have at least some of the now-present stimuli already nicely established as cues for being relaxed and calm, for thinking clearly, for verbalizing pertinently and coherently. These supports will not guarantee that on the examination you will think well, remember everything you have heard there, and stay serenely calm, but they do stack the cards in your favor. The test situation will be less jarringly different from the learning situation. Further, it will contain many cues for the responses you want.

14. BUILD A MORE COMPREHENSIVE, REALISTIC VIEW OF
     THE USES OF TESTS.

Our conception of tests shrinks, oftentimes, until finally we regard tests as having one function only, and that their most wretched. We see them as a rather harsh way of grading our work, and possibly ourselves.

We become panicky lest our inner weaknesses be exposed. This fear of tests is much the same as our fear in other situations. We become jittery when forced to play a new game. Will we make fools of ourselves? We are suddenly apprehensive about meeting the renowned scholar. Will he think us stupid? Or shallow? Or poorly informed? We dread parties. Will we make blunders, say the wrong thing, do the wrong thing, be disgraced in front of all those people? We shrink from doctors and even from dentists. They might discover something wrong with us. At a sudden question, we quake.

These fears are largely unwarranted. Certainly in examinations, your professor is not looking for anything very deep. Seldom does he draw any sweeping conclusion about you or your nature, no matter what you do on a test.

Tests are not a way of grading *you*. They are one way of partially grading your work. You can make them far more than that. You can make tests into things of horror, or you can make them into something immensely valuable.

You can learn to use tests toward many ends: as an aid for evaluating your present study techniques . . . as a way to ascertain where your information and thinking are strong, and where they are weak . . . as a clue to areas in which you might strive to improve . . . as a way to discover where you have been making mistakes, and how better to eliminate them . . . as an opportunity to learn how to adjust to "failure" (a set of skills indispensable for becoming a mature person and a happy one) . . . as one basis to help you select a major and an appropriate vocation . . . as a place to practice thinking and solving problems alone . . . as an opportunity to pick up skill in adult living. These too are uses of examinations. Surely you know this; but unhappily you tend to forget these possibilities if you are like most of us.

Examinations are not designed as instruments of torture; you need not let them function as such.

15. Mild amounts of anxiety can be tolerated.

Some days are too warm. Some days are too cold. And some days are anxious ones. Much can be said for learning to tolerate such inconveniences when not extreme and for learning to creditably carry on in the face of them.

You can reduce anxiety in many ways. Almost certainly, however, you cannot reduce anxiety to zero; nor is there any compelling reason that you should. High anxiety is disruptive to problem-solving,[7, 17, 95, 98, 99] to performance on various kinds of achievement tests[10, 16, 18, 78, 79, 85, 89, 98, 101] and college aptitude tests,[85, 89] to appropriate generalizing of concepts,[50] and to intellectual functioning in other respects.[1, 7, 41, 84, 86, 87–89, 111] It is also deleterious in other ways,[74, 102] even affecting how much one can see at a glance,[32] especially if one is working against time[73] or feels trapped and has no way of coping with the situation.[106]

However, mild anxiety is not particularly disruptive,[33, 59, 93, 98] and may in fact enhance academic performance if the individual is functioning far below his potential,[82] and sometimes under other circumstances too.[59, 97]

Often we become anxious in the face of impending
examinations, and still might do all right; then we worry,
and become anxious about being anxious—thereby setting
up a dangerous cycle and pushing anxiety to a damagingly
high level. The data suggest that we should try to prevent
anxiety from reaching high levels, but that small amounts of
anxiety are no cause for alarm.

16. THE FOREGOING ANALYSIS IS PERFORCE INCOMPLETE.

However, through understanding even these causes of
anxiety and fear, you can devise additional ways to reduce
the causes and thus reduce the contingent panic or despon-
dency.

Suppose even with patience and practice of these new
techniques, panic still persists. In such instances there may
be some deeply underlying, complex difficulty. You can
work out such problems more easily with a partner who is an
expert in the area of personality formation. Some social
agencies, clinical psychologists, and psychiatrists can offer
you effective assistance. These men and women have studied
intensively what sorts of things make people happy and what
sorts of things make them miserable. They understand many
complicated difficulties and their causes. Through their
training and experience, they often can help you find the
roots of various troubles and can help you devise ways to
reduce or eliminate them.

Sometimes counseling or psychotherapy makes no significant difference in one's academic performance,[5, 40, 45, 92, 110]

although it may have other significant effects,[5, 23, 76] and sometimes the improvement is only temporary;[29, 37] but sometimes the changes are quite dramatic, with significant improvement in one's course grades,[15, 19, 24, 28, 52, 61, 83, 90, 94, 103, 104, 108] as well as significant changes in one's self-concept, including heightened self-respect and increased joyousness and peace in one's interactions with others.[11, 28, 31, 61, 67] Such changes are especially pronounced when the style of counseling or psychotherapy is appropriate to the particular individual seeking aid,[11, 19, 29, 67, 104] and at least sometimes the changes are known to persist.[15, 67, 83]

Various of the books by psychologists, psychiatrists, and psychoanalysts afford at least a glimpse of what these people can help one achieve. Such books also can aid you in gaining a more complete understanding of yourself. At the end of the chapter are listed some by Frank, Freud, Horney, Lindner, Maslow, Menninger, and Rogers, which you might find of especial aid.

D. Grades Versus Education?

Most students value high grades. Grades make some difference in obtaining certain jobs and in being admitted to graduate school, though grades alone make less difference than is commonly believed. Most students also value the attributes we call "being highly educated." Valuing both grades and education poses a problem.

As is well-recognized, one can get very high grades without becoming educated. The activities practiced by people working primarily for grades seldom facilitate becoming educated. In fact, working primarily for grades almost eliminates our chances for becoming educated.

This does not mean grades and education do not mix! It means they do not mix that way.

Working for grades usually prevents getting an education. But *working for a fine education* does not prevent getting high grades. This last proposition is scarcely debatable, for many people have done just that. They strove skillfully and consistently to become highly educated, and ceased working for grades. As a result they developed those skills and habits which constitute being highly educated; as a sort of by-product, they made top-flight grades.

There are, you see, two alternative methods of making a high grade-point-average. One is to work for grades; the second is to strive to become educated. The second is probably a more effective way to achieve a high grade-point-average and the *only* way to become highly educated.

These two ways of going to school have other radically different results. The person who primarily works for grades usually finds studying a tedious series of chores, an onerous burden imposed upon him by someone else. When he graduates, the results of his studying often do not seem worth the effort. He wonders why he worked so hard and so long. He feels let down, somehow betrayed.

The person who, on the other hand, sets out to become educated, generally enjoys the process. He makes school and studying a stimulating series of experiences, fascinating and fun. When his schooling is finished, he is not disillusioned nor in doubt about the worth of his work. The results of his study often seem even more precious and satisfying than he had anticipated.

Getting grades and getting an education are incompatible if (perhaps *only* if) one works primarily for grades. They are highly compatible when one forgets grades and endeavors to become educated. One achieves, thereby, much of lasting pleasure.

E. Concluding Comments — Pointers Concerning the Use of These Suggestions

As we were noticing, the same skills and habits which facilitate becoming educated also facilitate getting high grades. Each technique in these chapters does double duty — working toward both ends.

However, developing these modes of response requires practice. Even to remember the techniques takes practice. When first starting, do not try to use all of these new methods simultaneously. Be satisfied with working on only a few. Practice a few one week, add some more the next week, and so on. They will become habitual, taking no more time and effort than commoner methods of study and with more gratifying results.

The prospect of trying to build new skills is frightening to some people. It takes so much time and effort. But are these such fearsome drawbacks?

Many of you now dance beautifully. How many lessons did you have from friends or from professionals? How many hours did you practice by yourself or with a companion? Probably you cannot recall. And in addition to all those hours, you practiced at every dance you attended. Some of us have devoted a large proportion of our life to perfecting these skills, and they are worth it to us.

Are other skills in living worth as much time and wholehearted effort as that devoted to dancing? Is becoming educated worth as much? Our entire life is colored by the extent to which we develop those skills and outlooks. So also are the lives of our friends and associates and the nature of the world of which we are a part. No time will be more suited to their creation and development than our years in college.

We should observe too that expending considerable time and effort on a project does not make it drudgery.

Having spent uncounted hours on becoming a more skilled dancer in no way ruined dancing for us, nor made it burdensome work.

Whether something is work or play depends very little upon the nature of that activity, or the amount of time and effort it entails. Rather, whether something is work or play depends primarily upon us—and how we approach the activity. When we tackle a project enthusiastically, because we are eager to learn and not because we feel obliged to do so, it is play. When we do not, it is work.

Becoming a skillful dancer was fun—despite the patience required, the slow progress made at first, and the energy and time still required. Becoming an educated person can be fun also.

Bibliography for Chapter 3

1. Amoroso, Donald M.; and Walters, Richard H. Effects of anxiety and socially mediated anxiety reduction on paired associate learning. J. Personality Soc. Psychol., 11, 388-396, 1969.
2. Anderson, Ruth I.; Straub, Lura Lynn; and Gibson, E. Dana. Word Finder. Englewood Cliffs, N.J.: Prentice-Hall, Inc., 1960.
3. Bahrick, Harry P. Discriminative and associative aspects of pictorial paired-associate learning: Acquisition and retention. J. Exper. Psychol., 80, 113-119, 1969.
4. Bartley, S. H.; and Chute, E. Fatigue and Impairment in Man. New York: McGraw-Hill Co., 1947.
5. Berg, Robert C. The effect of group counseling on students placed on academic probation at Rock Valley College, Rockford, Illinois, 1966-67. Diss. Abstr., 29 (1-A), 115-116, 1968.
6. Berlyne, D. E.; and Carey, S. T. Incidental learning and the timing of arousal. Psychonomic Sci., 13, 103-104, 1968.
7. Boersma, F. J.; and O'Bryan, K. An investigation of the relationship between creativity and intelligence under two conditions of testing. J. Personality, 36, 341-348, 1968.
8. Bowen, J. H.; Hussman, T. A.; and Lybrand, W. A. A review of the literature on induced systemic fatigue. Tech. Rept. No. 7, Proj.

DA-49-007-MD-222, Army Med. Res. & Devel. Div., Univ. of Maryland, March, 1952.

9. Broadbent, D. E. Neglect of the surroundings in relation to fatigue decrements in output. In Floyd, W. F.; and Welford, A. T. Symposium on Fatigue. London: H. K. Lewis and Co., 1953.

10. Bronzaft, Arline L. Test anxiety, social mobility, and academic achievement. J. Soc. Psychol., 75, 217-222, 1968.

11. Brown, Robert D. Effects of structure and unstructured group counseling with high- and low-anxious college underachievers. J. Couns. Psychol., 16, 209-214, 1969.

12. Buschke, Herman. Encoding for short-term storage. Psychonomic Bull., 1, 14, 1967.

13. Calfee, Robert C. Recall and recognition memory in concept identification. J. Exper. Psychol., 81, 436-440, 1969.

14. Calfee, Robert C; and Peterson, Richard E. Effect of list organization on short-term probe recall. J. Exper. Psychol., 78, 468-474, 1968.

15. Chestnut, William J. The effects of structured and unstructured group counseling on male college students' underachievement. J. Couns. Psychol., 12, 388-394, 1965.

16. Cowen, E. T.; Zax, M.; Klein, R.; Izzo, L. D.; and Trost, M. A. The relation of anxiety in school children to school record, achievement, and behavioral measures. Child. Devel., 36, 685-695, 1965.

17. Davis, William E. Effect of prior failure on subjects' WAIS Arithmetic subtest scores. J. Clinical Psychol., 25, 72-73, 1969.

18. Dember, W. N.; Nairne, F.; and Miller, F. J. Further validation of the Alpert-Haber achievement anxiety test. J. Abnorm. Soc. Psychol., 65, 427-428, 1962.

19. Dickenson, W. A.; and Truax, C. B. Group counseling with college underachievers. Personnel Guid. J., 45, 243-247, 1966.

20. Dominowski, Roger L. Concept attainment as a function of instance contiguity and number of irrelevant dimensions. Proceedings 76th Annual Conv. Amer. Psychological Assoc., 3, 41-42, 1968.

21. Dong, Tim; and Kintsch, Walter. Subjective retrieval cues in free recall. J. Verbal Learning Verbal Behav., 7, 813-816, 1968.

22. Edwards, A. S. Effects of the loss of one hundred hours of sleep. Amer. J. Psychol., 54, 80-91, 1941.

23. Finney, Ben C.; and Van Dalsem, Elizabeth. Group counseling for gifted under-achieving high school students. J. Couns. Psychol., 16, 87-94, 1969.

24. Flook, Alfred J. M.; and Saggar, Usha. Academic performance with and without knowledge of scores on tests of intelligence, aptitude, and personality. J. Educ. Psychol., 59, 395-401, 1968.

25. Frank, Jerome D. Persuasion and Healing: A Comparative Study of Psychotherapy. Baltimore: Johns Hopkins Press, 1961.

26. Freud, S. Psychopathology of Everyday Life. (Translated by A. A. Brill.) New York: Macmillan & Co., 1914.

27. Freud, S. Introductory Lectures on Psychoanalysis. (Translated by Joan Riviere.) London: G. Allen & Unwin, Ltd., 1922.

28. Gilbreath, Stuart H. Group counseling with male underachieving college volunteers. Personnel Guid. J., 45, 469-476, 1967.

29. Gilbreath, Stuart H. Appropriate and inappropriate group counseling with academic underachievers. J. Couns. Psychol., 15, 506-511, 1968.

30. Giorgi, Amedeo. Learning as a function of meaning levels with American and German Ss. Psychol. Rep.; 23, 27-39, 1968.

31. Goldman, Ruth K.; and Mendelsohn, Gerald A. Psychotherapeutic change and social adjustment: A report of a national survey of psychotherapists. J. Abnorm. Psychol., 74, 164-172, 1969.

32. Granger, G. W. Personality and visual perception: A review. J. Ment. Sci., 99, 8-43, 1953.

33. Grooms, R. R.; and Endler, N. S. The effect of anxiety on academic achievement. J. Educ. Psychol., 51, 299-304, 1960.

34. Hanna, Paul R.; Hanna, Jean S.; Berquist, Sidney R.; Hodges, Richard E.; and Rudorf, E. Hugh. Needed research in spelling. Elem. English, 43, 60-66 and 89, 1966.

35. Harari, H.; and McDavid, J. W. Cultural influences on retention of logical and symbolic material. J. Educ. Psychol., 57, 18-22, 1966.

36. Harkness, D. R. A surgical approach to large classes. J. General Educ., 17, 179-185, 1965.

37. Hart, Darrell H. A study of the effects of two types of group experience on the academic achievement of college underachievers. Diss. Abstr., 25, 1003-1004, 1964.

38. Haygood, Robert C.; Sandlin, J.; Yoder, D. J.; and Dodd, D. H. Instance contiguity in disjunctive concept learning. J. Exper. Psychol., 81, 605-607, 1969.

39. Heinrich, Barbara A. Motivation and long-term memory. Psychonomic Sci., 12, 149-150, 1968.

40. Hill, A. H.; and Grieneeks, L. An evaluation of academic counseling of under- and over-achievers. J. Couns. Psychol., 13, 325-328, 1966.

41. Hill, K. T.; and Sarason, S. B. The relation of test anxiety and defensiveness to test and school performance over the elementary-school years: A further longitudinal study. Monogr. Soc. Res. Child Devel., 2, #104, 1966.

42. Hodges, Richard Edwin. An analysis of the phonological structure of American-English orthography. Doctoral thesis. Stanford, Calif.: Stanford Univ., 1964, 635 pp. Diss. Abstr., 25, No. 10, 5788-5789, 1965.

43. Hodges, Richard Edwin. The case for teaching sound-to-letter correspondences in spelling. Elem. Sch. J., 66, 327-336, 1966.
44. Hodges, Richard Edwin; and Rudorf, E. Hugh. Searching linguistics for cues for the teaching of spelling. Elem. English, 42, 527-533, 1965.
45. Hogue, David W. The academic effect of counseling a group of underachieving college men. Diss. Abstr., 25, 5114-5115, 1965.
46. Horn, Thomas D. (Ed.) Research on Handwriting and Spelling. Champaign, Illinois: National Council of Teachers of English, 79 pp. 1966.
47. Horney, Karen. Self Analysis. New York: W. W. Norton & Co., 1942.
48. Horney, Karen. Our Inner Conflicts. New York: W. W. Norton & Co., Inc., 1945.
49. Horney, Karen. Neurosis and Human Growth: The Struggle toward Self-realization. New York: W. W. Norton & Co., Inc., 1950.
50. Katahn, Martin; and Branham, Lee. Effects of manifest anxiety on the acquisition and generalization of concepts from Hullian theory. Amer. J. Psychol., 81, 575-580, 1968.
51. Kintsch, Walter. Recognition and free recall of organized lists. J. Exper. Psychol., 78, 481-487, 1968.
52. Lichter, Sigmund J. A comparison of group counseling with individual counseling for college underachievers: Effect on self concept and academic achievement. Diss. Abstr., 27 (6-B), 2138-2139, 1966.
53. Liftik, Joseph; and Leicht, Kenneth L. Effect of number and relatedness of stimulus-term components on paired-associate learning. Psychonomic Sci., 13, 315-316, 1968.
54. Lindner, Robert M. The Fifty-Minute Hour. New York: Rinehart & Co., Inc., 1954.
55. Lovatt, D. J.; and Warr, P. B. Recall after sleep. Amer. J. Psychol., 81, 253-257, 1968.
56. Lybrand, W. A.; Andrews, T. G.; and Ross, S. Systematic fatigue and perceptual organization. Amer. J. Psychol., 67, 704-707, 1954.
57. MacKay, Donald G. Phonetic factors in the perception and recall of spelling errors. Neuropsychologia, 6, 321-325, 1968.
58. McGeoch, John A.; and Irion, A. L. The Psychology of Human Learning. New York: Longmans, Green, 1952.
59. McKeachie, W. J. Interaction of achievement cues and facilitating anxiety in the achievement of women. J. Appl. Psychol., 53, 147-148, 1969.
60. Mager, Robert F.; and McCann, J. Learner-controlled Instruction. Palo Alto, Calif.: Varian Associates, 1961.
61. Mandel, Harvey P.; Roth, Robert M.; and Berenbaum, Harris L. Relationship between personality change and achievement change as a function of psychodiagnosis. J. Couns. Psychol., 15, 500-505, 1968.

62. Mandler, George. Organization and memory. In Spence, Kenneth W.; and Spence, Janet T. (Eds.) Psychology of Learning and Motivation. Vol. 1. New York: Academic Press, 1967.

63. Mandler, George. Organized recall: Individual functions. Psychonomic Sci., 13, 235-236, 1968.

64. Mandler, George. Association and organization: Facts, fancies, and theories. In Dixon, Theodore R.; and Horton, D. L. (Eds.) Verbal Behavior and General Behavior Theory. Englewood Cliffs, N.J.: Prentice Hall, 1968.

65. Marshall, George R. Stimulus characteristics contributing to organization in free recall. J. Verbal Learning Verbal Behav., 6, 364-374, 1967.

66. Maslow, Abraham H. Toward a Psychology of Being. Princeton: D. Van Nostrand Co., Inc., 1962.

67. Mendelsohn, Gerald A.; and Rankin, Neil O. Client-counselor compatibility and the outcome of counseling. J. Abnorm. Psychol., 74, 157-163, 1969.

68. Menninger, Karl A. Man against Himself. New York: Harcourt, Brace & Co., 1938.

69. Menninger, Karl A. Love against Hate. New York: Harcourt, Brace & Co., 1942.

70. Meyer, G. An experimental study of the old and new types of examination. I. The effect of the examination set on memory. J. Educ. Psychol., 25, 641-661, 1934.

71. Meyer, G. An experimental study of the old and new types of examination. II. Methods of study. J. Educ. Psychol., 26, 30-40, 1935.

72. Montague, William E.; and Wearing, Alexander J. The retention of responses to individual stimuli and stimulus classes. Psychonomic Sci., 9, 81-82, 1967.

73. Morris, Larry W.; and Liebert, Robert M. Effects of anxiety on timed and untimed intelligence tests: Another look. J. Consulting Clin. Psychol., 33, 240-244, 1969.

74. Moses, Michael; and Marcia, James E. Performance decrement as a function of positive feedback: Self-defeating behavior. J. Social Psychol., 77, 259-267, 1969.

75. Norman, Donald A. Memory and Attention: An Introduction to Human Information Processing. New York: John Wiley and Sons, Inc., 1969.

76. Padgett, Harry G. Effects of group guidance and group counseling on the self concept and professional attitudes of prospective teachers. Diss. Abstr., 28 (10-A), 3976-3977, 1968.

77. Paivio, A.; Rogers, T. B.; and Smythe, P. C. Why are pictures easier to recall than words? Psychonomic Sci., 11, 137-138, 1968.

78. Phillips, B. N. Sex, social class, and anxiety as sources of variation in school achievement. J. Educ. Psychol., 53, 316-322, 1962.

79. Reese, H. W. Discrimination learning set in children. In Lipsitt, L. P.; and Spiker, C. C. (Eds.) Advances in Child Development and Behavior. Vol. 1. New York: Academic Press, 115-145, 1963.

80. Rogers, Carl R. Toward becoming a fully functioning person. In A. W. Combs (Ed.). 1962 Yearbook, Amer. Soc. for Curriculum Development. Washington, D.C.; National Education Assoc., 1962.

81. Rogers, Carl R. On Becoming a Person; A Therapist's View of Psychotherapy. Boston: Houghton Mifflin Co., 1961.

82. Rosmarin, Martin S. Reaction to stress and anxiety in chronically underachieving high-ability students. Diss. Abstr., 27 (5-B), 1630, 1966.

83. Roth, Robert M.; Mauksch, Hans O.; and Peiser, Kenneth. The non-achievement syndrome, group therapy, and achievement change. Personnel Guid. J., 46, 393-398, 1967.

84. Sarason, I. G. Effects on verbal learning of anxiety, reassurance, and meaningfulness of material. J. Exper. Psychol., 56, 472-477, 1958.

85. Sarason, Irwin G. Test anxiety and the intellectual performance of college students. J. Educ. Psychol., 52, 201-206, 1961.

86. Sarason, I. G.; and Minard, J. Test anxiety, experimental instructions, and the Wechsler Adult Intelligence Scale. J. Educ. Psychol., 53, 299-302, 1962.

87. Sarason, Irwin G.; and Palola, Ernest G. The relationships of test and general anxiety, difficulty of task, and experimental instructions to performance. J. Exper. Psychol., 59, 185-191, 1960.

88. Sarason, S. B.; Hill, K. T.; and Zimbardo, P. G. A longitudinal study of the relation of test anxiety to performance on intelligence and achievement tests. Monogr. Soc. for Res. in Child Devel., 29, #98, 1964.

89. Sassenrath, J. M. Anxiety, aptitude, attitude, and achievement. Psychol. in the Schools, 4, 341-346, 1967.

90. Schaar, William G., Jr. Changes in academic success and self-concept of low achieving community college freshmen. Diss. Abstr., 27 (9-A), 2750-2751, 1967.

91. Schulz, R. W.; Miller, R. L.; and Radtke, R. C. The role of instance contiguity and dominance in concept attainment. J. Verbal Learning Verbal Behav., 1, 432-435, 1963.

92. Semke, Charles W. A comparison of the outcomes of case study structured group counseling with high ability, underachieving freshmen. Diss. Abstr., 29 (1-A). 128, 1968.

93. Sinha, Durganand. A psychological analysis of some factors associated with success and failure in university education: Intelligence, anxiety and adjustment of academic achievers and non-achievers. Psychological Studies, 11, 69-88, 1966.

94. Smith, C. W.; and Walsh, W. Bruce. Effect of various institutional contacts upon the academic performance of the underachiever. J. Couns. Psychol., 15, 190-193, 1968.

95. Solso, Robert L. The effect of anxiety on cue selection in the A-Br paradigm. Psychonomic Sci., 13, 105-106, 1968.

96. Sperry, Bessie; Staver, Nancy; Reiner, Beatrice S.; and Ulrich, David. Renunciation and denial in learning difficulties. Amer. J. Orthopsychiat., 28, 98-111, 1958.

97. Spielberger, Charles D. The effects of manifest anxiety on the academic achievement of college students. Ment. Hyg., 46, 420-426, 1962.

98. Stakenas, Robert G. Evaluative stress, fear of failure and academic achievement. Diss. Abstr., 27 (2-A), 401, 1966.

99. Stevenson, H. W.; and Odom, R. D. The relation of anxiety to children's performance on learning and problem-solving tasks. Child Devel., 36, 1003-1012, 1965.

100. Sutherland, J. D. Three cases of anxiety and failure in examinations. Brit. J. Med. Psychol., 19, 73-81, 1941.

101. Sweeney, Christopher J. The effects of stress and achievement anxiety on academic test performance. Diss. Abstr., 29 (3-A), 820-821, 1968.

102. Tedeschi, James; Burrill, Dwight; and Gahagan, James. Social desirability, manifest anxiety, and social power. J. Social Psychol., 77, 231-239, 1969.

103. Thelen, M. H.; and Harris, C. S. Personality of college underachievers who improve with group psychotherapy. Personnel Guid. J., 46, 561-566, 1968.

104. Tresselt, M. E. A preliminary study on factors in learning in a how-to-study course. J. Psychol., 64, 91-93, 1968.

105. Tulving, Endel; and Pearlstone, Z. Availability versus accessibility of information in memory for words. J. Verbal Learning Verbal Behav., 4, 381-391, 1966.

106. Wachtel, P. L. Anxiety, attention, and coping with threat. J. Abnormal Psychol., 73, 137-143, 1968.

107. Wallace, William P. Influence of test trials on the development of subjective organization in free recall. J. Exper. Psychol., 81, 527-535, 1969.

108. Watson, Gladys H. An evaluation of counseling with college students. J. Couns. Psychol., 8, 99-104, 1961.

109. Watts, Graeme H.; and Anderson, Richard C. Retroactive inhibition in free recall as a function of first- and second-list organization. J. Exper. Psychol., 81, 595-597, 1969.

110. Winborn, B. B.; and Schmidt, L. G. The effectiveness of short-term group counseling upon the academic achievement of potentially superior but underachieving college freshmen. J. Educ. Res., 55, 169-173, 1962.

111. Wrightsman, Lawrence S., Jr. The effects of anxiety, achievement motivation, and task importance upon performance on an intelligence test. J. Educ. Psychol., 53, 150-156, 1962.

chapter 4

Developing ability to concentrate: reducing fatigue

A. Distraction: Its Frequency and Repercussions

The "human memory still exceeds any machine memory both in overall capacity and in speed and flexibility of retrieval."[63] The human memory is a spectacular asset. So is our capacity to learn. Sometimes, though, when our efforts to learn and remember seem to get us nowhere, we wonder whether we have any abilities whatsoever along these lines.

Of the difficulties interfering with our efforts to learn and remember, poor concentration is outstanding.[3, 10, 58, 96] In fact, when a large group of students were asked to list five of their difficulties in studying, over 80% listed poor concentration.[10] Poor concentration was mentioned more often than any other difficulty, far surpassing even lack of interest.

Distressing enough in itself, inability to concentrate is rendered yet more distressing by the fatigue which accompanies it. Almost always, poor concentration and fatigue go hand in hand, accentuating each other.[40] Poor concentration leads to fatigue. Fatigue leads to poor concentration.

Both poor concentration and fatigue are caused in large part by conflict. We try to study, but simultaneously we are half set to abandon the whole business and do something else. We are inclined to jump up and tell someone to make less noise. We debate going out for the evening. We try to figure out some personal problem. We do all these things and simultaneously we try to study. We attempt to make incompatible reactions at the same time. This is what conflict means.

As a consequence we become tired. Studying, or anything else done with much conflict, is highly fatiguing. Even an hour of such studying leaves us weary, more weary by far than an hour of tennis. This is small wonder. Fatigue always results when we tear against ourselves.

What can be done about this? How can we reduce conflict, thus becoming better able to concentrate and less subject to fatigue? The problem can be tackled in many ways.

B. *Some Common Sources of Distraction and Some Ways to Reduce Them*

1. QUIET IS NEITHER NECESSARY NOR SUFFICIENT FOR CONCENTRATION.

Have you debated the merits of playing the radio while studying? If so, some information uncovered by Fendrick[32] might interest you. He had several groups of students study in quiet rooms. Others studied in rooms where lively music was played. On the average, for students of all levels of college aptitude, comprehension and retention of reading were decreased when exciting music was played. (Rate of reading, however, was not affected adversely, on the average, a fact which could lure one into believing he was doing as well with the music present as with it absent.) Similar results have been found in other research.[69, 88]

Many students also are distracted in the presence of talking, noise, and other extraneous stimuli. One is more apt to be distracted when the task is very tedious[13, 46] or difficult[12, 14, 17, 28, 47] or the material is relatively unorganized,[19] as well as when the extraneous stimuli are erratic[13, 16, 78, 95] or in the same sense modality as the information being processed.[12, 14] A quiet place for study can help. However, quiet definitely is not essential for avoiding distractions.

You can learn to not be distracted.[43, 56, 78, 86, 95] If you develop skill in an activity under relatively quiet circumstances, before the distraction sets in, you can carry your skill over better to distracting circumstances than if you try to start under the distracting circumstances.[15, 16, 46]

The data above and others[28, 45] suggest a second way to become impervious to potential distractors: Practice relatively easy but interesting tasks under potentially distracting circumstances; then when you are adept at ignoring the extraneous stimuli, shift to more difficult or less intriguing tasks.

You can become free from distractions even in noisy rooms; and you can be mightily torn by distractions even in quiet rooms. Quietness is neither necessary nor sufficient for concentration and freedom from distraction.

This fact is nicely illustrated by the experience of a friend. This girl lived in a sorority, not the quietest place in the world. To complicate matters further, her room became a gathering place. On many of the occasions when she found studying desirable, her room was filled with her friends, playing bridge, chatting and laughing. She seldom sent them away. She simply excused herself from the conversation, curled up in a chair, and studied. Other people would stop by. She greeted them, invited them in, and then went on with her work. She said this racket in no way distracted her, and probably it did not. She rarely was tired or cross. She made high grades—better than Phi Beta Kappa quality. Her concentration seemed in no way impaired.

Many experiments show the same thing: One can work efficiently in noisy surroundings, even on complex tasks.[2, 6, 7, 12, 23, 30, 42, 44, 53, 64, 65, 68, 69, 86, 93, 95]

A particularly enlightening experiment was performed by Hovey.[44] He had 171 people take two forms of an intelligence test, in which considerable speed and concentration were imperative for fine performance. The first form was taken in a quiet room, the second in a room equipped with many "distractors": seven bells, five buzzers, a 550-watt spotlight, a 90,000-volt rotary spark gap, a phonograph, two organ pipes of varying pitches, three metal whistles, a 55-pound circular saw mounted on a wooden frame, a well-known photographer taking pictures, and four students doing acrobatics. Sometimes there was quiet; sometimes one or two of these "distractors" were operating; sometimes several of them were going simultaneously. This is somewhat less peaceful than the typical college library. But even with this horrendous welter of extraneous stimulation, the group did as well as when the room was continuously quiet. In fact, they showed some improvement on the second test, although a trifle less than that of a control group who performed both times in a quiet room.

The results of another experiment are possibly even more spectacular.[2] The students were doing addition problems. Two groups of students actually did *better* work in noisy surroundings than in quiet rooms. They solved the problems both more rapidly and more accurately in the noisy room. These students had been shown a graph, reputedly the results of a previous experiment, showing that fast work is facilitated by noise.

Two other groups were shown a graph supposedly demonstrating the opposite results, that noisy surroundings retard mental work. These students did significantly worse in noisy surroundings than in quiet ones. Another group, shown no graphs, had no consistent differences in their performance under quiet and noisy conditions.

The behavior of these groups shows that distractedness depends upon much more than the presence or absence of noise. *The same external pattern can act as either a distractor or a facilitator, or as neither.* Whether something acts as a distractor or not depends largely upon our expectations, upon our own internal organization.

To gain additional insight into the nature of distraction and its causes, let us look at some other experiments, introduced by Morgan in 1916.[62]

He had individuals translate numbers into letters and letters into numbers according to a code system. The conditions were alternatingly quiet and noisy—the noise being furnished by a variety of bells, buzzers, and phonograph records. Accuracy of the work was not affected in any significant way. Speed was somewhat impaired with onset of either noise or quiet, but even this impairment did not long persist. The poorest workers were most disrupted by these changes; the best workers were affected little.

In another experiment the subjects engaged in different kinds of activities (addition and number-perception tasks) and had different kinds of "distractors" (the blast of a Klaxon horn and reputedly humorous stories told in a loud voice). Results were essentially the same. The onset of either noise or quiet acted as a temporary distractor, but recovery was rapid.[33]

Thus we see that one can rapidly learn not to be distracted, and can work as well under what generally are assumed to be distracting conditions as under quiet conditions.

Moreover, concentration in the presence of many extraneous stimuli does not necessarily tax one's system. The onset of the "distractor" sometimes is[39, 62] and sometimes is not[33] accompanied by an increase in energy expenditure. Sometimes, in fact, good work takes even *less* energy after the "distractor" has been present for a time than it took before the "distractor" began.[33, 62] However, even if the energy expenditure were increased by 60% (the most reported by these investigators), this would have no great effect on the general bodily economy of a student—because only trifling amounts of energy are needed for reading, thinking, and other mental activities.

One other study would probably interest you. Engineers of the United States Signal Corps tested precision instruments, working singly in well sound-proofed rooms. These rooms were specially constructed to eliminate all noise from outside the room and practically all noise too from the person within the room. The conditions seemed almost perfect for effortless concentration. However, after about half an hour, the men suffered acutely from "nervous exhaustion" and could not continue work. The apparently peaceful setup, singularly free of all noise and all other external distractions, was acutely distracting. Men could not work in it for long.

A recent experiment with college students had similar results.[8] Working conditions again were arranged to be unusually free of varying external stimuli. Here again these conditions were not conducive to high quality intellectual endeavor. In fact, the students did considerably poorer intellectual work than usual.

The experiments we have just discussed and others[14, 22, 25, 27, 55, 61, 83] eloquently demonstrate that the intensity, the number, and the nature of the external stimuli do not alone determine whether one is distracted. Whether one is distracted or not depends largely upon the nature of one's self — one's own internal stimuli and one's personal habits.[1, 2, 18, 35, 61, 71, 80, 91]

You, not the external stimuli, determine whether you will be distracted. *Distractions, it appears, are basically from inside ourselves, not from outside.*

The most efficacious way, then, to eliminate distractions is this: Instead of attempting to change the external world, change yourself.

Let us try to analyze more clearly what it is about ourselves which makes us distracted, and how we can change. Since the inner distractions differ from person to person, you must make most of the analyses for yourself. However, we can point out the kinds of things to look for and the kinds of approaches to use in combating the difficulties.

2. OUR RESENTMENTS DISTRACT US AND SENSITIZE US TO
   OTHER POTENTIAL DISTRACTORS; BUT WE CAN
   REDUCE THESE.

When people talk near our study room, many of us are disturbed. Why? The noise from talking is not great; and even if it were very great, not everybody would be distracted. Clearly we are not distracted by the noise *per se;* rather we are distracted by some of our reactions to the talking.

Often we feel the talking is inconsiderate. We feel abused and resentful. Why, we wonder, don't people treat us with more consideration? We are trying to work; therefore, they should keep quiet.

This is the way we often feel; and when we do, these feelings disrupt and distract us. What can we do about this? Tell the talkers to be quiet? You may *feel* that is a good plan. But do you *think* so? Probably you care about those people. Do you really want them to abandon activities they value? Or be obliged to go somewhere else—just because you happen to be studying? We may have a starry-eyed notion of what you are like, but we doubt that you would often want people to reshuffle their lives merely for your convenience. What do you think?

Let us consider this matter a little further. Do you like to have those whom you love be happy? Do you want them to be as happy as possible? Do you want to accord them as much freedom as possible? Remember, these questions do not involve the relative importance of your studying versus their activities; for, with practice, you can learn to study well even while they are talking. Do you really want them to keep still? Are you pleased by forcing people whom you cherish to drop pursuit of their interests? Or have to rearrange their lives because of you? Whenever you study well or pursue your other interests while permitting other people to continue their own activities, you increase their freedom and your own. Is this something you value?

Really think about these questions. If you do, you will become far less distracted in the presence of talking and laughing. Much of your annoyance will be broken up; much of your inclination to subdue people will be gone too. With these changes, distraction evaporates. You will have a new ability to study with concentration.

The same sorts of feelings often are aroused by interruptions, making them notoriously distracting. Someone calls to you or comes barging into your room while you are trying to study. You are annoyed. Without thinking, you make flash emotional responses. You are irritated at "the gross lack of consideration." And you are hurt—"People just don't care at all! They don't care about me and they don't care about what I am doing. At least, they sure don't show it." But wait! That impression cannot be accurate. That person must care about you, or he would not be there. He would not have interrupted you unless he wanted to be with *you*. He must want to communicate with *you*. Is that such a crime? From some standpoints, it would have been better had he chosen a different moment. There is much in favor of good manners. However, you can eliminate most of the losses from other people's inept timing.[56] What moment a person arrives will usually not matter much, for it will not be very disturbing *if* you learn to avoid resentment at the "intrusion." When he leaves, you can return to work and become engrossed without any additional lost time—unless you go on feeling annoyed.

To become better able to concentrate, we need not change other people nor their behavior. We need to change ourselves. To do this, try out the ideas offered above. They can give you, and your friends, new freedoms.

3. WISTFULNESS LEADS TO DISTRACTION; THIS TOO WE
   CAN REDUCE.

The sound of people laughing, chatting, having a good time together, may arouse civil war within you. You become torn between continuing to study and going to join them. Wistfulness creeps in. Conflict storms. Here again, it is the stimuli from these internal responses (not the talking itself) which distract you. In this instance, your conflict and wistfulness are the distractors, and it is these feelings you need to reduce in order to concentrate.

How can you reduce this conflict and wistfulness? For one thing, remember that this is an instance when you can have your cake and eat it too. You can study at that particular hour and have the joy of others' companionship at some other times. You are not committing yourself to a life of solitude and eternal studying merely because you devote this particular time to study. We should remember this. Unfortunately we forget it and as a consequence are caused needless worry and misery.

Many students have greatly reduced their conflict by another system: They earmark definite hours for study and other hours for recreation. This frees them from the almost perpetual conflict of trying to decide whether to study or whether to play. It also enables them to really believe that they too are going to have fun later on.

Still another way to combat internal distraction is this: Whenever you decide to study or decide to do anything else, practice sticking to your decision until your self-appointed job is completed. Establishing this as a habit greatly reduces the conflict now elicited by conversation and other trivial stimuli; thus it eliminates much of the distraction.

4. FEAR OF REJECTION AND OTHER CONFLICT-AROUSERS
   ARE POTENT DISRUPTERS; THEY NEED NOT CONTINUE
   TO EXIST.

Sometimes the real distractor is a nagging, almost unverbalized fear: Unless I stop studying and join other people, I may lose their friendship. Perhaps they will think I'm stuffy.

This raises some questions. Would *you* consider a person

stuffy just because he studied during some of the times you felt sociable? Do you withdraw *your* friendship and respect that easily? Is there any reason to believe others care less about you, or are so much less civilized than yourself? No sound basis exists, really, for thinking other people will drop you or withdraw their friendship on such slight provocation. A few may, but not many. Friendship is not that superficial, and you *know* this if, for a moment, you can stop feeling only and start thinking too.

Many students cannot study when company is present, and company is "always" present. Are you like that? If you are, you may suffer from the fear sketched above, a fear of losing friends. Or you may unwittingly feel obligated to drop whatever you are doing and join people who come to visit, albeit their presence was unexpected.

A part of the essence of friendship is this: One deeply wants his friend, or anyone else whom he esteems, to have as extensive freedom as possible for living his own life in his own way. Try giving your friends a chance to show this. If you have many things which need doing soon and few opportunities in which to do them, generally you can chat for a few minutes and then excuse yourself, making arrangements to meet at some other time. Such behavior is not only forgivable; it is deeply understandable. Further, such behavior is highly desirable—in the eyes of friends. To a great extent, friends want you to do whatever you think is best.

5. THE THREAT OF DEVASTATION DISRUPTS US.

For several decades now students have been trying to study and start their adult life under the continuing threat or actuality of extensive devastation. This is difficult. Today more efficacious tools for peace and abundant living exist than ever before; more efficacious tools for massive destruction or even obliteration of any life also exist.

If you are troubled by the specter of a thermonuclear disaster, as almost any sane, compassionate human being would be, the following books and article may prove especially worth looking into: Osgood's "An Alternative to War or Surrender," Hocking's "The Freedom to Hope," and Russell's "New Hopes for a Changing World." Particularly sustaining, they are suggestive of possible creative solutions to our new human dilemma.

6. YOUR RESPONSES TO A ROOMMATE'S MANNERISMS CAN DISTRACT YOU.

Is your roommate perfect? Most of us when asked this question could give plenty of reasons why our roommate is terribly annoying. He drums on the desk, or snaps his fingernails, or taps a pencil, or cracks his knuckles. Sometimes we are aroused to near-frenzy by such behavior. We go all to pieces and cannot study at all while such noises are going on.

Why are these trivial sounds so highly distracting? Here again it is not our roommate's behavior, but our own response, which shatters concentration.

A major source of our trouble is this: We are annoyed with ourself for being annoyed by him and his behavior. Then, naturally, we become annoyed with him for making us annoyed with ourself. (In many such cases, we notice only our annoyance with him.) Annoyance creates a great flood of internal stimuli which overwhelm and woefully disrupt us.

We sometimes become annoyed too because we feel our roommate's behavior is silly and thoughtless. His behavior *is* thoughtless—in the sense that it occurs without thinking. However, his behavior is not thoughtless in the more usual sense: Such behavior does not mean the person values your welfare lightly. As a matter of fact, unless your roommate expended great effort and unless he also possessed extraordinary skill in making and breaking habits, he could not possibly eliminate pencil-tapping and other such mannerisms — no matter how deeply he cared about you and longed to please you! He cannot eliminate those habits any better than you can cease twisting a lock of hair, or stop stammering occasionally, or quit blushing slightly. The reactions are made unconsciously. The person is not aware of making the reaction nor of the exact conditions which evoke it. He is aware only that he has made the reaction after it is done.

In a charming parody, Lewis Carroll pointed up the essential absurdity of irritation over these automatic reactions.

> "Speak roughly to your little boy,
> And beat him when he sneezes;
> He only does it to annoy,
> Because he knows it teases."[21]

That, of course, is ridiculous. Sneezing is not done to annoy us. Neither are the other reactions about which we have spoken. They do not mean that someone is indifferent to our wishes. What, then, do they mean?

These mannerisms signify tension. You are often tense, especially when working under pressure. Well, so is your roommate. Perhaps you "let off steam" by twisting a lock of hair; he "lets off steam" by drumming his fingers, or tapping his pencil, or acting in other similar ways. Such behavior merely shows that your colleague is overwrought. He is, for example, working very rapidly, or thinking hard, or worried.

The next time a pencil starts tapping or knuckles start cracking, try to remember these things. Say to yourself,

"Poor guy! He sure is tense tonight." If you can do this, life will run more smoothly for you, and also for your associates. Your world will be freer of annoyances and freer too, therefore, from distraction.

7. LET US SUMMARIZE — DISTRACTION OFTEN IS CAUSED BY SOME EMOTIONAL RESPONSE WHICH WE CAN MODIFY OR ELIMINATE.

Here is a résumé of the potentially revolutionizing ideas we have been examining. Whether or not we are distracted depends rather more upon us, our own internal stimuli and learned reactions, than upon external stimuli *per se*. The real distractions are not from without, but from within ourselves. More specifically, our distractions spring from such responses as these: a feeling that someone is being thoughtless and inconsiderate; a conflict between two action tendencies; an unspoken fear of losing the respect of others, or their friendship; a misinterpretation of situations with resultant irritation. These are only examples. Other reactions may be more characteristic of you. You must figure out for yourself what *you* are like, for many other emotional reactions also are distracting.

This, in turn, means: To greatly reduce or eliminate distractions, we need to change ourself. We need to break up the sorts of emotional response sketched above and learn different patterns of response.

How? The general approach is this: (1) Try to analyze the situations in which you cannot concentrate. Examine your feelings. Determine what really is distracting you. (2) Reinterpret the situation as rationally as you can, more rationally than we usually do. Often then you will perceive the external stimuli differently. Almost immediately they will be less potent distractors. (3) Set out to build new responses to these "distracting" stimuli. Let your brain have a voice here too, rather than permit your life to be tyrannized by flash emotional responses.

If you can have patience with yourself and persevere in your attempts, you can learn these arts.

Other means too are available for enhancing your ability to concentrate. We turn now to them.

8. WHEN POTENTIAL DISTRACTIONS ARE PRESENT, LAUNCH YOURSELF PARTICULARLY ENERGETICALLY INTO YOUR WORK.

For example, try at those times especially to actively search for new implications and new applications of what you read. Actively sort what you already know from what you did not, rather than passively wait for facts to sink in and ideas to occur to you. Various other ways whereby you can get started energetically studying were presented on pages 36, 52-69 of Chapter 2 (Starting Study and The Use of Books).

With these approaches, you sometimes will succeed in working effectively while former distractions are present. Each time you succeed, you are getting more stimuli established as cues for effective studying. You are making formerly distracting stimuli become cues for what you want to do. In the future, their presence actually will facilitate rather than hinder your studying. You will be developing increasingly great abilities to concentrate.

9. KEEP A PAD OF PAPER ON YOUR DESK AND JOT DOWN CERTAIN ONES OF YOUR DISTRACTING THOUGHTS.

Somehow it is just when we try to study that suddenly

we recall dozens of things we should have done. We remember the button not sewn on our coat. The button has been loose for days, but we forget it until we start to study. We remember letters which are not written and should be, questions we meant to ask a friend but forgot, phone calls to be made, a suit to be pressed, nails to be filed, books to be returned, a host of other neglected "duties." To make things still more complicated, it is when studying mathematics, for example, that ideas start popping for our English paper.

When thoughts of those kinds occur during study, write a brief note of them. This is a small thing to do, but it greatly increases your power to concentrate.

Without some such technique, you are attempting the impossible: You are trying to talk to yourself about your studies; simultaneously you are trying to talk to yourself about utterly unrelated matters, such as what you wish to do later. These are incompatible responses; doing both at once is a logical impossibility. Under such circumstances, concentration is impossible.

10. DIVIDE YOUR STUDIES INTO DEFINITE SUB-PARTS.

When starting to study, specify the particular skills you are going to acquire in this session or the units of material you are going to master. For example, specify a certain number of pages to be read . . . a definite number of math problems to be solved . . . a particular task to be accomplished in writing a term paper (e.g., outlining the paper, or arranging the bibliography, or polishing the phrases). You work until that part is done (regardless of time). This method of tackling your studies facilitates concentration.

Concentration is hindered, you recall, by specifying merely the number of minutes to study and failing to specify the job to be accomplished. Studying by the clock necessitates watching the clock while studying. Obviously this precludes becoming wholly absorbed in your studies. You cannot, under those conditions, build habits of studying wholeheartedly with real concentration.

Possibly you are so pressed for time you dare not do anything but allot a certain amount of time to each subject. One neat solution is to set an alarm or timer. This sounds a bit silly; but it helps. Setting an alarm gives you at least a chance of building habits of concentration. You can study without one eye and "half your mind" on the clock.

A useful variation is this: Set a goal for yourself of having completed a certain number of problems or pages or other parts in a certain amount of time. This can help appreciably when you are first learning to concentrate. Set a timer to go off when you should be half done (or have done a quarter, or some other fraction of your choosing). On various occasions you will be making your self-set goal; this heartens you. When you are not making it, this too can spur you on. When you note that you are a bit behind, try remembering your time-goal and throw yourself into your work with new fervor and interest; often (to your surprise) you will still manage to finish in the allotted time what you had hoped and intended. It becomes a game and a challenge.

11. SET REASONABLE TASKS FOR YOURSELF.

It is folly to try to do a week's assignments in one evening. The only results of such practices are apt to be vague fears, intensified anxieties, and a berating of oneself for failing a self-assigned task. Such emotions further impair our ability to concentrate.

12. ARRANGE EACH STUDY PERIOD SO THAT DIFFERENT
    TYPES OF STUDYING FOLLOW ONE ANOTHER.

For example, suppose you have two somewhat similar courses, such as sociology and psychology, and a third course that is quite different, such as mathematics. First study sociology, then mathematics, then psychology; or else, psychology, mathematics, sociology.

Or suppose you wish to read two chapters and review another chapter during some study period. Do not do all the reading first and then all the reviewing. Instead, interweave those activities. If you are reading and reviewing in ways like those sketched in Chapters 2 and 3, reading and reviewing will be quite different activities and refreshing changes from each other.

You can devise many other interleaving systems of your own. The basic idea is to arrange your study period so that you get variety *while* studying. Alternate many different sorts of activities. This enables you to study more easily for long periods of time, with the need for far fewer rest periods. In addition, interference effects can be thereby reduced—especially the kinds of interference in which learning one thing impairs retention of something else previously learned or impedes subsequent learning of something new.[11, 31, 34, 36, 54, 59, 66, 81, 82, 87, 89, 90, 92]

13. MAKE THE MOST OF REST PERIODS.

The purpose of rest periods is to provide relief from doing the same thing for too long. Naturally, then, your activity during rest periods should be as different as possible from that involved in the studying you were doing. If you have been writing a term paper, "resting" by writing a letter will not be very refreshing. Better far would be washing dishes, telephoning a friend, walking around the block, or doing some gardening. You can think of other activities which also take only a little time, and are a change from studying.

Often you can do a couple of items from the list of neglected "duties" which occurred to you while studying. This has a twofold value: it relaxes you by being a different sort of activity; and it relaxes you by eliminating one more small, but pestering, worry. You will have completed one more thing you wanted to get done.

14. DEVISE A SCHEDULE, UNLESS YOU ARE STRENUOUSLY OPPOSED TO THE IDEA.

If you find concentration difficult or are troubled by vague anxieties, a schedule can help considerably. One of the best kinds is this: parts of various days are reserved for social activities; other periods for taking care of various obligations; others for studying; and some parts of each day are left unscheduled.

Be sure to schedule time for social activities. To most people, social activities are just as important as study. Take that into account when making your schedule. This way of arranging one's week decreases the fear that all of life is going to be spent poring over books, that never will one have any fun. Such fears haunt many a student while he is trying to study. The fears are no less intense because they are irrational. Having certain hours reserved for social activities can be deeply reassuring. While you are studying you *know* gay times are coming and thus you can study with a greater enthusiasm and concentration.

Equally important is to leave a significant amount of time unscheduled. Many people, when first making a schedule, designate almost every waking hour for some particular activity. Consequently they feel enslaved—as indeed they are. Further, a student's life is rather chaotic. Many unforeseen things come up. A schedule must leave time free for attending to them.

Devising a schedule appropriate to you will take some trial and error. If your first schedule turns out to be impracticable and you cannot abide by it, revise it so you can.

Scheduling can work like a charm in cutting down on tensions, worries, and daydreams. But in order for the system to work, the earmarked periods must be held inviolate. They must always be used for their designated purpose and other activities re-directed to the free times.

15. CAST YOURSELF FOR A WORTHY ROLE WHEN
    STUDYING.[4, 5, 24, 26, 85]

Greater self-respect and better grades often appear together.[9, 20, 48, 49, 50, 51, 84, 94] You can increase your self-respect in various ways, some of which we have touched upon already; others are discussed later. This is simply one more.

You are many things. For one: You are a student. Define "student" in a way worthy of you and consistent with your goals. When you become discouraged or your "mind begins to wander," remind yourself of this role.

Many of you have been pummelled by strong forces leading you to see yourself as weak, or lazy, or stupid, or distraught. You need not cooperate on that project. Think of yourself in new ways which are worthy of your many wonderful capacities. "I *am* a potential doctor, by George!" "I *will* become a perceptive reader." We are not suggesting you try to hypnotize yourself. We are suggesting you devise for yourself and *live* a role you conceive to be worthy of your best potentialities.

You can become an increasingly expert student. You can learn how to learn. Squirrel monkeys can learn to learn;[73, 75] so can macaque monkeys;[37, 38, 79] so can chimpanzees and gorillas and orangutangs,[60, 74, 76] and even pigeons.[29] That is, members of all those species can get better and better at learning, making increasingly fewer errors on successive tasks, mastering new tasks and solving new problems increasingly swiftly. So can people.[52, 70, 72] And so can you.

Never forget what you have excellent reason to believe: You can learn increasingly well. You can learn, and change, and grow. You can become more nearly the person you long to be.

16. You are on scholarship.

Some of you realize that your attendance at a university or college is being made possible through a scholarship or fellowship you were awarded. However, in actuality all of you at any university or college are there on scholarships. Only a tiny part of the expenses of your advanced education are borne by you or your family. In the state colleges of California, for example, the cost per student was almost $500 per semester (1967-68), of which the student's fees were $61.50 for the term.

The situation is similar throughout the country. If you are a student at a state university or college, a major part of your expenses are covered by other citizens through taxes. If you are attending a private university or college, again most of the cost of your education is covered by other people through their endowments, trust funds, and other gifts to the university or college. These are almost incredible gifts.

Universities and colleges are almost incredible worlds. One such place anywhere would be worthy of wonder. For hundreds and thousands to exist in a country is a marvel. The remarkable libraries of books, and movies, and paintings, and films, and artifacts of other cultures; the lovely buildings and grounds—and some spots are truly beautiful; the projectors and screens and slides and microscopes and telescopes and other doorways to let you see worlds you have not seen before; the cafeterias and dormitories; the auditoriums and other carefully designed rooms with special lighting for art and engineering and other studies, special acoustics and special seating, for drama, music, speech, seminars; special supplies for music, botany, physics demonstrations, and other courses; the many kinds of laboratory equipment for dozens of kinds of courses; all of these and much more are made available to you through the care and generosity of former students and other citizens. The gifts are immense.

One of my favorite professors (my husband) wrote about this to his students. In connection with the prosaic matter of laboratory supplies, he noted:[57]

"To carry on research requires considerable material and equipment. Even simple investigations of the kind you will be doing here require considerable material and equipment—some of which is very expensive. Most of what you will need will be furnished to you as a gift from people you probably never will meet. Regardless of whether you are at a private university or college or are at a state university or college, the major expense of your education is being borne by people who do not know you and will probably never meet you. But nonetheless they are investing their resources in you, to enable you to better develop your abilities and realize your potentialities. Remember this as you accept and use their gifts."

These people, strangers to you, make no gain directly from your life becoming enriched and happier—nor from your becoming educated in any other sense. They are playing it on faith, that somehow this will be a better world when you are better educated; they are offering their gifts on trust to you. We have a high responsibility to these individuals. If we accept their gifts, we must keep faith and not betray that trust. The gifts are inestimably precious to many millions of persons. To be a recipient of such a gift is a privilege and a great honor. To be a student is a splendid thing.

When you are distraught and frantic, discouraged or filled with gloom, these facts are worth recalling. Many persons care tremendously about you, are backing you, and deem your undertaking as a student one of great merit.

C. Concluding Comments and a Forecast of Things to Come

To study with the results we value deeply, we must answer three questions: (1) Where am I? (2) Where do I want to be? (3) What is necessary to get there? The solution of any problem rests upon answering the same three questions.

Chapter 1 dealt with "where you want to be," with what sort of person you may long to become. Chapters 2, 3, and 4 indicated various routes for reaching those goals and steps which aid one to follow those routes. So far, "where you now are" has been only lightly touched. Chapter 5 treats that aspect of our problem in some detail.

The importance of this step should not be underestimated. No matter where we are trying to get, we must start from where we are. It helps tremendously to note where that is! Largely because of a failure to recognize this fact and because of impatience with its implications, we spend much time in futility. We try to brush our teeth in the fireplace — because the living-room is where we happened to be when we desired to clean our teeth. Of course you will not do that, exactly. You will, however, behave in strictly analogous fashions. You will try to leap to some goal which simply cannot be reached directly from where you happen to be. That you are so behaving will often not be clear to you. That the results are poor will be all too clear, however.

Let us turn now to where you are at present. Let us consider the aspects of your current position which hinder you in achieving your goals, and try to formulate some additional steps for leaving there and moving to positions from which your goals can be achieved more readily.

Bibliography for Chapter 4

1. Amoroso, Donald M.; and Walters, Richard H. Effects of anxiety and socially mediated anxiety reduction on paired associate learning. J. Personality Soc. Psychol., 11, 388-396, 1969.
2. Baker, K. H. Pre-experimental set in distraction experiments. J. Gen. Psychol., 16, 471-488, 1937.
3. Baker, R. W.; and Madell, T. O. A continued investigation of susceptibility to distraction in academically underachieving and achieving male college students. J. Educ. Psychol., 56, 254-258, 1965.
4. Battle, E. S. Motivational determinants of academic task persistence. J. Personality Soc. Psychol., 2, 209-218, 1965.
5. Battle, E. S. Motivational determinants of academic competence. J. Personality Soc. Psychol., 4, 634-642, 1966.
6. Bee, Helen L. Individual differences in susceptibility to distraction. Percept. Mot. Skills. 23, 821-822, 1966.
7. Berlyne, D. E.; and Carey, S. T. Incidental learning and the timing of arousal. Psychonomic Sci., 13, 103-104, 1968.
8. Bexton, W. H.; Heron, W.; and Scott, T. H. Effects of decreased variation in the sensory environment. Canad. J. Psychol., 8, 70-76, 1954.
9. Bhatnagar, K. P. Academic achievement as a function of one's self-concepts and ego-functions. Educ. Psychol. Rev., 6, 178-182, 1966.
10. Bird, C.; and Bird, D. M. Learning More by Effective Study. New York: Appleton-Century-Crofts, Inc., 1945, p. 24.
11. Blankenship, A. B.; and Whitely, P. L. Proactive inhibition in the recall of advertising material. J. Soc. Psychol., 13, 311-322, 1941.
12. Boggs, David H.; and Simon, J. Richard. Differential effect of noise on tasks of varying complexity. J. Appl. Psychol., 52, 148-153, 1968.

13. Broadbent, D. E. Noise, paced performance, and vigilance tasks. Brit. J. Psychol., 44, 295-303, 1953.
14. Broadbent, D. E. Some effects of noise on visual performance. Quart. J. Exper. Psychol., 6, 1-5, 1954.
15. Broadbent, D. E. Effects of noises of high and low frequency on behavior. Ergonomics, 1, 21-29, 1957.
16. Broadbent, D. E. Effect of noise on an "intellectual" task. J. Acoustical Soc. Amer., 30, 824-827, 1958.
17. Broadbent, D. E. S-R compatiblity and the processing of information. Acta Psychologica, 23, 325-327, 1964.
18. Broadbent, D. E.; and Heron, Alastair. Effects of a subsidiary task on performance involving immediate memory by younger and older men. Brit. J. Psychol., 53, 189-198, 1962.
19. Buschke, Herman. Verbal noise and linguistic constraints. Psychonomic Sci., 12, 391-392, 1968.
20. Caplin, Morris D. The relationship between self concept and academic achievement and between level of aspiration and academic achievement. Diss. Abstr., 27 (4-A), 979-980, 1966.
21. Carroll, Lewis. Alice in Wonderland. New York: Grosset & Dunlap, Inc., 1946, p. 63.
22. Chiles, W. Dean. Effects of high temperatures on performance of a complex mental task. USAF WADC Tech. Rep., No. 58-323, 1958.
23. Cofer, C. N.; and Dorfman, P. W. Free recall of trigrams in the presence of distractors: A replication. Psychonomic Sci., 14, 197, 1969.
24. Coombs, Robert H.; and Davies, Vernon. Self-conception and the relationship between high school and college scholastic achievement. Sociol. Soc. Res., 50, 460-471, 1966.
25. Craddick, Ray A.; and Grossmann, Klaus. Effects of visual distraction upon performance on the WAIS Digit Span. Psychol. Rep., 10, 642, 1962.
26. Crandall, Virginia C.; and McGhee, Paul E. Expectancy of reinforcement and academic competence. J. Personality, 36, 635-648, 1968.
27. Davis, F. B. Fundamental factors of comprehension in reading. Doctoral Dissertation. Cambridge, Mass.: Harvard Univ., 1941.
28. Davis, Gary A.; Train, Alice J.; and Manske, Mary E. Trial and error versus "insightful" problem solving: Effects of distraction, additional response alternatives, and longer response chains. J. Exper. Psychol., 76, 337-340, 1968.
29. Eck, Kenneth O.; Noel, Richard C.; and Thomas, D. R. Discrimination learning as a function of prior discrimination and nondifferential training. J. Exper. Psychol. 82, 156-162, 1969 (pigeons).
30. Egeth, Howard. Selective attention. Psychol. Bull., 67, 41-57, 1967.

31. Eschenbrenner, A. John, Jr. Retroactive and proactive inhibition in verbal discrimination learning. J. Exper. Psychol., 81, 576-583, 1969.

32. Fendrick, P. The influence of music distraction upon reading efficiency. J. Educ. Res., 31, 264-271, 1937.

33. Ford, A. Attention-automatization: An investigation of the transitional nature of mind. Amer. J. Psychol., 41, 1-32, 1929.

34. Frost, Robert R.; and Jahnke, John C. Proactive effects in short-term memory. J. Verbal Learning Verbal Behav., 7, 785-789, 1968.

35. Grim, Paul F.; Kohlberg, Lawrence; and White, Sheldon H. Some relationships between conscience and attentional processes. J. Personality Soc. Psychol., 8, 239-252, 1968.

36. Hamilton, C. E. The relationship between length of interval separating two learning tasks and performance on the second task. J. Exper. Psychol., 40, 613-621, 1950.

37. Harlow, Harry F. The formation of learning sets. Psychol. Rev., 56, 51-65, 1949.

38. Harlow, Harry F. The development of learning in the rhesus monkey. American Scientist, 47, 459-479, 1959.

39. Harmon, F. L. The effects of noise upon certain psychological and physiological processes. Arch. Psychol., 23, No. 147, 1933.

40. Henley, W. E. Fatigue. New Zealand Med. J., 50, 212-221, 1951.

41. Hocking, William Ernest. The freedom to hope. Saturday Review, 46, 12-15 and 50, 1963.

42. Houston, B. Kent. Inhibition and facilitating effect of noise on interference tasks. Percept. Mot. Skills, 27, 947-950, 1968.

43. Houston, B. Kent; and Jones, Thomas M. Distraction and Stroop color-word performance. J. Exper. Psychol., 74, 54-56, 1967.

44. Hovey, H. B. Effects of general distraction on the higher thought processes, Amer. J. Psychol., 40, 585-591, 1928.

45. Jerison, Harry J. Performance on a simple vigilance task in noise and quiet. J. Acoustical Soc. Amer., 29, 1163-1165, 1957.

46. Jerison, Harry J. Effects of noise on human performance. J. Appl. Psychol., 43, 96-101, 1959.

47. Jerison, Harry J.; and Wing, S. Effects of noise on a complex vigilance task. USAF WADC Tech. Rep. TR 57-14, AD 110700, 1957.

48. Johnson, Edward G., Jr. A comparison of academically successful and unsuccessful college of education freshmen on two measures of "self". Diss. Abstr., 28 (4-A), 1298-1299, 1967.

49. Jones, John Goff. Relationships among identity development and intellectual and nonintellectual factors. Diss. Abstr., 28 (3-A), 941, 1967.

50. Jones, John G. The relationship of self-perception measures and academic achievement among college seniors. J. Educ. Res., 63, 201-203, 1970.

51. Jones, John G.; and Strowig, R. Wray. Adolescent identity and self-perception as predictors of scholastic achievement. J. Educ. Res., 62, 78-82, 1968.

52. Keppel, Geoffrey; Postman, Leo; and Zavortink, Bonnie. Studies of learning to learn. VIII, The influence of massive amounts of training upon the learning and retention of paired-associate lists. J. Verbal Learning Verbal Behav., 7, 790-796, 1968.

53. Kirk, R. E.; and Hecht, E. Maintenance of vigilance by programmed noise. Percept. Mot. Skills, 16, 553-560, 1963.

54. Kothurkar, V. K. Effect of similarity of interpolated materials on short-term recall. Quart. J. Exper. Psychol., 20, 405-408, 1968.

55. Kryter, K. D. The effects of noise on man. J. Speech Dis., Monogr. Suppl., No. 1, 1950.

56. MacMillan, Donald L. Resumption of interrupted tasks by normal and educable mentally retarded subjects. Amer. J. Mental Deficiency, 73, 657-660, 1969.

57. McBlair, William. Experiments in Physiology (Second Ed.). Palo Alto, California: National Press Books, 1968.

58. McQuary, J.
Educ. Res., 48, 393-399, 1955.

59. Melton, A. W.; and Von Lackum, W. J. Retroactive and proactive inhibition in retention: Evidence for a two-factor theory of retroactive inhibition. Amer. J. Psychol., 54, 157-173, 1941.

60. Miles, R. C. Discrimination-learning sets. In Schrier, Allen M.; Harlow, Harry F.; and Stollnitz, Fred. (Eds.) Behavior of Nonhuman Primates. Vol. 1. New York: Academic Press, pp. 51-95, 1965.

61. Mitchell, Adelle H. The effect of radio programs on silent reading achievement of ninety-one sixth grade students. J. Educ. Res., 42, 460-470, 1949.

62. Morgan, J. J. B. The overcoming of distraction and other resistances. Arch. Psychol., 5, No. 35, 84 pp., 1916.

63. Norman, Donald A. Memory and Attention: An Introduction to Human Information Processing. New York: John Wiley and Sons, Inc., 1969.

64. Oltman, P. K. Field dependence and arousal. Percept. Mot. Skills, 19, 441, 1964.

65. Oltman, Philip K. Activation and cue utilization. Diss. Abstr., 26, No. 8, 4800, 1965.

66. Osgood, C. E. A study of the causes of retroactive inhibition. Amer. Psychologist, 1, 258-259, 1946.

67. Osgood, C. E. An Alternative to War or Surrender. Urbana: University of Illinois Press, 1962.

68. Park, James F., Jr.; and Payne, M. Carr, Jr. Effects of noise level and difficulty of task in performing division. J. Appl. Psychol., 47, 367-368, 1963.

69. Poock, Gary K.; and Wiener, Earl L. Music and other auditory backgrounds during visual monitoring. J. Indus. Engr., 17, 318-323, 1966.

70. Postman, Leo; Keppel, Geoffrey; and Zacks, Rose. Studies of learning to learn. VII, The effects of practice on response integration. J. Verbal Learning Verbal Behav., 7, 776-784, 1968.

71. Reese, H. W. Manifest anxiety and achievement test performance. J. Educ. Psychol., 52, 132-135, 1961.

72. Reese, H. W. Discrimination learning set in children. In Lipsitt, Lewis P.; and Spiker, Charles C. (Eds.) Advances in Child Development and Behavior. Vol. 1. New York: Academic Press, pp. 115-145, 1963.

73. Rumbaugh, Duane M. The learning and sensory capacities of the squirrel monkey in phylogenetic perspective. In Rosenblum, Leonard A.; and Cooper, Robert W. (Eds.) The Squirrel Monkey. New York: Academic Press, pp. 256-317, 1968.

74. Rumbaugh, Duane M.; and McCormack, Carol. The learning skills of primates: A comparative study of apes and monkeys. In Starck, D.; Schneider, R.; and Kuhn, H. J. (Eds.) Progress in Primatology. Stuttgart: Gustav Fischer, pp. 289-306, 1967.

75. Rumbaugh, Duane M.; and McQueeney, J. A. Learning set formation and discrimination reversal: Learning problems to criterion in the squirrel monkey. J. Comp. Physiol. Psychol., 56, 435-439, 1963.

76. Rumbaugh, Duane M.; and Rice, C. Learning-set formation in young great apes. J. Comp. Physiol. Psychol., 55, 866-868, 1962.

77. Russell, Bertrand. New Hopes for a Changing World. New York: Simon & Schuster, 1951.

78. Sanders, A. F. The influence of noise on two discrimination tasks. Ergonomics, 4, 253-258, 1961.

79. Schrier, A. M. Learning-set formation by three species of macaque monkeys. In Starck, D.; Schneider, R.; and Kuhn, H. J. (Eds.) Progress in Primatology. Stuttgart: Gustav Fischer, pp. 307-309, 1967.

80. Shapiro, M. B.; Slater, P.; and Campbell, D. The effects of distraction on psychomotor slowness in co-operative, depressed, and schizophrenic subjects. Brit. J. Soc. Clin. Psychol., 1, 121-126, 1962.

81. Shuell, T. J. Retroactive inhibition in free-recall learning of categorized lists. J. Verbal Learning Verbal Behav., 7, 797-805, 1968.

82. Slamecka, Norman J. Proactive inhibition of connected discourse. J. Exper. Psychol., 62, 295-301, 1961.

83. Smith, Kendon R. Intermittent loud noise and mental performance. Science, 114, 132-133, 1951.

84. Sparling, Joseph J. The etiology of self esteem in childhood and adolescence. Diss. Abstr., 29 (3-A), 820, 1968.

85. Stillwell, Lois J. An investigation of the interrelationships among global self concept, role self concept and achievement. Diss. Abstr., 27 (3-A), 682, 1966.

86. Treisman, Anne M.; and Riley, Jenefer G. A. Is selective attention selective perception or selective response? A further test. J. Exper. Psychol., 79, 27-34, 1969.

87. Twining, P. E. The relative importance of intervening activity and lapse of time in the production of forgetting. J. Exper. Psychol., 26, 483-501, 1940.

88. Uhbrock, Richard S. Music on the job: Its influence on worker morale and production. Personnel Psychol., 14, 9-39, 1961.

89. Underwood, B. J. Associative inhibition in the learning of successive paired-associate lists. J. Exper. Psychol., 34, 127-135, 1944.

90. Underwood, B. J. The effect of successive interpolation on retroactive and proactive inhibition. Psychol. Monogr., 59, No. 273, 1945.

91. Wagman, Morton. University achievement and daydreaming behavior. J. Couns. Psychol., 15, 196-198, 1968.

92. Watts, Graeme H.; and Anderson, Richard C. Retroactive inhibition in free recall as a function of first- and second-list organization. J. Exper. Psychol., 81, 595-597, 1969.

93. Wilbanks, William A.; Webb, Wilse B.; and Tolhurst, Gilbert C. A study of intellectual activity in a noisy environment. U.S. Naval School of Aviation Medicine, Research Report NM 001 104 100, Report 1, October 31, 1956.

94. Williams, Robert L.; and Cole, Spurgeon. Self-concept and school adjustment. Personnel Guid. J., 46, 478-481, 1968.

95. Woodhead, M. M. The effect of bursts of noise on an arithmetic task. Amer. J. Psychol., 77, 627-633, 1964.

96. Wrenn, C. G.; and Larsen, R. P. Studying Effectively. Stanford, Calif.: Stanford Univ. Press, 1943, pp. 1-3.

chapter 5

Personality characteristics which handicap us; some ways to change them

A. A Consideration of Infantile Habits, Their Causes and Consequences

The students left their lecture room, beaming, jubilant. They radiated a buoyancy somewhat rare. What was the occasion? An inspired lecture they had been blessed to hear? It might have been, for students sometimes look that way on such occasions. Or was there, perhaps, a marvelously stimulating class discussion in which they had been eager participants? Or a film in which they had lost themselves and found new understandings? It could have been any of these—and some of you will leave many classes in the manner described, fired with new ideas, aglow with new insights, inspired.

It could have been any of these; but as a matter of fact, it was not. The occasion for exuberance was a simple announcement: "Professor X is in the hospital. Class will not meet this week." That was the good news. Professor X, incidentally, was popular with his students, admired and liked with an uncommon devotion.

This incident spotlights some of our difficulties in becoming educated. Here are a few of them.

Were those students wholeheartedly eager to get an education? Are we?

What does such behavior signify? Does it merely reflect our natural liking of holidays? And what does a "natural liking of holidays" imply regarding our fondness for our chosen line of work—in this case, studying? If we deeply enjoy holidays and also deeply enjoy our work, we should be radiant and enthusiastic when holidays end, as well as when they begin. Were those students? Would you be?

Did the students perhaps feel somewhat like slaves, unexpectedly set free?

Was their reaction consistent with an unambivalent fondness for their professor? Or did it perhaps reflect some hostility and resentment?

From one incident it is foolhardy to draw many conclusions about anyone. But one incident does properly start a flow of questions worth pondering. What are those students like, deep inside? What is school like to them? What are they becoming as a consequence of their ways of going to school? More important, what are *you* like? How are you going to college? What will you be like in the future as a result of your current actions?

What any student is like depends partly upon his experiences in school. Put in other words, the nature of our personality is a *result* in part of how we go to school. But "information," without which they would have been wiser. They lacked the serenity and deep self-respect they sorely needed. They were racked by anxieties which led to sudden flashes of rage. With these handicaps, they did their best. They tried; but their attempts were almost doomed to partial failure. Our teachers often were in no happier a situation; nor were our friends.

As a result, we were subjected to many unfortunate experiences — experiences which caused us to develop some habits not healthy even in a child, and still more lamentable in adults. The personalities of most adults are peppered with these "infantile habits," as they are technically called. Even your personality probably is.

Unfortunately, getting older is no guarantee we will become more mature, nor more civilized — a sobering matter Overstreet discusses brilliantly in *The Mature Mind*. Infantile habits can persist a lifetime. Indeed, these modes of behavior often become stronger with passing years, despite the heartaches they engender both in the possessor and in his associates.

In a real sense, it is not your fault if you have many infantile habits; but it definitely is your responsibility if you *keep* them. You can break up those habits and build more satisfying ones.

Having infantile characteristics does not mean you are a weakling, or disgusting, or anything else remotely like that. You have many endearing qualities, too, and many remarkable skills. You might have all of these infantile characteristics and still be a truly wonderful person, although not *as* wonderful, nor as happy, as you otherwise could be.

Neither do these characteristics mean you are peculiar. These are extremely common habits, so their possession is normal, albeit highly unfortunate from many standpoints.

further, the nature of our personality is also a *cause* of how we go to school and college.[4, 18, 27, 112, 184]

This brings us to a fact of vital import: Some personality characteristics gravely limit our ability to get what we wish to attain and what we otherwise *could* attain from college and the university. We are handicapped by some of our own habits.

To get the most we can from college, we must become able to recognize disadvantageous characteristics in ourselves, and then learn to do something about them.

These same personality characteristics which handicap us in college, also handicap us in the rest of life. They jeopardize or cause us to lose many things we cherish and otherwise could have—deeper friendships, more steady employment, happer family relationships, more vivid enthusiasms, peace with ourselves, and many more.

As one example, let us consider the causes for discharging people from their jobs. Over a period of months, some 4,000 office workers were discharged from 76 large firms. Why? Few were fired because they were technically inept. Inadequate technical skill was listed as a cause for dismissal for only 10.1% of these people. The other 89.9% were discharged because of personality inadequacies—especially carelessness, lack of initiative, and inadequate skills in cooperation.[79]

Much of our unhappiness is caused not by the nature of the world but by the nature of ourselves and our own habits. These habits often are begun in childhood.

Most of us had parents who tried very hard to help us. They tried to start us off well in life, but they were woefully trained (or untrained, depending upon your viewpoint) for their difficult job. They lacked much information they should have had. They had much folklore, disguised as

What does their possession mean? It simply means you have some unvanquished problems, the effects of which have long distressed you. That is all—but it is enough.

The object of this chapter is to make it easier for you to recognize these limiting characteristics and their effects, and to offer some leads whereby you can better overcome them.

This chapter may be rather rough going. To look squarely at ourselves is always difficult and takes great courage. We fear what we may find, and we have little enough self-respect and confidence anyway. And yet we must scrutinize our own actions and learn to recognize inner hindrances in order to cope with them more adequately. The likelihood of solving any problem (including, of course, personality difficulties) is increased greatly by recognizing the nature of the problem.

Let us, then, plunge into an examination of these characteristics which jeopardize our happiness and our success in living.

B. Growing Away from Slave Attitudes and Hostility Toward Instructors

1. DO YOU HAVE SOMETHING OF A SLAVE ATTITUDE?

Do you eagerly count the number of days to the next week-end? Or the number of weeks before the end of the term? Do you even count the number of terms left to go before you graduate? During vacations do you gleefully anticipate the beginning of school? Or do you regard its commencement ruefully? School, for many students, is piteously like a jail sentence—to be endured as best one can.

We feel abused and terribly sorry for ourselves: In class

we listen casually, take as few notes as possible, do as little work as possible. We sometimes even reach the point of complaining because too many ideas and facts are presented. Assignments are resented. When we read the textbook, we feel we have done the *instructor* a gracious favor. When we turn in a paper, we feel positively noble. We may even react in ways like those sketched in the opening paragraphs of this chapter—feeling pleased by our instructor's illness. The slave driver is gone; for the moment we feel more free. Have you perchance had such experiences?

Probably you have, for apparently almost all of us possess at least some trace of this "slave attitude." Almost all of us also possess some buried antagonisms toward our professors.

To understand our problem, we should note that antagonisms and slave attitudes, self-debasement and apathy are interlocked.[15, 19, 55, 60, 111, 131] They are an instance of reciprocal causation.

2. HOSTILITY AND FEELING ENSLAVED INCREASE EACH OTHER.

In studying human behavior, you will find many such cases of reciprocal causation. In its simplest form, reciprocal causation consists of this: A causes an increase in B, and B in turn causes an increase in A. For example, Andy treats Tom in a hostile fashion. Andy's hostile behavior toward Tom increases Tom's hostile behavior toward Andy; and Tom's hostile behavior toward Andy, in turn, increases Andy's hostile behavior toward Tom. A vicious circle is set in motion, increments in either half of the circle bringing increments in the other half.

Similarly, our hostility and slave attitudes are reciprocally linked; each increases the other. In this case, however, the reciprocal pattern is more complicated than in the example of Tom and Andy. Between our hostility and slave attitudes is an intervening chain of events. The relationship is diagrammed in Figure 4, with each arrow signifying "leads to an increase in."

As is shown in the last step of the diagram, feeling abused by someone makes us more hostile toward him. You realize this, of course. But perhaps you have not realized that the reverse is also true: *Feeling hostile toward someone will cause us to feel abused by him.*

Strengthening any link in the chain above ultimately strengthens all of the links. It works this way: Feeling hostile toward professors (for example) leads to greater anxiety and guilt feelings. The anxiety is increased very greatly if the hostility does not seem "justified," for in our culture unprovoked hostility rarely is condoned and generally is condemned. This condemning attitude becomes part of ourselves, so we are anxious about our hostilities. Consequently, we set out to concoct excuses to justify our hostility. (Psychologists call this rationalizing.) We say to ourselves that

> Hostility toward the professor
> ↓
> Anxiety and guilt feelings about this hostility
> ↓
> Need for rationalizing our hostility,
> attempting to justify it
> ↓
> Saying "He abuses me" and finding
> supporting "evidence" for the statement
> ↓
> Feeling deeply abused: i.e.,
> having a slave attitude.

Figure 4. Reciprocal relationship between hostility and slave attitudes.

the professor is mean, that he makes unreasonable assignments, gives unfair tests, and in other ways too abuses us; then we look for and find "evidence" supporting our accusations. The more we do this, the more deeply abused we come to feel. As a consequence, our hostility becomes even greater, which creates still more anxiety, and still more need for rationalizations, and so on and on, ad infinitum. Our hostility increases our feeling of being abused and enslaved. This in turn increases our hostility. Matters become ever worse and worse. We are caught in a spiralling circle of hostility and feeling enslaved.

As the diagram shows too, *being* abused is not necessary for *feeling* abused. We can, and often do, feel gravely mistreated without actually being mistreated at all. Deep hostilities toward someone are caused by many conditions other than being mistreated.

3. THE CAUSES OF HOSTILITY FOR SOMEONE OFTEN ARE
   FAR REMOVED FROM THAT PERSON AND HIS ACTIONS.

Let us consider, for example, some common causes of hostility toward professors. Such antagonism can arise from a great variety of conditions. The antagonism can arise from a general distrust of people with authority: We may have learned to view any powerful person with rancor and suspicion, and professors are powerful. Or hostility toward professors can grow from our own inner insecurities: We feel, for instance, that anyone with much intelligence will view us as stupid; we dislike that view and we dislike anyone we imagine to have it. The hostility can also stem from a generalized resentment of a world which often runs counter to our needs and cherished hopes. Hostility toward our professor can result too from antagonisms built up against some other individual and then transferred to the professor.

When we have the habit of making a particular emotional response to one pattern of stimuli, subsequently that emotional response can be evoked by other rather different stimuli without our having had any experiences with these other stimuli. Psychologists call this phenomenon displacement, transference, or generalization. Displaced antagonisms occur frequently in life and have also been repeatedly demonstrated in the laboratory.

For example, white rats were trained to fight each other whenever an electric shock was turned on in the floor of their cage. Then each rat was put into a cage with a celluloid doll, and no other rat. When the shock was turned on, half the rats attacked the doll, although they had had no previous experience with any doll. Rats without training to fight each other almost never showed hostility toward the dolls, even when they were shocked.[118]

Transference of emotional responses likewise has been frequently demonstrated with people. For example, a small boy was caused to have fear responses cued, through learning, to the sight of a small white rat.[189] As a result of this learning, fear was also evoked by (transferred to) the previously neutral stimuli from a rabbit, cotton wool, a fur coat, and the experimenter's hair, even though the child had had no adverse experiences with these objects. Another child, previously fearful of a white rat, rabbit, fur coat, feather, and cotton wool, learned to have responses of interest and fondness cued to the rabbit. This new response of interest and fondness was then evoked by each of the other stimuli mentioned—without any intervening experiences with them.*

---

*This is one of the earliest experimental studies ever made of the nature of emotion, being reported in 1924 by Mary Cover Jones under the title "A Laboratory Study of Fear: The Case of Peter" in the Pedagogical Sem., 31, 308-315.

Many other reports of transference also are available.[5, 40, 55, 57, 58, 99, 119]

The psychoanalytic literature is replete with instances in which stimuli have evoked some emotional response — not because of experiences the individual had had with those objects or persons, but because of his having learned to make that emotional response to other somewhat similar stimuli. Here is one other illustration, taken from a marvelously enlightening book by Reik.[143] A man had intense hostility toward his mother. This hostility engendered in him considerable uneasiness and feelings of guilt. One day a woman, whom the man never before had seen, slipped and fell at some distance from him. He, of course, was in no way accused of causing her fall. Nonetheless he protested, in a quite desperate way, that he had not pushed the woman and had not caused her to fall. Apparently the strange woman in an unhappy predicament aroused much the same feelings of uneasiness and guilt as were originally cued to his mother.

From these examples of transference, you can start building clearer notions of the significance of this remarkably widespread phenomenon. See if you can spot instances in which you transfer emotional responses evoked by one person, object, or event to another "innocent bystander." When you become able to see transference in your own behavior, many reactions which now seem strange will be more comprehensible. "Love at first sight," sudden immediate dislike for a person whom you have just met, bewildering flare-ups, and many other confusing phenomena will become more intelligible. You will understand better, too, your partial antagonisms toward professors.

To the extent that this hostility for professors and its accompanying slave attitude are present, they spoil what could be wondrously joyous, edifying experiences. Even when present in small degrees only, they preclude studying with wholehearted delight. When present to a considerable extent, they make studying an onerous burden and ruin our college years.

Antagonisms toward professors and a slave attitude toward school predispose us toward similar responses outside school. They impair our ability to enjoy thoroughly our vocation; they dilute our delight in social affairs; and they contaminate many other aspects of life as well.

Are you doomed to that fate? Certainly not, for you can do much toward breaking up this pattern of "hostile slavishness."

Two major modes of attack are available: You can work on reducing your slave attitude, or you can work on reducing your antagonism toward profesors. Because reciprocally linked, partial success on either project will alleviate the other condition too. Anything you do to reduce your hostility toward professors will reduce your slave attitude toward school and your feelings of abuse; this, in turn, will further reduce your hostility. Likewise, any reduction in your slave attitude will reduce your hostility for professors (and other people also); this, in turn, will further decrease your feelings of being abused. Any case of reciprocal causation can work in a vicious circle; but the circle can be reversed and it will then work in your favor. By tackling the problem with partial success at *either* end, you reverse the circle so it goes in the opposite, desired direction.

Let us tackle this circle at both ends. Here are some of the ways you can alleviate both your slave attitudes and your hostilities. You, we hope, will think of other ways too.

4. DEVELOP THE HABIT OF TAKING ASSIGNMENTS FOR
   WHAT THEY ARE: EFFORTS TO HELP YOU GROW.

Often we feel that assignments are some low trick, perpetrated by professors to make life miserable. Actually the opposite is more nearly the case.

Assignments are intended to help us learn. They are offered to help us understand the confused and confusing world of which we are a part . . . to help us become equipped to deal with that world more skillfully than we otherwise could . . . to assist us in developing new technical competencies . . . to aid us in building the habits we need for interacting with our fellow inhabitants with greater mutual enjoyment. To facilitate our achieving those goals, assignments are designed — often after hours of thought and study. Try to see them this way.

5. TRY ALSO TO TAKE LECTURES FOR WHAT THEY ARE: ATTEMPTS TO SAVE YOU TIME AND MUCH WORK.

Progress cannot be made if each of us must repeat, step by step, what other people have done. Somehow we must be enabled to pick up where they left off, and carry on from there.

Through lectures and discussions a gifted, educated person is trying to help you do that. He is trying to help you reach more quickly than did he the point where he now is, so that you may start near where he is finishing. In an hour, he passes on to you facts and ideas which he spent years accumulating and reworking into a more accessible form. This material you need not dig out and organize for yourself. He has done that; and he shares the results with you. He offers you concepts and principles, many of which he gained only after years of study and research, years of pondering and testing. He presents to you techniques he has found most satisfactory for tackling certain problems, and helps you master these techniques. He tells you of ideas which he has found illuminating. He shows you sources of information he has found helpful. All of these and more he gives you freely — in the hope that by so doing he can spare you at least some of the work he had to do, and leave you free to start from there.

Is it so very hard to remember that that is what lectures are? Probably not, if once you see them in that light.

6. MOST OF YOUR PROFESSORS ARE DEEPLY FOND OF YOU.

Is that surprising? It really should not be. You realize, of course, that for their services they often are paid far less per hour than, for example, the men who repair your plumbing or who help keep your car running or who build your roads. Many of your professors have been offered positions through which they could make considerably more money with their current skills than they make by teaching. But they continue to teach. They continue largely because, as you say, "they like their job." That, in large part, means they like you and your colleagues. They deeply value contact with you and helping you in your quests.[54, 74, 95, 121]

Most of your professors also have many interests apart from teaching. Many activities they find delightful and worthwhile. Yet hours they could spend playing chess, or engaging in sports, or dancing, hours they could be traveling, or reading, or talking with their friends, they spend instead preparing lectures for you. Hours far beyond what are needed to hold their job, they spend trying to make things more understandable to you. Unless they are badly confused as to what they most cherish, they must be deeply fond of you.

7. CAN YOU LEARN TO SEE YOUR PROFESSORS AS PARTNERS IN A COOPERATIVE ENTERPRISE?

Can you see them as colleagues working with you to achieve goals you both cherish? They can be wonderful partners with you in your effort to develop new skills and become more nearly the person you long to be.

No one, of course, can cooperate all by himself. Cooperation always takes at least two. If cooperating with you is made impossible, what other forms of interaction are accessible? This is worth some thought. Suppose you regard your teachers as antagonists and act accordingly. Do you not thereby almost compel them to become antagonists?

Try to see your professors as partners. Learn to regard yourself as a collaborator (not as a receptacle nor yet as a slave). You will discover, then, that professors *are* your partners, working with you in a deliciously exciting game of discovery and building.

8. Let us look now at that atrocity called a textbook.

Is it really so atrocious? Certainly it has flaws, many of them. Having been created by human beings, your textbook is bound to be noticeably less than perfect. It may, however, have many advantages too.

In any area of investigation there are dozens, even hundreds or thousands, of books available. From this great reservoir, your particular textbook was chosen as the one most apt to be of greatest help to you. It is the book which, in the opinion of your professor, can best help you discover the greatest amount about that area of investigation. It is the book he thinks is especially apt to open new vistas to you, to answer soundly your questions, to incite you to ask further questions, and to afford you exciting ideas. Terrible though this book may seem, your professor thinks it is more apt to accomplish these goals than many other books.

No book, of course, can do all these things perfectly.

But any book can do them better when you see these possibilities and view the book in this way.

9. ARE YOU IN COLLEGE MAINLY BECAUSE SOMEBODY ELSE THINKS YOU SHOULD BE?

Many students labor under that impression. Seldom, however, does a person attend college only because somebody else advocates it. How about you? Are you in college solely, or even primarily, because your parents or someone else desired it? Try examining this matter and see what you believe.

Suppose your primary reason for attending college actually is that someone else thinks you should do so. Suppose *you* do not share that opinion. If this is the case, you would be wise to withdraw. If on the other hand, you too think college offers opportunities for a net gain by *your* standards, then you should keep that fact in mind.

Sometimes we feel (consciously or unconsciously) that we are doing someone a great favor by attending college, that we are forced to do this favor, and that that is our main reason for attending college. These nagging impressions contribute much to our feeling enslaved, wretched and rebellious. When weighted by such millstones, no one can enjoy his school years nor profit from them as deeply as he otherwise could.

This furnishes another clue to how you can alleviate resentfulness and feelings of enslavement: Decide for yourself whether you should be in college. Is it worthwhile by your standards? If you decide to stay, remember that you are going to college primarily to attain goals of value to you by your standards and not merely to pacifiy or please somebody else.

10. Do what you can to understand your parents
    better.

This may seem a miserably oblique attack on the problem of learning to study better; yet it is highly effective. It
goes far toward freeing us from slave attitudes and hostilities
in general.

Long ago scientists discovered that many antagonisms
toward professors (and toward other people in positions of
authority) are caused in large part by early antagonisms
toward one's parents. These antagonisms toward our parents
are generalized; they become displaced to other persons in a
somewhat similar position.

This transference of resentment illustrates the principle
mentioned a few pages ago: When emotional responses are
established to one class of stimuli, they tend to generalize to
other somewhat similar stimuli, and, subsequently, to be
evoked by them. Displacement of resentment from our
parents to our teachers is a particularly common reflection
of that principle and also a particularly important contribu-
tor to difficulties in school.*

Therefore, although it seems roundabout, we can
markedly reduce hostility toward instructors and our
feelings of being enslaved, by reducing resentment and antagonism toward our parents.

You probably love your parents and are grateful to
them for many things. You also have many antagonisms
toward them. By stern injunction and awesome threats, you
were compelled to follow courses far different from your
choice. You did these things as you were ordered; but you

---

*For an especially provocative discussion of this phenomenon, look up
Sutherland's analysis of several such instances. Sutherland, J. D. Three cases
of anxiety and failure in examinations. Brit J. Med. Psychol., 1941, 19, 73-
81.

did them feeling dreadfully abused and sorry for yourself. You were laughed at by them for awkward creative attempts, and sometimes were patronizingly instructed to do things their way. You were ridiculed for mistakes in grammar, for mispronouncing words, for mistreating your sister, for ignoring folkways and mores, for breaking things they cherished, for reading books instead of playing outdoors, for playing outdoors instead of practicing. For a thousand actions which were ill-conceived or clumsily executed, you were shamed. Often your interests were scoffed at. As a result of such psychological hardships, you have many habits of doing things reluctantly and with grave misgivings. As a result also, you have many buried antagonisms toward your parents. Your love for them became shot through with resentments.

Reducing these resentments is difficult. It cannot be achieved in a day or a week, nor by firm resolutions against feeling resentful. It can be achieved only through building a new set of emotional responses. To help you on this difficult project, the next section is offered.

C. *Alleviating Hostility Toward Parents and Others*

Some of us had miraculous luck in the nature of our father and mother, drawing parents wondrously tender and skillful, adroit in helping us develop fine, healthy responses to them, to ourselves, and to other persons. Few, however, have such fortune.

More commonly, as we were just noting, resentments abound against many things one's parents have done and still do. This is almost inevitable—but we need not go on forever being gnawed by these antagonisms. Resentments and antagonisms can be vanquished.

1. WHEN RESENTMENTS SURGE, DO NOT TRY TO SHAME
   YOURSELF OUT OF THEM.

Such attempts are depressing.[45] They also are futile. In
fact, they are worse than futile, for being shamed increases
rather than decreases hostile antagonisms.[52, 55, 75, 176] Becoming *less* ashamed and *less* guilt-ridden will reduce our
hostility considerably. This is not such a paradox.

Guilt-feelings, you recall, drive us to justify our hostility.
The more ashamed we feel about something, the harder we
work to justify it. The more ashamed we feel for partially
hating someone, the harder we work to justify our hostility.
We try to prove the person is despicable and therefore
deserves our hostility. We search for, and find (!), additional
"reasons" for feeling antagonistic.

Further, the more ashamed we feel, the less assurance
we have of our own worth. The less inner respect we have
for ourselves, the harder we try to show that other people
are even worse. Thus we build greater and greater hostilities
within ourselves.[44, 53, 55, 75, 76, 151, 152, 155, 176]

This then would be a first step: Do not make your
hostilities an occasion for treating yourself harshly, nor for
feeling you or someone else is despicable. Accept your present hostilities as an almost inevitable reaction to the things
which happened to you — to being hurt and ashamed and in
many other ways sorely frustrated.

Although they were almost bound to occur, these hostilities need not haunt your life forever. Here is a second step
toward reducing them.

2. TRY TO UNDERSTAND THE PROBLEMS YOUR PARENTS
   FACE.

The problems parents face are numerous and complex.
No matter how large their income, for example, they have

financial difficulties. Everyone has, but that does not lighten the burden. They worry too about their status in the community—what other people think of them and you. They are apprehensive about possibly losing a job, or not getting a promotion, or missing a commission for which they have striven. They are distressed by the specter of your being called to war, or in other ways killed or damaged. They are worried about mistakes they made with you. Almost certainly they are troubled deeply by signs that youth is lost, forever, and old age irrevocably encroaching.

And those are but a few of the problems your parents face. If you ask about these, you may be astounded by what your folks confide.

3. REGARD EMOTIONAL OUTBURSTS AND "LACK OF CONSIDERATION" AS SYMPTOMS OF ANXIETIES AND OTHER INNER TENSIONS.

One result of their many worries and anxieties is that your folks make mistakes. They hurt you unwittingly.

How do *you* behave when apprehensive and worried? If you are like most people, you become less able to behave with the reasonableness and gentleness you desire. When worried (or ill or fatigued), your voice has an edge not intended and not often understood. The edge may be wholly unrelated to rage or to the person you are addressing; but the hearer fails to realize this and is hurt. When anxious, you are apt to be stubborn or curtly short in discussions. You are prone to flare up "for no reason at all." You make harsh remarks and behave inconsiderately, without even noticing what you are doing.[11, 160, 199]

Your parents are human too and probably respond to anxiety in these same ways. Such responses mean the person is tense. Not necessarily is he tense from rage at you nor from lack of love. He is tense, more usually, from worry and feelings of failure, from conflict or anxiety. Even the violent chest-beating of gorillas, so commonly construed as vicious rage, turns out to be merely a mode of showing excitement—fight tendencies sometimes, but also flight tendencies, or bewilderment, or general tension from any of multifarious conflict situations.[163]

Understanding better the expression of tension and its various sources, we are less hurt by flare-ups, harsh voices, or "unreasonableness." We are more able to treat the person appropriately, with the consideration and kindness he deeply needs.

4. REMEMBER THAT RAGE AND CONTEMPT ARE NOT
   NECESSARILY AIMED AT YOU, NOR CAUSED BY YOU,
   EVEN THOUGH MADE IN YOUR DIRECTION.

Sometimes, of course, the person is angry when he "sounds" angry. He makes genuinely angry responses, and in your direction. These angry responses may or may not be intended for you or caused by you.

The boss criticizes your dad unjustly. When your dad gets home, he explodes—more like a volcano than like a cannon. The lava is not aimed; it simply is there, scalding anyone near. Or the neighbors scoff. Or friends act cool. Or relatives make belittling remarks. Any of a thousand other events occur which hurt your parents deeply. In their turmoil and pain, they do what people usually do when hurt: They lash out at anyone handy—oftentimes at their children, or husband, or wife. You might be amazed by how much that is cruel stems from the person's being hurt, and responding blindly. Quite possibly all cruelty is caused in part by the "cruel" person's being hurt.

Whether we caused the wound or not, we are behooved—in our own interests even—to do what we can to reduce the hurt and give the person peace and a sense of being valued. This is far more adequate protection than is counter-hostility.

5. YOUR PARENTS OFTEN FEEL THEY ARE PARTIAL FAILURES.

They may make a great deal of money. They may have a job with prestige. They may have a lavishly furnished home and many friends. And *still* they feel they are partial failures. There were so many things they wanted to do—and never did; so many things they wanted to be—and never were; so many attributes they wished to have—and never developed. And now it is too late. Life has more than half gone. Probably they do not feel complete failures, for there is much of which to be proud and much for which to be pleased. Yet, there is so much, so very much, that could have been—and wasn't.

Maybe, they hope fervently, maybe you can do better. Maybe you, their child, can do and have and become what they did not. That is the great hope of most parents. But then again, perhaps you will be like them and have a life like theirs—no better. That is a deep fear. It is a fear mounting almost to terror in many parents, a terror nonetheless real because unverbalized, hidden from their own recognition except for disrupting flashes.

This fear leads them to watch anxiously your development and your actions. (Other factors do also, but this is a main one.) They apprehensively chivy you around and often-times quite unpredictably bawl you out. You, they feel, must not turn out as they did! In their great anxiety and yearning, they do all manner of things which make life rougher for you—while attempting, ironically, to make life smoother for you than it was for them.

6. YOUR PARENTS MAKE MANY MISTAKES, BASED ON
   POPULAR MISCONCEPTIONS, IN TRYING TO HELP YOU
   GROW.

They try to secure for you a life better than that they had. But their attempts often are misguided, based largely on folklore and other common misconceptions. They labor under a mass of misinformation handed down from generation to generation. Long before they could think, they were bombarded by beliefs which they accepted uncritically. Their way of looking at the world, its people, and "human nature," is shot through with these beliefs, beliefs which are largely mistaken but which are widely accepted, nonetheless, as facts. (This can happen also to you and me; our beliefs too can become an unsorted hodge-podge of fact and misconception.)

Your parents may have the impression, for example, that unless they often "took you down a notch," you would become conceited, insufferably smug. But would you really have become conceited and smug? "Of course! Everybody knows this!" The phrase "everybody knows this" is a way of saying, "I've heard this all my life"; and that, in turn, is a way of saying, "This is a part of the folklore." To a highly sophisticated person, that means "Watch out! Folklore is often mistaken. Better look twice." Most people, however, are not highly sophisticated. They do not think of questioning the truth of what is commonly believed. They unreflectively accept the folklore and have, as a consequence, all sorts of mistaken convictions.

Your parents may have the conviction that children are small savages, in the most unfavorable sense. Being small savages, they must be treated accordingly: Children must be curbed, watched closely, directed almost continuously, punished severely—else they will not learn what society expects of them and will not care. When adolescent, they may do awful things in their inexperience unless parents are ever alert and devise numerous restrictive measures. Or your parents may have the conviction and fear that unless they do everything possible for their offspring, follow his every whim, let him virtually rule the household, they will not be loved by their "child" or will have caused his growth to be forever stunted.

Sadly enough, this list could be extended greatly, and still it would not exhaust the misinformation with which most parents take up their difficult profession.

Most of the information they really needed was not a part of their equipment. Information concerning personality formation, the making and breaking of habits, what one can reasonably expect of a growing individual—much of this information they did not have.

Your parents' predicament (unless they are very unusual) is rather like that of a wanderer lost in a desert country, a desert country utterly unlike what he expected. In his quest for water and shade, he is given a map. But the map omits most of the crucial landmarks. Worse, it includes numerous directions for "right paths" which do not lead to the promised oasis. Instead they lead the weary stranger ever farther and farther from his objectives.

7. Often your parents realized their methods were working out poorly. But what else was there to do?

Contrary to what we expect from fairy tales, most of us have rather limited imaginations and resourcefulness. Many people cannot conceive what they *could* be doing other than what they *are* doing. Your parents probably never meant to make you feel left out, to have you feel enslaved, or caged in. Without some training or some model, they simply could not imagine what else they could do besides follow their current procedures.

Often your folks are acutely aware that *their* parents made terrible blunders, and they want desperately to do better by you. But just where did their parents err? They do not know, and (vaguely) they know they do not know. This too makes them apprehensive, while in no way making them more skillful.

They know they are piteously unprepared for their job; but this simply leads to more anxiety, and is often glossed over because of the pain involved in recognizing it. Squashing this recognition, in turn, precludes seeking help and leads to still more unresolved and unrecognized difficulties, to more problems, more anxieties, and more tensions—with their customary disquieting results.

Can you get some feeling for their predicament? The marvel becomes not that your parents made so many mistakes, but that they managed to do as well as they did.

If we can remember these things, we can understand our folks better and will have less hostility toward them.

8. Your parents had many dreams about you shattered.

What is it like to have bright dreams of some event, to work and struggle for that event, to have the event finally occur, and then to find out the reality is not at all as one had dreamed? Can you imagine what that is like? Probably you can, for at least in a small way that has happened to you.

You maybe worked hard to get to college. And you had such bright, glorious hopes. What fun college would be! What successes you would have! What wonderful things you would do! What exciting things you would learn! These played a part in your dreams, waking and sleeping. Then you got to college. And college, you now find, is quite altogether different from your dreams. Such discrepancies are disconcerting and saddening. You can see how you are responding.

Our parents likewise dreamed of having us, but their dreams were far more elaborate and of longer duration, and to make those dreams come true, they worked far harder. They dreamed of how cute we would be, of how much fun we would be, of the joy we would be to play with and talk with and watch, of how we would adore them and help them. Finally we arrived. And we weren't particularly cute or fun. We interrupted their sleep—and we kept right on doing so. We broke things they cherished. We messed up our clothes. Even when we became older, we spilled on our little outfits, all freshly washed and ironed, tore clothes it took them long to make or earn, lost our sweaters and toys and books, made a shambles of the rooms they had swept and dusted. This was not part of their dream. We often prevented their going out with companions they enjoyed. We gave them a mass of new responsibilities for which they were utterly unprepared. We were fairly stupid companions for a while. Then when we became capable of talking and playing with them in a companionable way, we left home for most of the day, or all of it, to spend our time with other people.

This is not the way we were supposed to be. And our parents are disappointed. So they cling to us when we want to have freedom; they try to force us into the mold of their dreams; they do the many other things we find deeply annoying.

9. Yet despite all of this, your parents brought much of value into your world.

Despite all the handicaps under which they worked, they did much to comfort you, to open new worlds of interest to you, to help you gain skills in living as an adult, to give you a place of refuge—with them or with one of your siblings. It is quite remarkable how much good your parents created, along with the psychological hardships on which we tend to dwell. These contributions are worth noticing too.

10. Take advantage of opportunities to reassure your parents of their worth.

As we were observing a bit ago, parents have many anxieties. They have made mistakes which trouble them greatly. They have a host of shattered dreams. They often feel their life has been more or less a failure. As a consequence, they have emotional outbursts, and do much which you (and they) regret. Remember that rages and contempt stem largely from these tensions and deep anxieties. Then do what you can to mitigate these anxieties, thus removing many of the sources of the behavior you lament.

You cannot wholly undo what has happened to your folks. No one can. But you can give your parents the understanding all people crave.

You can show them the sympathy and love you feel. You can notice their endearing qualities . . . respect their opinions . . . listen attentively to their ideas . . . express appreciation for the many little (and big) things they do for you in your daily role as parents . . . accept their mistakes for what they usually are—misguided attempts to help you grow . . . offer them little services when they so desire. You can show them the courtesies all human beings deserve and need. In these and many other ways, you can communicate to your parents that they are valued.

11. TREATING OTHERS KINDLY DECREASES YOUR
    HOSTILITY TOWARD THEM.

Much of our hostility toward people is caused by our own shabby treatment of them. We previously explored how this comes about. We noticed that often we try to justify our abuse of someone by "proving" he deserved such treatment. To some extent we come to believe our "proof"; and thus we see the mistreated person as more despicable, and dislike him even more.

In addition, something else happens. When we feel ashamed and rather sick inside because of our own poor actions, we tend both to hate ourselves and also to hate the other person who partially occasioned such feelings. To make sad matters worse, we fear retaliation from the mistreated person; and most of us hate what we fear.

In all those ways, our shabby treatment of a person increases our own hostility. We set up devastating circles. Because we dislike someone, we mistreat him; and because we mistreat him, we dislike him more. But this circle can be reversed.

We can treat a person as kindly as we know how. We become, as a consequence, more serene inside, enjoy that person's company more, and like him more. With deepened respect for ourselves and deepened liking of him, we become able to treat him with still more consideration, and thus we like him still more. A new sort of circle is set in motion. You can do this with anyone. You can do it with your dad and mother, with your professors, with roommates and classmates and friends.

While leading your own life as a free and self-reliant

individual, you need not be callous and indifferent to other people. You still can heed their needs and wishes and do much to brighten their worlds. In so doing, your buried antagonisms will melt, like ice-fields in spring, slowly. But melt they will. A wistfulness may remain even when you are adept in treating others well. A yearning for things-which-might-have-been may still be present; but animosity will be largely gone.

D. *Breaking Habits of Dependency, Projection, and Irresponsibility*

Habits of dependency, of projection, and of denying responsibility for our own life hinder our studying and hinder our other attempts at growth. Such habits are more common than we ordinarily realize.

Most of us tend to project our own inadequacies onto other people. We blame incidental or external factors for outcomes we ourselves largely caused. For example, when we do not understand a lecture, "it's the professor's fault," we say, "he doesn't explain things well." When we do poorly on a test, often we say (and come to believe) that that is the professor's fault too—"he didn't teach properly"; or it is the examination's fault—"the test wasn't fair"; or the reader's fault—"he doesn't grade fairly"; or the book's fault—"it was confused"; or our parents' fault—"they interrupt too much."

If you are like many people, doing poorly is regarded as almost anyone's or anything's fault, except your own. Your contribution to frustrating events is treated, quite generally, as a factor of negligible importance.

Do you expect the professor to order your life for you? To make detailed assignments, preferably daily ones? To see to it that you do them? Do you ask him to analyze your errors for you and tell you where to do things differently, and how to do them differently? Do you do this even before you have tried to figure these matters out for yourself? Many students do. You would not be unusual if you even expect the professor to make everything clear, to "*give* you an education," while you do relatively little except be there.

When we have few habits of accepting responsibility, we place ourselves in an intellectual strait jacket and stunt our growth — a matter examined in Chapter 1, pages 23-26.

What can we do about this? How can we develop the skills of accepting responsibility? Here are some leads which can help you get started.

1. LEARN TO RECOGNIZE SOONER EVENTS WHICH ARE TURNING OUT POORLY.

This is difficult, since most of us have learned to *not* recognize when events are going poorly. We have learned to pretend, as long as possible, that nothing is wrong — especially when we are partly responsible.

This partial blindness makes our task harder. By the time we finally notice that all is not well, so much has happened that we cannot ascertain where our mistake occurred. We decide we are stupid and have not much insight. We become more disheartened, and more afraid to accept responsibility, and more dependent.

How can we become able to recognize sooner when events are turning out poorly? Our first step should be to develop a willingness to be mistaken. Let us turn now to that.

2. DEVELOP A WILLINGNESS TO BE MISTAKEN, TO ADMIT IMPERFECTION.[16, 75, 76]

This is essential for recognizing well our mistakes. It also is essential for becoming more independent, more capable of responsibility — better able to try for what we care about.

When not willing to admit we are imperfect, we tend to avoid any activity in which we might fail to excel. Life is sharply restricted. When badly afraid of making mistakes, we are less able to make our own decisions, less able (therefore) to take charge of our own life. We stand by while someone else takes authority, or we delegate authority to someone else. Then, when things go wrong, we point to him. He made the mistake. He is responsible for the mess we are in, not we. Or so we say, rather illogically.

What we overlook is this: When we delegate responsibility to someone else, we still are responsible for any subsequent mistakes. We have merely pushed our mistake nearer to the beginning of the causal sequence. After all, we are the ones who permitted (or even forced) the other person to make the decisions and choose the actions which worked out poorly. The outcome is our "fault" as much as his. We blind ourselves to this fact; but it is nonetheless a fact.

No matter what we do, we cannot avoid mistakes. We can become better, however, in recognizing our mistakes, and thus avoid repeating the same mistakes over and over. But to do this, we must reduce our fear of errors.

We can reduce our fear of errors. We can become more willing to admit mistakes and to make our own decisions. Remembering the following facts will help.

a) No one is omniscient. Therefore, everyone will make mistakes, a lot of them.

b) Fifty million Frenchmen can be wrong. So can one hundred million Americans. If we say what they say, and do what they do, we still have no guarantee of being right. We must not be lulled into believing all will be well merely because we adopt a popular course of action.

c) Other people's love and respect for us are rarely contingent upon our having a perfect or near-perfect performance. Indeed, the reverse is more often true — their love is partially contingent upon our making mistakes, upon our being "human."

You are familiar probably with James Thurber's essays and drawings. A part of his charm lies in describing the absurd things he has done and said. Far from trying to cover up his mistakes, he publishes them — and Thurber is one of our most beloved authors. You can observe this same phenomenon in your own more immediate worlds. Being right is not necessary for being beloved. Having a terrifically high "batting average" is not necessary for being respected.

These are facts which intellectually you know, but which emotionally you tend to forget. They are worth remembering.

d) A person's willingness to be mistaken increases with his basic confidence. Paradoxical though this seems at first, the greater the confidence we have in our own value, the greater our ability to see and admit our mistakes.

Therefore, whatever reminds us that we are precious (and all people are), that our existence is worthwhile and our contributions appreciated, whatever increases our self-respect will also increase our ability to accept our mistakes. This is one place where you probably can do more for others than you can do directly for yourself. Even so, there is much you can do to increase your own self-respect. The rest of this section and Section E point out some ways by which you can increase your self-esteem.

3. RECOGNIZE THE FUTURE.

We are human beings. In some ways we are special. One of our most especially human potentials is high capacity for recognizing the future: for knowing there is a future — not just a present and past — for realizing that *which* future materializes is dependent upon us, for realizing that what happens later is linked to what happens now, for planning and slanting our actions in terms of these coming days, and weeks, and centuries.

Some persons have developed little more skill here than have typical members of other species. Other persons have made themselves highly adroit. One part of this skill consists of a willingness to defer gratification, to work for future satisfactions though it means sometimes foregoing an immediately possible gratification. This ability to defer gratification turns out to be related to social responsibility. Persons of greater responsibility are able on occasion, and willing, to postpone some certain immediate gratification for the sake of a better future, relatively irresponsible people being unable or unwilling to forego small immediate rewards even for the sake of larger later gratifications.[120]

4. Practice making your own decisions.

We become so accustomed to waiting for suggestions and orders or to asking other people what to do, that we hardly realize we could be making our own decisions and determining our own courses of action. Rather than relying upon our adviser to tell us what courses to take, we could make out at least a tentative program by ourselves. Rather than asking our friends to tell us what professor is "best," we could ask our friends what they like and dislike about various professors and make our own decisions here. Rather than studying only when compelled to do so by a test, we could plan our own work. We overlook many opportunities for leading our own life more fully. Watch for opportunities to make your own decisions and to take responsibility for your own life; then accept these opportunities.

5. WHENEVER YOU SPOT AN UNFORTUNATE OCCURRENCE,
   SEE HOW YOU CAN BEHAVE DIFFERENTLY IN ORDER TO
   FACILITATE DIFFERENT, MORE VALUED OUTCOMES.

Instead of searching for ways other people should change or the world should change, see how you could change. Look for the role you played in causing things to be as they are. Look for new ways of behaving which would be more apt to enhance what you value. Then set out to modify your behavior accordingly. This is worthwhile even though the respects in which you can behave differently seem insignificant. At the very least, you thereby will contribute "insignificantly" to what you value, rather than contribute to what you dislike. Further, you will have gained new skill in accepting responsibility and will have become more free.

6. PRACTICE BEING THE PERSON YOU WISH TO BECOME.

All too often we act in ways we do not want as part of our personality, and fail to practice the habits we do want as part of our self.

In a radio skit, a comedienne (Gracie Allen) remarked that she didn't like dogs. Dogs are too stupid. They cannot even learn to fetch sticks. She knew, because she had tried to teach a dog that trick. She threw a stick and said "Fetch"—but the stupid dog just sat there. One hundred times she threw the stick, each time saying "Fetch." Did that silly beast learn to go get it? He did not! He just went on sitting there, laughing at her, she said, while she lugged the stick back in her mouth. The audience laughed.

Imagine expecting the dog to learn anything under those circumstances! The audience thought this absurd. It is absurd. And yet we often behave in much the same way as Gracie. We expect ourselves (and others) to learn highly complicated tricks by merely watching someone else do them.

How many times have you watched a professor develop a logical line of thought? How many times have you watched him find examples of complex principles, watched him integrate materials from various fields, watched him do all manner of complicated tricks? How many times have you watched, and done little more? And have you ever wondered why you were so slow in acquiring his skill in reasoning? Why you became so little better in following up ideas or working independently? Have you even concluded (à la Gracie's reasoning) that you must be a pretty stupid animal?

The major trouble here, and many other places too, is this: Watching is not sufficient for learning. Even very attentive watching while somebody does his tricks will not enable you to do those tricks. You must actively practice them.

Richly suggestive in this connection is an experiment by Thompson.[183] The task was to assemble a mechanical puzzle. One group watched while the experimenter assembled the puzzle and partially described what she was doing. After each demonstration, the learner tried to assemble the puzzle; thus he gained some practice in tackling the task. With this method, an average of sixteen trials was required before the learners could assemble the puzzle correctly.

Another group did not have the benefit of watching the experimenter assemble the puzzle. Instead, the subject himself tried to solve the puzzle and described what he was doing. Mistakes in his description were corrected by the experimenter. This group took 25% *fewer* trials on the average than the first group, who had more demonstrations but less active practice.

Still another method was tried: The experimenter solved the puzzle while the subject passively watched what he saw being done. (While watching, he was counting aloud by two's.) How well did those people develop skill in solving the puzzle? As you probably would expect, they did very poorly. In fact, they learned almost nothing about the puzzle. Even after 25 or more demonstrations of the solution, 22 of the 25 individuals still did not know how to assemble the pieces correctly.

Other methods also were used in this experiment. The most ineffectual is the one just described—that of passively observing skillful demonstrations. This might be what you would expect. And yet, how often do you try to learn under similar conditions?

Do you spend a major part of your time passively watching an expert demonstrate the skills you wish to develop? The comedienne's approach to dog-training and Thompson's demonstrations without practice, you may deem ridiculous. No less ridiculous is the same approach in college or life in general. But we do this. We really expect to get educated, if only we sit long enough and patiently enough in the right places and have the right teachers, ones who are sufficiently bright and conscientious. We place unwarranted reliance on living in the right house, being seen in the right places, happening to be in the right spot at the right moment—for the good things of life to come our way. We fancy that merely by becoming older, we will have more independence, more self-reliance, greater skill in making decisions, greater clarity of thought.

But neither you nor anyone else can learn new habits by watching someone else do the tricks or by any other such passive approach. You must actually do what you wish to learn.

If you wish to develop independence, you must practice drawing your own conclusions, practice making your own decisions, practice noticing and accepting your mistakes. In all of life, always do what you wish to learn. This accords with the crucially important, but often forgotten, principle of learning: We learn only what we do; and what we do, we become. Live, therefore, in the ways you desire to have as part of your personality. Practice being the person you wish to become.

7. TRY TO REMEMBER THE VALUES INHERENT IN HAVING MARKED ABILITY TO ACCEPT RESPONSIBILITY.

When we remember what can be won by an enterprise, we find it easier to embark upon and work for that enterprise. We can better tolerate the disappointment accruing from our first clumsy efforts and can continue to work for our goal.

Many of the values gained by developing heightened skill in accepting responsibility were sketched on pages 24-26 of Chapter 1. You might find it profitable to refer again to that section.

8. ALLEVIATE YOUR FEAR OF FAILURE.

To break up habits of dependency and projection, to gain new freedoms and deeper happiness, it is crucial to break up the fear of failure. But this is enormously complex. Because of its importance and complexity, the next section is devoted to this single matter.

E. Reducing Fear of Failure

1. WHAT DOES A FEAR OF FAILURE DO?

Very occasionally, fear leads to creative activity. Usually fear distracts and disrupts us. When intense, fear paralyzes.

Fear that we may fail acts as a strait jacket, despite which (*not* because of which) we sometimes manage to do well. Seldom can we perform as well as we could without the fear.[23, 33, 35, 37, 66, 92, 114, 140, 142, 145, 167, 168, 174]

By fear of failure we do not mean merely a dislike of failure, nor do we mean a striving to avoid failure. We are speaking, rather, of an apprehensive dread of failure and disgrace, a dark foreboding which ranges from mere anxiety to vast terror.

Let us look at this fear in operation. Do you yearn to be a witty conversationalist, but fear saying something stupid? What happens? Do you then speak more eloquently, and gracefully, with greater perceptiveness and sparkle? The opposite is more likely. When afraid of disgracing yourself, you are apt to keep very still, not even try to converse. Or else you become garrulous, with a spate of jumbled words tumbling out. Have you wished to be an adroit ballroom dancer? Perhaps you even took lessons, but then became gripped by fear. You started to worry about being awkward, about doing poorly, about being a social failure. What happened then? We are apt to do just what we feared. We lose the beat; we step on our partner's toes; we become stiff and clumsy, and make still more mistakes. Have you ever wanted to be loved? But fearful of failure and rebuff, shut yourself off from others by walls steely strong and cold—announcing that *you* did not care about such silly things? Do you ever sit down to study and suddenly find the thought charging madly about that you cannot possibly ever "get" this stuff, that you are going to disgrace yourself this time for sure? Did that fear improve the quality of your studying? Has fear of failure ever helped you much yet? Often we fail because we fear failure.[9, 92, 124, 175] Far from spurring us on to greater achievements, fear of failure actually is a major cause of our doing poorly.

Do not confound "desire to succeed" with "fear of failure." They are radically different.[8, 9, 35, 51, 92] They are no more the same than a fear of the dark is the same as a love of bright sunshine. Not only is a desire to succeed very different from a fear of failure, but neither one is a cause for the other. You can value and desire success without fearing failure. You can fear failure and, instead of desiring success and striving for it, desire only to avoid failure, desire to *withdraw* from the whole appalling situation.

2. HOW DID WE GET THESE NAGGING, GNAWING FEARS?

We were not born with them, nor with many other fears. Only a few stimuli evoked startle or fear responses in us as infants: Being dropped, loud noises, flashes of light, sudden intense changes in stimulation—these apparently are all.[84, 85, 189] The other stimuli which now evoke fear responses in us do so through learning.

We learned to fear failure. We learned it through experiences such as these: We tried new activities, but our attempts were clumsy, inept; they elicited sniggers and sharp rebuffs. We made mistakes and were called stupid, and dumb, and in other ways ridiculed. People whose esteem we deeply needed seemed to make their love contingent upon our being successful. "That's Mother's dear little boy," greeted some of our finest actions. We wondered fearfully if we were expected to always do that well and we were troubled because we knew we couldn't. If we fell below standards, we were asked, "How do you expect *anyone* to love a person like *you?*" Other disconcerting threats were levied concerning what would happen should we fail to meet the criteria set up for us. We would be a disgrace to the whole family . . . a disappointment to our parents and friends . . . unworthy of the time and effort lavished upon us. As one result, our own self-respect became contingent upon uniform success.

Simultaneously we were caused to gravely mistrust our ability to reach any worthwhile criterion. ("High school may be a cinch, but just wait until college! You'll flunk, unless you do a lot better than this." "You do the most idiotic things for a supposedly bright person." "How could anyone be so stupid!" "You're not half as good as you think." You can extend the list.)

Sometimes we were trained to have fantastically high criteria for success, high absolutely and high relative to our own capacities. We were expected to be as good as the best person we knew, in everything or in certain specified endeavors. Anything less, we felt, would be profoundly disappointing to our parents or our teachers or even ourselves. We knew we never could do all this. We greatly feared what would happen when we failed.

One such episode makes little difference. A series of such experiences, or others of similar tone, will create a fear of failure, ranging from mild anxiety to downright terror.

3. AVOID TREATING YOURSELF IN WAYS WHICH CREATE FEAR.

Unless your life has been very unusual, many people many times have treated you in ways like those sketched above. More tragic, you do these same things to yourself! You treat yourself in ways bound to accentuate your fear of failure. Take another look, if you will, at Section 2 above. Can you learn to avoid doing those things to yourself? To the extent that you can, you will greatly mitigate your fear of failure. To the extent that you continue to exert such pressures on yourself, you will deepen your fear of failure. The results of this fear are manifold. Let us look at some of the effects on studying, and at how we ourselves make the fear worse.

When we fear failure, we tend to reject anything which does not fit our current beliefs. New, divergent views show we were mistaken on something. This confirms our fear of incompetency. Illogically, we let it prove to us that we are inadequate. We were stupid, we tell ourselves, to have been misinformed or to have drawn the wrong conclusion. We do not tell ourselves that we are bright for seeing our mistakes and getting them corrected.

We try to write a term paper. Suddenly we are gripped by fear of failure. Is the paper going to be any good at all? Will it seem hopelessly naive, ridiculously puerile? Anything from a faint misgiving to blind panic seizes us. We do not look at our first drafts with sympathy, setting out to save the good and eliminate the weaknesses. We tear the whole thing up. We try to do mathematics. More misgivings assail us. We tell ourselves that any dope could do those problems. But *we* can't! We stare at some textbook, read and reread pages, and despair of ever understanding the material. We call ourselves dumb, and decide we are just no good at anything the least bit complicated.

We suffer from strange moods and emotional states which we do not understand, but which are all too understandable in terms of the way we have been treated by others and by ourselves. We become obsessed by grades. We may even think about them continuously—a response utterly incompatible with what we mean by "studying." We look at long tasks and scurry in the opposite direction, feeling "bored" or slightly sick. These are some of the repercussions of *fear* of failure. None of them helps you study effectively.

Fear of failing in school even results in not studying. We avoid studying in order to have an excuse for failure and prevent harsh self-criticism for failure. "Failure" is not necessarily an "E" or "F"; any grade at all can be construed as failure, depending upon the individual's own standards and his demands upon himself.

Let us consider Bill. To Bill any grade below "B" is psychological failure; it means the person is dumb—*if* he tried. Of course if he didn't try, that's different. Bill is afraid he would make "C's" even if he did try. Consequently, he does not try. He gets a "C" and jauntily remarks, "Well, I didn't crack a book all term." He got the "C," he says, because he "didn't try" and not because he was "stupid." To give himself this out, he avoids studying. Do you ever do this? Do you ever attempt to protect yourself from failure by not trying? Most people do, at least occasionally; some people do habitually.

We cannot change the whole world, but we can change ourselves. We can refrain from making fun of ourselves; we can stop threatening ourselves; we can stop taking errors or failures as "proof" that we are stupid. Although we cannot stop everyone else from trying to frighten us, we can at least stop frightening ourselves. We can avoid deepening our fear of failure.

In other ways too we can at least partially free ourselves from this fear of failure. Some ways of achieving this are discussed below.

4. TREAT YOURSELF WITH MORE RESPECT.

Although you are not perfect and never will be, by your own or anyone else's standards, you are extremely valuable. You may not be "the grandest tiger in the jungle," but through fulfilling the potentialities you do have, you can do tremendously worthwhile things and make many contributions to our world. These facts are worth remembering. Can you do so? That is a part of what we mean by "Treat yourself with more respect." Other parts are these.

Recognize your special assets and use them to their utmost. Recognize also your shortcomings. Regard shortcomings not as proof of some malignant inferiority, but as places where you can apply your skill in learning to become a somewhat different person. Similarly, regard mistakes as clues to where you profitably can do differently in the future—not as evidence that you are "worthless."

Bear in mind the things you have done well, and not merely those you have done poorly. Encourage yourself. Tell yourself you have done well, when you have. In short, treat yourself in the ways you treat your friends, and wish they would treat you.

5. STRIVE FOR IMPROVEMENT, NOT PERFECTION.

Guard against making your self-respect contingent upon a perfect performance, or the equal of the most skillful person you know. Similarly, do not define "success" as achievement of your highest ideals. Such "success," if you have much imagination, is impossible. You are bound to fail and learn to fear failure in everything you try.

Instead, define success as *moving nearer* to your ideals. Whenever you evaluate your performance, do not note merely how far you are from where you aim to be. Note also how far you have progressed from where you began. The direction in which you are moving is at least as important as where you are at the moment. Indeed it is a better indication, than your present position, of where you are heading and what you will become in the future.

When fear of failure bids fair to swamp you, try recapturing this outlook. Remind yourself: "At least I can try. And I can try to improve. No matter how low I rate myself, nor how slim the chances for success appear to be, I can try for what I hold dear. I can do my best with what I have." In all of life, no man or woman can do better.

6. WHENEVER YOU CARE TREMENDOUSLY ABOUT
   SOMETHING, TRY FOR IT—REGARDLESS OF THE
   APPARENT ODDS AGAINST SUCCESS.

For each person, some entities are so precious they are worth trying for, even when the try seems doomed to failure. Which things these are for you, you will have to decide for yourself. In general, they are whatever you care most about in life, whatever you deem most dear.

In such circumstances, the attempt itself is valuable. You may lose a large part of what you were striving for, but you will not have lost by default. Nor will you have betrayed yourself and what you cherish. At the very least, you will win the profound satisfaction of knowing you slanted your life toward the entities you hold most valuable. You will have lived for your ideals. You will have won the self-respect, the sense of peace and achievement, which come from being true to oneself and one's own ideals. These are notable successes.

In other respects too, many attempts are bound to have partial success. Let us suppose, for example, that you endeavor to become highly educated. You study wholeheartedly in an all-out try for that goal. You try to become as skilled a thinker, as understanding, as informed, as broad and deep in your interests, and as responsible as is possible for you in your world. Through practicing the habits necessary to attain those goals, you inevitably develop at least some of the attributes you value. Whenever you practice being the person you wish to become, you do become a little more that person.

7. IF YOU INTENSELY FEAR FAILURE IN SOME ACTIVITY,
   WHOLEHEARTEDLY TRY THAT ACTIVITY.

Let us return to Bill to clarify the significance of this.
You will recall that when Bill studies little and gets a "C," he
says that is all right because he did not try. That approach
has a flaw: The lingering suspicion haunts him that even *had*
he tried, he still would have made a low grade. So Bill has
lost after all. Despite not studying and thereby rationalizing
low grades, Bill still has only a tenuous grasp on his self-
esteem.

Fear of failing in a situation probably never can be
alleviated by avoiding the situation and by declining to try.
Such an approach leaves one feeling much as though he
actually had tried and failed. It also prevents discovering
that one's fears were sometimes groundless. Fear of failure
can be alleviated only when one dives in and tries.

At best one succeeds. If Bill were to study
wholeheartedly, he *might* make a "B" or even an "A." He
thus would allay, at least somewhat, his misgivings about his
intelligence and other abilities.

At "worst," he fails to make a "B" or an "A". He gets the
grade he dreaded. Would this merely confirm his gloomiest
suspicions about himself, thus making matters worse than
ever? No, for even this outcome is no worse and causes him
to think no more lowly of himself than what he was fearfully
thinking anyway.

Furthermore, even this outcome *could* lead to a marked
improvement in Bill's situation. Suppose in response to his
low grade, Bill set out to modify his ways of studying. He
then could end with new, more satisfying approaches to
learning. Or he could revise his demands upon himself so
they accorded more closely with his present abilities. He
could build a new view of his role in the world, such that he

sees he is valuable even though unable to do certain things successfully. He could discover new ways of responding to failure which remove its sting.

Failure seldom is as awful as we feared. Few events are. Only rarely is an event as grim in actuality as in our horror-stricken imaginings. By trying and "failing," Bill will discover (at least in part) the truth of that important fact.

He might discover also that studying to the best of his abilities has intrinsic values, values quite apart from getting high grades or some other extrinsic reward. He could learn, in short, that though an activity failed to achieve some of the goals for which it was intended, other valued goals were achieved through it. When we try, "failure" is almost never as complete as we feared.

In all these ways, a defeat can lead to triumphs, with our chances for happiness being better than ever—and far better than they could have been had we declined the challenge and not tried.

8. DEVELOP YOUR RESPECT FOR OTHER PEOPLE.

The greater the extent to which you actively recognize the value of other individuals, see their contributions and special assets, and treat them with genuine consideration, the greater your respect for those individuals becomes. And, in general, the more skillfully and extensively you do these things with other people, the better you can do them with yourself.[20, 22, 32, 61] In other words, there is marked transfer here. A deep respect for other persons and deep respect for yourself often (perhaps always) are reciprocally linked.[31, 44, 52, 53, 75, 76, 115] Hence, increasing your active respect for others will increase your esteem for yourself. Enhanced self-esteem, in turn, reduces your fear of failure.

F. Other Habits Which Handicap Us and Some Ways to Change Them

1. THE MERE PROSPECT OF RIDICULE IS TERRIFYING TO MANY PEOPLE.

What is your greatest fear or worry? One thousand normal men and women were asked that question.[69] The fear they mentioned most often was "criticism of others." Similarly, they regarded their "most difficult tendency" as being too self-conscious, worrying about what others will think of them, and being too sensitive—reported in that order. They considered their "worst habit" to be worrying over other people's opinion of them. For both men and women, these were the most frequent replies. The replies reflect a fear of ridicule, pervasive and strong.

Much of your life, too, is spoiled by this same fear. Seldom do we realize how great is its influence.

Have you started to compliment someone and then not done so, lest someone scoff? Have you started to offer someone a seat on the bus or trolley, and hastily quashed the impulse from fear of condescending smiles by other passengers? Those are people whom you do not even know by name and probably never will meet again—yet you fear their opinion. Have you started to help someone and then refrained, lest somebody call you a "sucker"? Or an "apple polisher"? Or ask you what you were after? Other people too suppress kindness with a frequency which might astonish you. They too fear ridicule.

And what about your interests? Do you enjoy concerts, but become apologetic when people discover you sometimes attend them? Do you attend fine plays or read classics, but carefully not mention this lest people think you are silly? Would you like to read more, but squelch the interest? You do not want to be called stuffy, or queer, or highbrow. And how about studying? Do you hide that too? To be caught studying brings blushes of shame to many a collegian. To admit actually liking to study is almost unthinkable.

What happens to your ideas? Have you started to present an idea—and then stifled it from fear of ridicule? Have you started to build a new line of thought—only to drop it quickly when someone barked, "*No* one believes that!"?

All these actions we avoid because someone *might* scoff. Much which would be gentle and considerate . . . much which would develop an uncommon breadth and depth of interests . . . much which would enhance our skill in thinking . . . much which would be creative and novel . . . we abandon from fear of ridicule. We abandon actions which are the very essence of being civilized. We place in jeopardy values unspeakably dear to us—all to avoid the mere *possibility* of ridicule, or teasing, or loss of other people's esteem.

"We dread the blows we never feel

And what we never lose is yet by us lamented!"[65]

Fear of ridicule is a force of tremendous strength, a force which can rule, and thereby ruin, life.

We hide this from ourselves. We camouflage from ourselves that we are quashing actions primarily because someone might scoff. Often we cover up by saying emphatically (too emphatically) that we too consider the activities "silly" and "pointless." You know what happens next. We come to believe our rationalizations, with the result that many activities are spoiled for us. Many valued activities we no longer can bring ourselves to do at all; many others we do sporadically and with faint heart.

Quite probably you study little and do that studying listlessly, largely because of this fear of being ridiculed. We have a deeply rooted fear of losing status, of being labelled a "bookworm" or being given some other equally ignominious title.

Is the laughter of others really so terrible? Do you care more about avoiding the possibility of ridicule than you care about attaining various other values? Do you, for example, really value more deeply not being laughed at than you value finding the world increasingly fascinating? Or being free from boredom with yourself, now and in the years to come? Or having an increased fund of information and greater skill in thinking? Or being able to make a more sizable contribution to your fellow men? Do you care so much about avoiding occasional scoffs? These are questions each of us should answer for ourself.

When you find yourself drawing back from something largely because someone might laugh were you to go ahead, pause for a moment. Examine what rests on the other side of the balance. It is your choice. Make it. Look at what you are choosing, and at what you are choosing to reject, while still you have the choice. Not always will you choose to do what your first automatic impulse dictates.

Quite possibly you do not care very much about avoiding laughter—but only *feel* as if you do and automatically act in the ways you were trained as a child. Very possibly you value other people's friendship and respect far more than you value avoidance of their laughter. You may have these entities confused. Avoiding people's laughter and having their friendship are not the same thing, nor does either one cause the other.

Laughter at your actions does not necessarily mean contempt of you nor of your actions. Often people laugh from surprise. Often too, laughter and even ridicule are affectionate roughhouse. They are clumsy ways of expressing attention and affection in a culture that discourages many other modes of expressing affection. Such laughter (though not always so perceived) is rather like Christopher Robin's "Silly old Pooh!" followed by, "I love you so"; except we do not add that last phrase because it is too sentimental (and people might laugh!).

Extremely often too, laughter is a defense of the laugher's self-respect. It is a defense of his right to do things in the way he sees fit. *Much disparaging laughter and much ridicule are occasioned by the person's feeling that pressures are being exerted on him to change, that he is being threatened.* Belittling other people and their activities is a way of retorting, "My ways of going at life are all right! *I* am all right! I'll prove it by showing that you and your ways are silly." This points the way to a solution.

We can largely avoid laughter and ridicule by following this humane expedient: Never try to force another person to adopt your ways. Communicate in words and actions that you regard his cherished ways as fine for him, though perhaps not for you. This you can do in many ways. Here are some of them.

Keep your own interests and develop them, but in addition share with other people their interests and enthusiasms. . . . Never belittle and never make fun of their actions or ideas. . . . Treat their preferences and tastes with the deep respect any person's preferences deserve. . . . Respect people as unique individuals. . . . Remember that they too need to feel important in others' eyes. . . . Express whatever admiration you feel. . . . If you defend your actions and interests, make extremely clear that you are defending them *only* as right to you and for you, and not as best or right for anyone else. . . . Never behave as though your actions should be models. . . . Never flaunt your achievements, nor in any other way (and here we return to our starting point) try to force other people to adopt your practices.

Without developing some such skills as these, you can

sedulously avoid every activity your associates might ridicule, but you will not have their friendship.

When you do develop practices and attitudes like those sketched above, you can do almost anything, no matter how strange the activity seems to some people, and still win and hold their friendship and esteem. You can go to concerts; you can read a lot; you can even study for hours and hours—and rarely will anyone laugh. You can do pretty much as you please and seldom be ridiculed—so long as you do not try to force other people to do likewise nor imply your way of living is the only way worth much. In giving other people the freedom to live their lives in their own ways and encouraging them to do so, undreamt-of freedom becomes possible for you and deep friendship too.

Curiously, this approach often results in your associates' adopting many of your attitudes and coming to share many of your interests. Unadulterated, un-forcing enthusiasm is singularly contagious.

2. CONFLICT AND ANXIETY DURING STUDY HAVE OTHER
    ROOTS TOO WHICH WE CAN ERADICATE.

In addition to those already discussed, other fears impair our skill in studying. One of the most common is a fear that making high grades will impair our social success. Making high grades, we fear, will jeopardize our chances of being popular or holding school offices, or will in some other way cause us to be left out. These fears are very real, but are largely unwarranted.

Pertinent data now are available. The data show that something very like the opposite of our fears actually is the case. During college years, people with high grades are in no way handicapped socially. In fact, people making grades of Phi Beta Kappa caliber participate in *more* college activities and other extracurricular activities than do the average students.[10, 80, 158, 180, 181, 198] They also have more than their share of school offices (are elected to more presidencies of groups, and so on). Similarly, individuals with very high marks have just as many friends and acquaintances on the average as do students with lower grades. High grades and social success in college are not negatively correlated. Instead, they tend to go together.[24, 73, 82, 105, 172, 193, 195]

Comparably, university students participating in various sports (archery, fencing, wrestling, water skiing, etc.) 101 to 200 hours in a 32-week period made significantly higher grades on the average than those participating in sports only a little or not at all.[187]

Scholastic success and personal adjustment also are correlated, the student tending to be high on both or else on neither.[16, 17, 43, 50, 60, 71, 73, 86, 88, 90, 105, 133, 148, 165, 170, 172] For example, academically successful university and college students are found to be better integrated and freer of tensions,[48, 49, 60, 136, 156, 188] freer of anxieties,[48, 49, 136, 161] more self-controlled,[48, 49, 70, 71, 105, 136] more self-sufficient, independent and responsible,[70, 71, 111, 196] and in general better socialized,[49, 60, 86, 94, 105, 111, 133, 136, 172, 195, 197] on the average, than those with low grades or academically unsuccessful. (As you might guess, college and university students who are married do as well academically as those not married,[83, 159] and those working part-time do as well as those not employed.)[166, 185]

Results are comparable for grade school,[14, 34, 41, 123, 125, 137, 139] junior high school,[3, 25, 41, 138, 162, 179] and high school.[36, 46, 63, 67, 77, 89, 91, 117, 128, 138, 154, 171, 182, 190]

At all levels, young people high scholastically tend to be high in other ways as well, including psychological health and social accomplishments. The trends cut across age groups; and they cut across geographical locations and time. This is a remarkably stable phenomenon.

For students of five, ten, or fifteen years ago, and for students during the 25 years preceding that, the trends held; for students of the present, the trends still hold. Exceptions do exist,[127, 192] especially for art,[10] and never are the trends so strong that one can accurately predict individually. Still, in general, and across a wide span of time, young people of high scholastic achievement tend to be more popular, have better personal adjustment, and participate in more activities than those with low scholastic achievement.

After graduation, the trends continue. One expects success as an undergraduate and success as a graduate student to be correlated, and they are — substantial correlations being found between undergraduate grades and success in graduate work for law,[96] pharmacy,[43] education,[30] engineering,[101] and other fields.[78, 113] Similarly, substantial positive correlations usually are found between grades in high school and grades at the university or college,[59, 81, 87, 106, 122, 135, 136, 144, 153, 164] and from one year to the next,[68, 106] and from one term to the next,[129] suggesting again the salient role in academic success played by ones' intellectual and personality habits.

In more pervasive respects, the foregoing trends continue in the years after college: People who earned high grades have better chances of success than those who did not. What is construed as success depends upon the observer. But whether one takes as the criterion for "success" the amount of money one later makes,[21, 62, 64, 80, 101, 169, 186] rapidity of salary increases,[6, 101] being listed in *Who's Who in America*,[80, 97, 98, 173] the ratings of one's classmates,[80, 100] or creativity in science and engineering,[28, 29, 101, 177] success is positively correlated with grades in college. That is, by any of these criteria, people with high grades generally are more successful in later life than people with lower grades.

People with high grades generally are more successful after college, but not always. For example, in a study of engineering graduates over a 45-year period,[101] 25% of the persons with grade-point averages in the highest tenth of the graduates advanced to the top salary level, but so also did 9% of the persons with grade-point averages in the bottom tenth. High grades do not guarantee later success, nor do low grades guarantee failure. The trend simply is in that direction, and fairly markedly so. In another sense too, the data do not mean that high grades necessarily cause success. The relationship between high grades and later success might be caused by a third set of factors. For example, certain personality characteristics (such as enthusiasm for whatever one is doing, ability to work independently and efficiently, freedom from restricting fears, relatively high intelligence) could facilitate both making high grades and being successful outside college. People who develop these personality characteristics while in school would tend, as a consequence, to make high grades in college and would tend also to become successful after college. Other interpretations of the correlations also are possible. What the data do show, conclusively, is that making high grades is no hindrance to later success.

No evidence appears of a negative correlation between grades and subsequent success. Sometimes there is no relationship, and often the relationship is low, though significant; but where there *is* a relationship, the relationship between grades and later success is always positive.

At the extremes, the relationship holds most closely. The moderately good student is only a bit more likely to do well later than the moderately poor student. But the exceptionally excellent student is apt to be excellent in other ways as well, both in college and in later life.

High grades and social success in college tend to go together. High grades and vocational successes also tend to go together. These facts are slow to be recognized; but they are facts. Remembering them can allay at least some of your fear of studying.

3. FEAR OF SUCCESS CAN BESET ONE.

Akin to fear of ridicule and fear of making high grades is a more subtle anxiety: the fear of success.

Fear of success can be diffuse—a feeling that one is not worthy of success and should fail. This was touched upon in connection with feelings of guilt (see page 133-134). The fear of success can be vague, with no target; or fear of success can be highly specific: fear of success in one's vocation—one wants to be a doctor but also is afraid to be a doctor, or actor, or carpenter, or president, or engineer, or anything else a human being can strive toward; or a fear of social success—a fear of other people's thinking too highly of one with danger of disappointing them; a fear of having much responsibility and making inappropriate decisions and being destructively criticized; a fear of loving and being loved and of losing love—fear of success and fear of failure often go hand in hand. The kinds of fear of success are about as numerous as the kinds of people in the world.

Three variations of fear of success are notably common: a fear of success as an instance necessarily involving divergence from the commonplace, fear of success as an instance involving conformity to various norms and expectations, and fear of success as an instance involving creativity. When present in a student, these fears can dilute seriously what he gains from his years at the university or college; they can destroy his effectiveness as a student (and also as much else). In the next sections, we consider these three kinds of fear of success: fear of any deviancy from the norms or from the average, fear (oppositely) of any conformity, and fear of creativity.

4. FEAR OF DEVIANCY CAN PLAGUE ONE.

We live in a world rife with pressures toward conformity. We strive to adapt and sometimes, instead, succumb: We become preoccupied with fitting in, with being one of the gang, with at least escaping censure. We may become almost obsessed with being "normal," consumed with not being different.[39, 76, 191] A host of concomitant fears can assail us—among them fear of success. We dare not be outstanding in any way.

5. FEAR OF CONFORMITY IS COMMON.

Sometimes we over-correct for the urge toward conformity. Instead of becoming obsessed with being as "normal" as possible, we become obsessed with being as deviant as possible. We develop habits of doing things merely because it is not common or is not a socially customary way. We acquire a fear of any conformity: a feeling that if we conform in any respect, we will lose our identity and creativity. Feeling this way, we become engrossed with being different, hardly daring to do anything if it is commonly done. This is a tremendous hindrance to learning from others' experience, since a large part of what has been learned has been codified in terms of customs and norms. Not all differences from the norm help us become more alive; not all conformings with norms hinder our development. Not everything that people have discovered and codified leads into blind alleys or in other ways hinders human living. Indeed, much of it gives us ways to stay out of blinds and to avoid needless trial-and-error or senselessly circuitous routes. Avoiding all conformity narrows and binds as surely as adopting all-conformity.

6. FEAR OF CREATIVITY EXISTS, TOO.

There is a variant of the fear of success with particularly devastating implications: the fear that being very creative will lead to maladjustment, or neuroticism, or social ostracism. This is a fear singularly enervating. It can discourage one from even attempting to develop his special talents. It can discourage one from using some of his most human potentials.

Until recently few data were available on this matter. Now however, besides the studies mentioned on pages 232-236, extensive studies have been made of highly creative individuals from a wide variety of fields: viz., chemistry, physics, architecture, literature, engineering, mathematics, biology, anthropology, art, and others.[12, 13, 26, 42, 109, 110, 134, 146, 147, 157, 177, 194] The studies show us our old stereotypes were faulty; our old fears unwarranted.

Far from being unhappy, neurotic individuals, the highly creative are relatively less subject to repression, and suppression, and self-defensiveness; are more discerning, more flexible in their routes to goals, more open to richness of experience. They are relatively freer. They are neither rigid conformists, blindly bound by convention, nor blindly anti-social. Instead they are genuinely independent.

Nor do they generally become bitter introverts. Though seldom joiners of many civic or social clubs, and sometimes described as aloof or reserved,[13, 26, 146] in general the highly creative are as secure and sociable, as happy and comfortable with their fellow men, as a random sample of more ordinary people.[28, 29, 42, 109, 110, 134, 147, 194] They are very far from being out of touch.

Indeed, as is implied by the above and other data,[13, 102, 110, 116] notably creative persons are more completely in touch with the world than the average. Commenting upon Aristophanes' masterpiece, Lysistrata, Seldes[7] remarks: " 'The contemplation of things as they are, without substitution or imposture, without error or confusion is in itself a nobler thing than a whole harvest of inventions,' said Francis Bacon. The inventions in Lysistrata are very few, but the contemplation of things as they are is steady and unafraid. This is, of course, the distinction of the great classical writers, and the reason that they live."

MacKinnon[110] summarizes: "It is quite apparent that creative persons have an unusual capacity to record and retain and have readily available the experiences of their life history. They are discerning, which is to say that they are observant in a differentiated fashion; they are alert, capable of concentrating attention readily and shifting it appropriately; they are fluent in scanning thoughts and producing those that serve to solve the problems they undertake; and characteristically, they have a wide range of information at their command."

Apparent too is "another pervasive trait of the creative, his preference for complexity, his delight in the challenging and unfinished. . . ."[110]

Far from killing one's breadth of interests and diversity, becoming a highly skilled and creative person leaves one more diversified. One does not become a narrow specialist — not if top-flight. Instead one is more abundantly alive.

7. SOMETIMES WE ARE LOATH TO ADMIT WE DO NOT
   KNOW EVERYTHING.

That is rare, but a slight modification is common: We are loath to admit we do not know everything known by our associates. This characteristic may or may not mean low respect for other people. It almost certainly means very low self-respect. What are some results of this low self-esteem?

To such a person, books *have* to be vapid; lectures *must* be stating mainly platitudes; associates *cannot* be saying much that is new or significant; for if something were interesting or in any other way were worthy of close attention, careful notes, or intensive study, this would prove the individual did not already know everything worth knowing. It would prove also he had not thought everything worth thinking. Perhaps he had not even thought of everything his associates had. Such an admission is intolerable to a person already low in self-esteem.

People with very low self-respect are driven to prove, over and over again, that they are "as good as the next person," or better. They must "prove" this to themselves and to others too, in order to maintain even their current low level of self-respect. Therefore, they scoff at other people's choice of activities; they belittle other people's achievements; they criticize harshly and indiscriminately. About their own activities, they wax boastfully eloquent.

Clearly then, one way to reduce the just-try-to-tell-me-anything attitude is this: Decrease the self-contempt underlying the attitude.

With the problem so stated, you yourself will have promising ideas for its solution. Undoubtedly you know many ways of making a person feel more valued and worthwhile, of helping him gain more self-esteem and (as a consequence) gain greater receptivity to new ideas and information, an enhanced ability to learn. This knowledge you can apply to yourself as well as to your associates.

8. Rigidity handicaps us in many endeavors.

What does rigidity mean? This in part: We fall into stereotyped ways of behaving, overlooking changes in the external situation. We do the same thing over and over and over, although external conditions have changed and our stereotyped response is not working out well at all. We make many mistakes, and eliminate our mistakes more slowly. We even make the same mistake repeatedly. This type of habit seriously handicaps us in school and in other aspects of living.[2, 47, 107, 108, 130, 149, 150]

A particularly poignant example of the impact of rigidity turned up in a recent experiment.[141] University students were guessing whether a green light or red light would be shown on various trials. It was found that they required considerably more information before they would change a decision than they required to make the original decision. When they had once made a decision, they tended to cling to it—even though evidence to the contrary was presented and even though the original decision was based on very scanty or even nonexistent information.

Decreased ability to modify our beliefs or to change in other ways gravely limits our chances for growth. In its extreme form, rigidity paralyzes us and utterly precludes our growth.

An increase in rigidity and a decrease in adaptability often are caused in part by fear or hostility.[2, 56, 114, 126, 142, 151] The alleviation of intense fears or hostilities is at least as complicated as repairing a broken leg. For such difficulties, one is wise to collaborate with someone highly skilled along these lines—e.g., a clinical psychologist, psychiatrist, or psychoanalyst. Milder fears and hostilities you, of course, can reduce or break up by yourself. Many ways of doing this have already been offered in the preceding sections.

There are other techniques also for increasing flexibility. One is this: Be organized for receiving new information, thinking of yourself as a recipient and processor of information rather than primarily as a transmitter of information or as already completely informed.[1, 38, 104]

Another route toward increasing flexibility: Remember that entities with the same label always have marked differences. We touched upon this before. Let us examine more closely now its meaning for your life.

Are all science courses the same? Of course not, you say. Are two beginning chemistry courses the same? Never. Often, indeed, they are very different, far more different than we are apt to realize. Even the "same" course is very different when taught by different instructors. Radically different objectives and radically different skills may be involved.

The situation is analogous to sports. Tennis and badminton, for example, have many similarities. The similarities can mislead us into believing the games are essentially alike. Yet techniques advisable for one are utterly ineffective in the other. In tennis, letting your wrist "break" will ruin the shot; in badminton, it can be part of a beautiful smash.

Superficial similarities do not necessarily mean basic similarities. In sports we see this clearly; in other phases of life we often overlook it. Two people have similar skin color; we then act, sometimes, as though they had similar personalities. Two people belong to the same church; we then imagine they will behave in fundamentally similar ways. Two courses are offered by the same college department; we fancy that techniques effective in one will necessarily be effective in another. We blindly carry habits from one situation to another and expect them to work well or at least be appropriate to the new situation. This leads to senseless disappointments.

In studying, in playing, in interacting with people, be alert for the differences in similar entities. Watch for evidence on how well your habits are working out. If old successful habits are giving poor results, you are confronting a new situation with crucial differences from the old one—despite there being, perhaps, many resemblances between the two. When you get such evidence, modify your behavior. Such procedures are the foundation of flexible adaptability.

9. WE FIND IT DIFFICULT TO STUDY OR DO MUCH OF ANYTHING ELSE WHOLEHEARTEDLY.

While studying, you probably feel like loafing. While loafing you feel, often, as if you should be studying; the pestering thought keeps returning that "this is a waste of time." And how does it go at the movies? Or dancing? Or playing? Do you find yourself troubled then too by vague thoughts of work undone, of duties calling, or of other pleasures you wish you had chosen instead? So life goes.

Most of us have been so trained that we live in an almost perpetual state of conflict. Regardless of what we are trying to do, we are both doing it and not doing it at the same time. Almost continuously we feel ambivalent—liking and disliking the same activity. Only the rare adult can even play wholeheartedly.

These conflicts and ambivalence which infest our activities can be eradicated. How? How can you become free from inwardly tearing against yourself? How can you gain the ability to live with greater enthusiasm and delight? These problems are an underlying concern of this entire little book. All of its suggestions are slanted toward achievement of these goals too.

Another big step toward resolving conflict is this: Face your fears and try to reduce them. Reducing any anxiety or fear brings increments in peace throughout one's life and better chances for unalloyed enthusiasm.

Another approach is to develop these habits: For any

particular time and situation, decide what course of action all in all seems best to you. Then embark upon that course and stick to it until you get data you did not have at the time of your original decision. Change your course when and only when you do have new information upon which to base a new decision. With practice, you can make this a habit. When you do, you will have new skills in living unfettered by conflict and ambivalence.

Practice living with enthusiasm. Whatever you are doing at any moment, do that with all the enthusiasm you can muster. When you become able to engage in one activity wholeheartedly, you will be able to engage in others too more wholeheartedly. For example, learning to play tennis with enthusiasm and free from conflict will enable you to study more wholeheartedly. Similarly, learning to study with wholehearted enthusiasm enhances your ability to do other activities with wholeheartedness. You can build a basic, generalized skill for doing whatever you are doing with wholehearted enthusiasm.

To develop such a habit, launch yourself with vigor into anything you decide to do. Whatever you begin, at least begin with enthusiasm. Then carry on with all the verve and imagination at your command. Live every moment to the fullest extent of your resources.

> "A Moment's Halt—a momentary Taste
> Of *Being* from the Well amid the Waste—
>   And Lo!—the phantom Caravan has reach'd
> The Nothing it set out from—Oh, make haste!
>
> Ah, make the most of what we yet may spend,
> Before we too into the Dust descend;
>   Dust into Dust, and under Dust to lie,
> Sans Wine, sans Song, sans Singer, and—sans End!"[93]

G. *Toward Earning a Better Life — Concluding Comments*

Suppose a man were interested in becoming a skilled violinist. He might solicit instruction on fingering and bowing techniques. But no matter how elaborate the instruction, it would profit him little — if he had a broken arm. Obviously, he should do something about that arm.

When we start our college careers, most of us are in a similar predicament — except instead of a broken arm, we have battered personalities. The damage is such that we are handicapped gravely in our efforts to become educated, even though we have expert tuition.

Further, these characteristics continue to handicap us after college. They jeopardize happiness and success in all of living.

You are not compelled to live your entire life with such handicaps; for you can repair the damage. Many leads have been presented on what the difficulties are. Many leads on how you can alleviate these difficulties and build a new personality have also been presented. From here, however, you must carry on by yourself. The actual breaking of these unfortunate habits and the building of new ones is nothing anyone can do for you, no matter how fervently he may so desire. If it is to be done at all, you must do it for yourself.

Perhaps you should be forewarned: The job is not easy. The difficulty is rather the same, we imagine, as that encountered by a person thrown into deep water with millstones tied around his neck. The presence of the millstones (as of those personality characteristics) makes it very difficult to act in the ways necessary to get free. But the presence of the millstones also makes it extremely difficult to live in the only ways possible for a person not freed. That leaves little choice but to try to get free.

Though arduous, this is a peculiarly challenging, exciting endeavor. Eventually you may even find it fun to work on these characteristics and note your gradual progress. Certainly you will find the results a joy—the exhilaration of achievement and seeing what you can do . . . the satisfaction of growing toward your potentialities and of recognizing the possibilities of new growth . . . the joys of a real freedom . . . the refreshing beauty of peace with yourself and with your fellow men . . . the new capacities for living enthusiastically. These are not trifles. They can be yours. Through striving to grow, working to eliminate handicaps, exploiting opportunities to become truly educated (not merely informed), a significant beginning will be made.

You can create a life you never have known, but only glimpsed. You can become, ever more nearly, the person you long to be. You can help build the world of your dreams—a new reality.

"No end is visible or even conceivable to this kingdom of adventure."[103]

Bon Voyage!

Bibliography for Chapter 5

1. Adams, J. S. Reduction of cognitive dissonance by seeking consonant information. J. Abnorm. Soc. Psychol., 62, 74-78, 1961.
2. Adorno, T. W.; Frenkel-Brunswik, E.; Levinson, D. J.; and Sanford, R. N. The Authoritarian Personality. New York: Harper and Brothers, 1950.
3. Airoldi, Norman; Peterson, Barbara; and Webb, Dwight. Junior high school athletes excel in scholarship. Personnel Guid. J., 45, 1021-1024, 1967.

4. Alexakos, C. E.: Stankowski, W. M.; and Sanborn, M. P. Superior high school students' thoughts about the future and their later college achievements. Vocational Guid. Quarterly, 15, 273-280, 1967.

5. Allport, G. W. Basic principles in improving human relations. In Bigelow, K. W., Cultural Groups and Human Relations. New York: Bureau of Publications, Teachers College, Columbia Univ., 1951, pp. 8-28.

6. American Telephone and Telegraph Company, Personnel Research Section. College Achievement and Progress in Management. Bell Telephone Magazine, Spring 1962.

7. Aristophanes. Lysistrata: A New Version by Gilbert Seldes. New York: The Heritage Press, 1962.

8. Atkinson, J. W. An Introduction to Motivation. Princeton: Van Nostrand, 1964.

9. Atkinson, J. W.; and Feather, N. T. (Eds.) A Theory of Achievement Motivation. New York: Wiley, 1966.

10. Baird, Leonard L. The achievement of bright and average students. Educ. Psychol. Meas., 28, 891-899, 1968.

11. Barnard, J. W.; Zimbardo, P. G.; and Sarason, S. Anxiety and verbal behavior in children. Child Developm., 32, 379-392, 1961.

12. Barron, F. Creativity and Psychological Health. Princeton: Van Nostrand, 1963.

13. Barron, F. The psychology of creativity. In Barron, Frank, *et al.* (Eds.) New Directions in Psychology. Vol. 2, New York: Holt, Rinehart and Winston, 1965.

14. Bedoian, Vagharsh H. Social acceptability and social rejection of the underage, at-age, and average pupils in the sixth grade. J. Educ. Res., 47, 513-520, 1954.

15. Bennett, James Weldon. The interrelationship of college press, student needs, and academic aptitudes as measured by grade point average in a southern denominational college. Diss. Abstr. 29 (2-A) 474, 1968.

16. Berger, Emanuel M. Willingness to accept limitations and college achievement. J. Counsel. Psychol., 8, 140-146, 1961.

17. Berger, Irving L., and Sutker, Alvin R. The relationship of emotional adjustment and intellectual capacity to academic achievement of college students. Ment. Hyg., N.Y., 40, 65-77, 1956.

18. Bhatnagar, K. P. Academic achievement as a function of one's self-concepts and ego-functions. Educ. Psychol. Rev., 6, 178-182, 1966.

19. Bloxom, Bruce. Effects of anger-arousing instructions on personality questionnaire performance. Educ. Psychol. Meas., 28, 735-745, 1968.

20. Boshier, Roger. A study of the relationship between self-concept and conservatism. J. Soc. Psychol., 77, 139-140, 1969.

21. Bridgman, D. S. Success in college and business. Personnel J., 9, 1-19, 1930.
22. Brown, Robert D. Effects of structured and unstructured group counseling with high- and low-anxious college underachievers. J. Couns. Psychol., 16, 209-214, 1969.
23. Bruner, J. S. Affrontement et defense. (Threat and defense.) J. Psychol. Norm. Pathol., 58, 33-56, 1961.
24. Carew, Donald K. A comparison of activities, social acceptance and scholastic achievements of men students. Personnel Guid. J., 36, 121-124, 1957.
25. Carter, Harold D. Overachievers and underachievers in the junior high school. Calif. J. Educ. Res., 12, 51-56, 1961.
26. Cattell, R. B.; and Drevdahl, J. E. A comparison of the personality profile (16 P. F.) of eminent researchers with that of eminent teachers and administrators, and of the general population. Brit. J. Psychol., 46, 248-261, 1955.
27. Cattell, R. B.; Sealy, A. P.; and Sweney, A. B. What can personality and motivation source trait measurements add to the prediction of school achievement? Brit. J. Educ. Psychol., 36, 280-295, 1966.
28. Chambers, J. A. Creative scientists of today. Science, 145, 1203-1205, 1964.
29. Chambers, J. A. Relating personality and biographical factors to scientific creativity. Psychol. Monogr.: Gen. and Applied, 78, #584, 1964.
30. Colvin, Gerald F. The value of selected variables in predicting academic success in graduate education at the University of Arkansas. Diss. Abstr., 29 (1-A), 55-56, 1968.
31. Conner, Jack M. Development and growth of understanding self and others. Diss. Abstr., 29 (2-A), 477, 1968.
32. Coopersmith, Stanley. Studies in self-esteem. Sci. Amer., 218, 96-106, 1968.
33. Cowen, E. L. Stress reduction and problem-solving rigidity. J. Consult. Psychol., 16, 425-428, 1952.
34. Cowen, E. T.; Zax, M.; Klein, R.; Izzo, L. D.; and Trost, M. A. The relation of anxiety in school children to school record, achievement, and behavioral measures. Child. Devel., 36, 685-695, 1965.
35. Crandall, Virginia C. Personality characteristics and social and achievement behaviors associated with children's social desirability response tendencies. J. Personality Soc. Psychol., 4, 477-486, 1966.
36. Davids, Anthony. Psychological characteristics of high school male and female potential scientists in comparison with academic underachievers. Psychol. in the Schools, 3, 79-87, 1966.
37. Davis, W. E. Effect of prior failure on subjects' WAIS arithmetic subtest scores. J. Clin. Psychol., 25, 72-73, 1969.

38. Deutsch, Morton; Krauss, R. M.; and Rosenau, N. Dissonance or defensiveness? J. Personality, 30, 16-28, 1962.
39. Dingwall, E. J. The American Woman. New York: Rinehart & Co., 1957.
40. Dollard, J.; Doob, L. W.; Miller, N. E.; Mowrer, O. H.; Sears, R. R.; Ford, C. S.; Hovland, C. I.; and Sollenberger, R. T. Frustration and Aggression. New Haven, Conn.: Yale Univ. Press, 1939.
41. Dreger, Ralph M. General temperament and personality factors related to intellectual performances. J. Genetic Psychol., 113, 275-293, 1968.
42. Drevdahl, J. E.; and Cattell, R. B. Personality and creativity in artists and writers. J. Clin. Psychol., 14, 107-111, 1958.
43. Drinkwater, Ruby Straughan. The relationship between certain factors and academic success in the School of Pharmacy at Southwestern State College. Diss. Abstr., 28 (12-A), 4871, 1968.
44. Dubin, S. S.; Burke, L. K.; Neel, R. G.; and Chesler, D. J. Characteristics of hard and easy raters. U.S.A. Pers. Research Bureau Note, No. 36, 8 pp., 1954.
45. Earls, Jim H. Human adjustment to an exotic environment: The nuclear submarine. Archives General Psychiatry, 20, 117-123, 1969.
46. Easton, Judith. Some personality traits of underachieving and achieving high school students of superior ability. Bull. Maritime Psychol. Ass., 3, 34-39, 1959.
47. Ehrlich, H. J. Dogmatism and learning. J. Abnorm. Soc. Psychol., 62, 148-149, 1961.
48. Faunce, Patricia Spencer. Personality characteristics and vocational interests related to the college persistence of academically gifted women. Diss. Abstr., 28 (1-B), 338, 1967.
49. Faunce, Patricia Spencer. Personality characteristics and vocational interests related to the college persistence of academically gifted women. J. Couns. Psychol., 15, 31-40, 1968.
50. Faunce, Patricia Spencer. Withdrawal of academically gifted women. J. College Student Personnel, 9, 171-176, 1968.
51. Feather, N. T. Level of aspiration and performance variability. J. Personality Soc. Psychol., 6, 37-46, 1967.
52. Fey, W. F. Acceptance of self and others, and its relation to therapy-readiness. J. Clin. Psychol., 10, 269-271, 1954.
53. Fey, W. F. Acceptance by others and its relation to acceptance of self and others: a reevaluation. J. Abnorm. Soc. Psychol., 50, 274-276, 1955.
54. Fielstra, C. An analysis of factors influencing the decision to become a teacher. J. Educ. Res., 48, 659-667, 1955.
55. Frank, Jerome D. Persuasion and Healing: A Comparative Study of Psychotherapy. Baltimore: Johns Hopkins Press, 1961.

56. Frenkel-Brunswik, E.; and Sanford, R. N. Some personality factors in anti-Semitism. J. Psychol., 20, 271-291, 1945.

57. Freud, S. Psychopathology of Everyday Life. (Translated by A. A. Brill.) New York: Macmillan & Co., 1914.

58. Freud, S. Introductory Lectures on Psychoanalysis. (Translated by Joan Riviere.) London: G. Allen & Unwin, Ltd., 1922.

59. Gallessich, June Marie. Factors associated with academic success of freshmen engineering students of the University of Texas. Diss. Abstr., 28 (5-A), 1677-1678, 1967.

60. Garms, Joe D. Predicting scholastic achievement with nonintellectual variables. Diss. Abstr., 28 (8-B), 3460, 1968.

61. Gibson, John E. Are you an optimistic pessimist? Modern Living, July-August, 10 and 11, 1966.

62. Gifford, W. S. Does business want scholars? Harper's Monthly, 156, 669-674, 1928

63. Gill, Lois J.; and Spilka, Bernard. Some nonintellectual correlates of academic achievement among Mexican-American secondary school students. J. Educ. Psychol., 53, 144-149, 1962.

64. Gist, N. P.; Pihlblad, C. T.; and Gregory, C. L. Scholastic achievement and occupation. Amer. Sociol. Rev., 7, 752-763, 1942.

65. Goethe, J. W. Faust. (Translated by Bayard Taylor.) New York: Hartsdale House.

66. Gotoo, Keiichi; and Sugiyama, Yoshio. Experiments on the relationship between anxiety and psychological stress in serial rote learning. Jap. Psychol. Res., 2, 158-163, 1960.

67. Gough, H. G. Academic achievement in high school as predicted from the California Psychological Inventory. J. Educ. Psychol., 55, 174-180, 1964.

68. Grant, Ardyce Mary. Student academic performance as influenced by on-campus and off-campus residence. Diss. Abstr., 29 (4-A), 1104, 1968.

69. Hepner, H. W. Psychology Applied to Life and Work. New York: Prentice-Hall, 1942, pp. 7-8.

70. Holland, J. L. The prediction of college grades from the California Psychological Inventory and the Scholastic Aptitude Test. J. Educ. Psychol., 50, 135-142, 1959.

71. Holland, J. L. The prediction of college grades from personality and aptitude variables. J. Educ. Psychol., 51, 245-254, 1960.

72. Holland, J. L.; and Astin, A. W. The prediction of the academic, artistic, scientific, and social achievement of undergraduates of superior scholastic aptitude. J. Educ. Psychol., 53, 132-143, 1962.

73. Hopkins, J.; Mallison, N.; and Sarnoff, I. Some non-intellectual correlates of success and failure among university students. Brit. J. Educ. Psychol., 28, 25-36, 1958.

74. Hoppock, R. Job Satisfaction. New York: Harper and Brothers, Inc., 1935, p. 166.

75. Horney, Karen. Our Inner Conflicts. New York: W. W. Norton & Co., Inc., 1945.

76. Horney, Karen. Neurosis and Human Growth: The Struggle toward Self-realization. New York: W. W. Norton & Co., Inc., 1950.

77. Horowitz, Herbert. Prediction of adolescent popularity and rejection from achievement and interest tests. J. Educ. Psychol., 58, 170-174, 1967.

78. Hsia, Hsio-Hsuan. A study of selected intellective factors related to academic performance in graduate school. Diss. Abstr., 28 (9-A), 3508, 1968.

79. Hunt, H. C. Business demands more character education. The Pitmanite, April 1937.

80. Husband, Richard W. What do college grades predict? Fortune, 55, 157-158, 1957.

81. Iglinsky, Clyde L. Intellectual and non-intellectual factors affecting academic success of college freshmen. Diss. Abstr., 29 (5-A), 1423-4, 1968.

82. Jensen, Vern H. Influence of personality traits on academic success. Personnel Guid. J., 36, 497-500, 1958.

83. Jensen, Vern H.; and Clark, Monroe H. Married and unmarried college students: Achievement, ability, & personality. Personnel Guid. J., 37, 123-125, 1958.

84. Jersild, A. T., and Holmes, F. B. Children's fears. Child Devel. Monogr., No. 20, pp. ix-358, 1935.

85. Jersild, A. T., and Holmes, F. B. Some factors in the development of children's fears. J. Exper. Educ., 4, 133-141, 1935.

86. Johnson, Edward G., Jr. A comparison of academically successful and unsuccessful college of education freshmen on two measures of "self." Diss. Abstr., 28 (4-A), 1298-1299, 1967.

87. Johnson, Richard W.; Keochakian, Simon V.; Morningstar, Mona; and Southworth, J. A. Validation of freshmen orientation test battery. Educ. Psychol. Meas., 28, 437-440, 1968.

88. Jones, J. B. Some personal-social factors contributing to academic failure at Texas Southern University. In Sutherland, R. L.; Holtzman, W. H.; Koile, E. A.; and Smith, B. K. (Eds.) Personality Factors on the College Campus: Review of a Symposium. Austin, Texas: Hogg Foundation for Mental Health, 1962.

89. Jones, John Goff. Relationships among identity development and intellectual and nonintellectual factors. Diss. Abstr. 28 (3-A), 941, 1967.

90. Jones, John G. The relationship of self-perception measures and academic achievement among college seniors. J. Educ. Res., 63, 201-203, 1970.

91. Jones, John G.; and Strowig, R. Wray. Adolescent identity and self-perception as predictors of scholastic achievement. J. Educ. Res., 62, 78-82, 1968.

92. Karabenick, Stuart A.; and Youssef, Azkhour I. Performance as a function of achievement motive level and perceived difficulty. J. Personality Soc. Psychol., 10, 414-419, 1968.

93. Khayyam, O. Rubaiyat. (Fourth translation by E. Fitzgerald.) New York: Thomas Y. Crowell Co., 48 and 24 quatrains.

94. Kisch, Jeremy M. A comparative study of patterns of underachievement among male college students. Diss. Abstr. (8-B), 3461-2, 1968.

95. Kitson, H. D. Investigation of vocational interest among workers. Psychol. Clin., 19, 48-52, 1930.

96. Klein, Stephen P.; and Evans, Franklin R. An examination of the validity of nine experimental tests for predicting success in law school. Educ. Psychol. Meas., 28, 909-913, 1968.

97. Knapp, R. M. The man who led his class in college—and others. Harvard Graduate Magazine, 24, 597-600, 1966.

98. Knox, John B. Scholastic standing and prominence. School and Society, 65, 194-195, 1947.

99. Lacey, J. I.; Smith, R. L.; and Green, A. Use of conditioned autonomic responses in the study of anxiety. Psychosom. Med., 17, 208-217, 1955.

100. Langlie, T. A.; and Eldredge, A. Achievement in college and in later life. Personnel J., 9, 450-454, 1931.

101. LeBold, William K.; Thoma, Edward C.; Gillis, John W.; and Hawkins, George A. A study of the Purdue engineering graduate. Engineering Bull. Purdue Univ., 44, #1, 1-298, 1960.

102. Lee, Young-Hi Kwum. Creativity and sensitivity to diverse cues. Diss. Abstr., 28, (4-B), 1684-1685, 1967.

103. Leigh-Mallory, G. Diary at Camp IV on the 1922 Everest Expedition. Quoted by Ullman, J. R., in Kingdom of Adventure, p. 102. New York: William Sloan Associates, Inc., 1947.

104. Leventhal, H. The effects of set and discrepancy on impression change. J. Personality, 30, 1-15, 1962.

105. Lewis, Leslie. A multivariate analysis of variables associated with academic success within a college environment. Diss. Abstr., 27 (12-A), 4134, 1967.

106. Leyman, Laretha. Prediction of freshman and sophmore grade-point averages of women physical education major students. Educ. Psychol. Meas., 27, 1139-1141, 1967.

107. Luchins, A. S. Classroom experiments on mental set. Amer. J. Psychol., 59, 295-298, 1946.

108. Luchins, A. S. Proposed methods of studying degrees of rigidity in behavior. J. Personality, 15, 242-246, 1947.
109. MacKinnon, D. W. The nature and nurture of creative talent. American Psychologist, 17, 484-495, 1962.
110. MacKinnon, D. W. What makes a person creative? Saturday Review, 45, 15-17, and 69, 1962.
111. McDonald, Robert L.; and Gynther, Malcolm D. Nonintellectual factors associated with performance in medical school. J. Genetic Psychol., 103, 185-194, 1963.
112. McKeachie, W. J. Motivation, teaching methods, and college learning. In Marshall R. Jones (Ed.) Nebraska Symposium on Motivation, 1961. Lincoln, Neb.: Univ. Nebraska Press, 1962.
113. Mann, Sister M. Jacinta. Relationship among certain variables associated with college and post-college success. Diss. Abstr., 19, No. 2, 253-254, 1958.
114. Marquart, D. I. The pattern of punishment and its relation to abnormal fixation in adult human subjects. J. Gen. Psychol., 39, 107-144, 1948.
115. Maslow, A. H. Cognition of being in the peak experiences. J. Genet. Psychol., 94, 43-66, 1959.
116. Maslow, A. H. Toward a humanistic biology. Amer. Psychologist, 24, 724-735, 1969.
117. Metha, Perin H. The self-concept of bright under-achieving male high school students. Indian Educ. Rev., 3, 81-100, 1968.
118. Miller, N. E. Theory and experiment relating psychoanalytic displacement to stimulus-response generalization. J. Abnorm. Soc. Psychol., 43, 155-178, 1948.
119. Miller, N. E.; and Bugelski, R. Minor studies of aggression: II. The influence of frustrations imposed by the in-groups on attitudes expressed toward out-groups. J. Psychol., 25, 437-442, 1948.
120. Mischel, W. Preference for delayed reinforcement and social responsibility. J. Abnorm. Soc. Psychol., 62, 1-7, 1961.
121. Moore, E. H. Professors in retirement. J. Geront., 6, 243-252, 1951.
122. Morgenfeld, George R. The prediction of junior college achievement from adjusted secondary school grade averages. Diss. Abstr., 28 (8-A), 2987-2988, 1968.
123. Moriarty, A. Coping patterns of preschool children in response to intelligence test demands. Genet. Psychol. Monogr., 64, 3-127, 1961.
124. Moulton, R. W. Effects of success and failure on level of aspiration as related to achievement motives. J. Personality Soc. Psychol., 1, 399-406, 1965.
125. Murphy, L. B. The Widening World of Childhood: Paths toward Mastery. New York: Basic Books, 1962.

126. Murthy, Vinoda N. Attempted suicide and goal-setting behaviour. Transactions All-India Inst. Ment. Health, 6, 69-78, 1966.

127. Musselman, Gerald C.; Barger, Ben; and Chambers, Jay L. Student need patterns and effectiveness in college. J. Clin. Psychol., 23, 108-111, 1967.

128. Newlon, Robert E. Relationship between self-actualization and educational achievement at the high school level. Diss. Abstr., 29 (5-A), 1453, 1968.

129. O'Donnell, Patrick I. Predictors of freshman academic success and their relationship to attrition. Diss. Abstr., 29 (3-A), 798, 1968.

130. Oléron, Pierre; and Bonneaud, Colette. Sur les rapports entre abstraction et plasticité. (Concerning the relation between abstraction and plasticity.) Année Psychol., 54, 357-366, 1954.

131. Oskamp, Stuart. Relationship of self-concepts to international attitudes. J. Soc. Psychol., 76, 31-36, 1968.

132. Overstreet, H. A. The Mature Mind. New York: W. W. Norton & Co., 1949.

133. Pace, Lawlis T. Roommate dissatisfaction in a college residence hall as related to roommate scholastic achievement, the College and University Environment Scales, and the Edwards Personal Preference Schedule. Diss. Abstr., 28 (8-A), 2989, 1968.

134. Parloff, Morris B.; Datta, Lois-Ellin; Kleman, Marianne; and Handlon, Joseph H. Personality characteristics which differentiate creative male adolescents and adults. J. Personality, 36, 528-552, 1968.

135. Passons, William R. Predictive validities of the ACT, SAT and high-school grades for first semester GPA and freshman courses. Educ. Psychol. Meas., 27, 1143-1144, 1967.

136. Pawlick, K. Educational prediction from objective personality test dimensions. In Cartwright, D. S. Criterion predictions from objective personality factor measurements. Symposium at Amer. Psychol. Assoc. Convention, New York, September 1961.

137. Phillips, B. N. Sex, social class, and anxiety as sources of variation in school achievement. J. Educ. Psychol., 53, 316-322, 1962.

138. Pierce, James V. Personality and achievement among able high school boys. J. Indiv. Psychol., 17, 102-107, 1961.

139. Porterfield, O. V.; and Schlichting, Harry F. Peer status and reading achievement. J. Educ. Res., 54, 291-297, 1961.

140. Postman, L.; and Bruner, J. S. Perception under stress. Psychol. Rev., 55, 314-323, 1948.

141. Pruitt, Dean G. Informational requirements in making decisions. Amer. J. Psychol., 74, 433-439, 1961.

142. Rao, N. C. S. Experimental study of the effects of psychological stress on rigidity in problem solution. Indian J. Psychol., 29, 97-102, 1954.

143. Reik, T. Listening with the Third Ear. New York: Farrar, Straus, & Co., 1949, p. 304.

144. Richards, James M., Jr.; Holland, John L.; and Lutz, Sandra W. Prediction of student accomplishment in college. J. Educ. Psychol., 58, 343-355, 1967.

145. Robbins, P. R. Level of anxiety, interference proneness, and defensive reactions to fear-arousing information. J. Personality, 31, 163-178, 1963.

146. Roe, Anne. A psychological study of physical scientists. Genet. Psychol. Monogr., 43, 121-235, 1951.

147. Roe, Anne. A psychological study of eminent psychologists and anthropologists, and a comparison with biological and physical scientists. Psychol. Monogr., 67 (2), #352, 1953.

148. Rogers, William Alfred. Intellective-nonintellective characteristics and academic success of college freshmen. Diss. Abstr., 28 (3-A), 973-974, 1967.

149. Rokeach, M. Generalized mental rigidity as a factor in ethnocentrism. J. Abnorm. Soc. Psychol., 43, 259-278, 1948.

150. Rokeach, M. Prejudice and rigidity in children. Amer. Psychologist, 3, 362, 1948.

151. Rose, Anna Perrott. The Gentle House. Boston: Houghton Mifflin, 1954.

152. Rothaus, Paul; and Worchel, Philip. The inhibition of aggression under non-arbitrary frustration. J. Personality, 28, 108-117, 1960.

153. Rothney, J. W. M.; and Sanborn, M. P. Wisconsin's research-through-service program for superior high school students. Personnel Guid. J., 44, 694-699, 1966.

154. Ryan, F. R.; and Davie, James S. Social acceptance, academic achievement, and aptitude among high school students. J. Educ. Res., 52, 101-106, 1958.

155. Ryan, James H. Dreams of paraplegics. Arch. Gen. Psychiat., 5, 286-291, 1961.

156. Ryle, Anthony; and Lunghi, Martin. A psychometric study of academic difficulty and psychiatric illness in students. Brit. J. Psychiatry, 114, 57-62, 1968.

157. Sallery, Robert D. H. Artistic expression and self-description with Arabs and Canadian students. J. Soc. Psychol., 76, 273-274, 1968.

158. Salley, Ruth E., and Weintraug, Ruth G. Students records of entrance and graduation. Sch. & Soc., 69, 404-406, 1949.

159. Samenfink, J. Anthony; and Milliken, Robert L. Marital status and academic success: A reconsideration. Marriage Fam. Liv., 23, 226-227, 1961.

160. Sarason, S.; Davidson, K.; Lighthall, F.; Waite, R.; and Ruebush, B. Anxiety in elementary school children. New York: John Wiley, 1960.

161. Sassenrath, J. M. Anxiety, aptitude, attitude, and achievement. Psychol. in the Schools, 4, 341-346, 1967.

162. Sattabanasuk, Thirapan. Junior high student performance and related student and parent characteristics. Diss. Abstr., 29 (4-A), 1052-1053, 1968.

163. Schaller, George B. Mountain gorilla displays. Natural History, 72, 11-16, 1963.

164. Schoemer, J. R. The college pushout. Personnel Guid. J., 46, 677-680, 1968.

165. Schofield, William. A study of medical students with the MMPI: III. Personality and academic success. J. Appl. Psychol., 37, 47-52, 1953.

166. Scoville, Wilber E. Effects of employment on the academic performance of selected college freshmen. Diss. Abstr., 27 (12-A), 4140, 1967.

167. Sears, R. R. Initiation of the repression sequence by experienced failure. J. Exper. Psychol., 20, 570-580, 1937.

168. Sears, R. R. Success and failure. In McNemar, Q., and Merrill, M. A. Studies in Personality. New York: McGraw-Hill, 1942.

169. Seifer, Daniel M. Relationships of selected personal characteristics to income achievement of college graduates. Diss. Abstr., 27 (9-A), 2694-2695, 1967.

170. Sinha, Durganand. A psychological analysis of some factors associated with success and failure in university education: intelligence, anxiety and adjustment of academic achievers and non-achievers. Psychol. Studies, 11, 69-88, 1966.

171. Shaw, Merville C.; and Grubb, James. Hostility and able high school underachievers. J. Counsel. Psychol., 5, 263-266, 1958.

172. Slocum, John W., Jr. Group cohesiveness: A salient factor affecting students' academic achievement and adjustment in a collegiate environment. Diss. Abstr., 28 (3-B), 1176-1177, 1967.

173. Smith, H. A. College records and success in life. Educ., 47, 513-529, 1927.

174. Smith, J. G. Influence of failure, expressed hostility, and stimulus characteristics on verbal learning and recognition. J. Personality, 22, 475-493, 1954.

175. Spielberger, C. D. The effects of manifest anxiety on the academic achievement of college students. Ment. Hyg., 46, 420-426, 1962.

176. Tanay, Emanuel. Psychiatric study of homicide. Amer. J. Psychiatry, 125, 1252-1257, 1969.

177. Taylor, C. W.; and Ellison, R. L. Biographical predictors of scientific performance. Science, 155, 1075-1080, 1967.

178. Tedeschi, James; Burrill, Dwight; and Gahagan, James. Social desirability, manifest anxiety, and social power. J. Soc. Psychol., 77, 231-239, 1969.

179. Tenopyr, Mary L. Social intelligence and academic success. Educ. Psychol. Meas., 27, 961-965, 1967.

180. Terman, Lewis M. The discovery and encouragement of exceptional talent. Amer. Psychologist, 9, 221-230, 1954.

181. Terman, Lewis M.; and Oden, Melita H. Genetic Studies of Genius. Vol. V, The Gifted Group at Mid-Life. Stanford, Calif.: Stanford Univ. Press, 1959.

182. Thomas, Robert Jay. An empirical study of high school drop-outs in regard to ten possibly related factors. J. Educ. Sociol., 28, 11-18, 1954.

183. Thompson, L. The role of verbalization in learning from demonstration. Doctoral dissertation. New Haven, Conn.: Yale University, 1944.

184. Thompson, O. E. High school students' values: Emergent or traditional. Calif. J. Educ. Res., 12, 132-144, 1961.

185. Trueblood, Dennis L. Effects of employment on academic achievement. Personnel Guid. J., 36, 112-115, 1957.

186. Van Voorhis, W. R.; and Miller, A. C. The influence of college training upon success after college as measured by judges' estimates. J. Educ. Psychol., 26, 377-383, 1935.

187. Varnes, Paul R. An investigation of college intramural athletic and recreational participation and academic success. Diss. Abstr., 29 (3-A), 825, 1968.

188. Wagman, Morton. University achievement and daydreaming behavior. J. Couns. Psychol., 15, 196-198, 1968.

189. Watson, J. B. Psychology from the Standpoint of a Behaviorist. New York: J. B. Lippincott Co., 1924, pp. 232-233.

190. Werts, Charles E. The many faces of intelligence. J. Educ. Psychol., 58, 198-204, 1967.

191. Whyte, W. H. The Organization Man. New York: Simon & Schuster, 1956.

192. Williams, Dale E. A study of selected personality and occupational aspiration variables associated with achievement level. Diss. Abstr., 27 (12-A), 4143-4144, 1967.

193. Willingham, Warren W. College performance of fraternity members and independent students. Personnel Guid. J., 41, 29-31, 1962.

194. Windholz, George. The relation of creativity and intelligence constellations to traits of temperament, interest, and value in college students. J. General Psychol. 79, 291-299, 1968.

195. Wyer, R. S., Jr. Behavioral correlates of academic achievement. II. Pursuit of individual versus group goals in a decision-making task. J. Educ. Psychol., 59, 74-81, 1968.

196. Wyer, R. S.; and Terrell, G. Social role and academic achievement. J. Personality Soc. Psychol., 2, 117-121, 1965.

197. Wyer, R. S.; Weatherly, D.; and Terrell, G. Social role, aggression, and academic achievement. J. Personality Soc. Psychol., 1, 645-649, 1965.
198. Young, C. W. Scholarship and social adjustment. Sch. & Soc., 43, 607-608, 1936.
199. Zimbardo, P. G.; Barnard, J. W.; and Berkowitz, L. The role of anxiety and defensiveness in children's verbal behavior. J. Personality, 31, 79-96, 1963.

Index of people
referred to or quoted*

Numbers in *italics* refer to pages on which
bibliographical data are listed.

*The accuracy and completeness of this index is attributable largely to
the care and skill of Sally and Cecil Burchfiel; their assistance on this and
other aspects of completing the third edition was invaluable.

259

Subject index